T0300502

Institutional and Technological Change in Japan's Economy

Institutional and technological change is a highly topical subject. At the theoretical level, there has been lively debate in the field of institutional economics, and technological change has become a key issue in endogenous growth theory. At a practical policy level, arguments about how Japan and the Japanese economy should plan for the future have been particularly prominent.

In this book, leading economists and economic historians of Japan examine a range of key issues concerning institutional and technological change, making extensive use of discipline-based analytical tools and drawing important conclusions as to how the process of institutional and technical change has actually worked in the Japanese context. In focusing on issues which are currently being much debated in the country itself, these chapters make a major contribution to a broader understanding of the world's second-largest economy.

Janet Hunter is Saji Professor of Economic History at the London School of Economics and Political Science. She is the co-editor of a volume on the application of new institutional economics to developing economies, and has published widely on modern Japanese economic history, particularly on the development of the female labour market. She is currently working on the history of communications.

Cornelia Storz is Professor of Japanese Economics at the Faculty of Economics and the Centre for Japanese Studies, University of Marburg. Her research focuses on the comparison of economic systems, genesis and change in institutions (especially institutional change in Japan), comparative institutional analysis, and entrepreneurship and the modern Japanese economy.

Routledge Contemporary Japan Series

Institutional and Technological Change in Japan's Economy

Past and present

**Edited by
Janet Hunter and
Cornelia Storz**

Routledge
Taylor & Francis Group

LONDON AND NEW YORK

First published 2006
by Routledge
2 Park Square, Milton Park, Abingdon, Oxon OX14 4RN

Simultaneously published in the USA and Canada
by Routledge
711 Third Ave, New York, NY 10017

Routledge is an imprint of the Taylor & Francis Group

© 2006 Janet Hunter and Cornelia Storz, selection and editorial matter;
the contributors, their own chapters

Typeset in Times New Roman by
Newgen Imaging Systems (P) Ltd, Chennai, India

British Library Cataloguing in Publication Data
A catalogue record for this book is available from the British Library

Library of Congress Cataloging in Publication Data
A catalog record for this book has been requested

ISBN 978 0 4153 6822 3

Contents

Figures

Tables

Contributors

Sigrun Caspary has since 1997 been an Associate Professor at the Institute for Comparative Research into Culture and Economic Systems at the Faculty of Management and Economics of Witten/Herdecke University. She holds a PhD in Japanese Studies with Economics and Political Science from Bonn University. Her working, research and teaching experience includes the Yamaichi Bank, Frankfurt (1997), Hitotsubashi University (1992–97), the Institute of International Economic Studies, Tokyo (1996) and Trier University (1992–93). Her recent work on international M&A with Japanese participation extends her previous research on the international aerospace industry, Japanese industrial policy and industrial districts.

Kerstin Cuhls is Project Manager at the Fraunhofer Institute for Systems and Innovation Research (ISI) in Karlsruhe. She obtained her doctorate from the University of Hamburg, lectures at the Hochschule Bremen and has acted as the scientific project coordinator for the German–Japanese foresight projects. As well as foresight and Delphi work, her research focuses on innovation strategies, research and development strategies, and comparison of Japanese and German research and technology policies. Her most recent publications are 'Evaluating a Participative Foresight Process: "Futur – the German research dialogue"' (with Luke Georghiou) (*Research Evaluation*, 2004) and *Participatory Priority Setting for Research and Innovation Policy* (with Michael Jaspers) (IRB Verlag, 2004).

Katalin Ferber graduated in economic history from Karl Marx University in Budapest, Hungary, and has worked as a comparative economic historian in various countries. She is currently Associate Professor at Waseda University in Tokyo. Her primary research interest is the comparison of the Japanese financial and fiscal system and its counterparts in Central Europe. Her recent publications include an article on the origins of the Deposit Fund in Japan (*Japanese Studies*, September 2002), and she is the author of *Origins of the Contemporary Japanese Economic and Financial System* (in Hungarian) (Budapest: Balassi Kiado, 2006).

Harald Fuess works at Sophia University in Tokyo. He grew up in France and Germany, studied at Princeton (BA), Tokyo and Harvard Universities (MA,

PhD), and taught Japanese history, culture, gender and business in the United States, Germany and Japan. He edited *The Japanese Empire in East Asia and Its Postwar Legacy* (Iudicium, 1998) and authored *Divorce in Japan: Family, Gender and the State, 1600–2000* (Stanford, 2004), as well as various articles and book chapters on fatherhood. His current research is on the history of beer in modern Japan.

Janet Hunter is Saji Professor of Economic History at the London School of Economics and Political Science. She received her PhD from Oxford University, and previously taught at the University of Sheffield. She has published widely on modern Japanese economic history, particularly on the development of the female labour market, and is now working on the economic history of communications. She is the author of *Women and the Labour Market in Industrialising Japan* (RoutledgeCurzon, 2003).

Ilona Koester received a master's degree in Japanese Studies and a PhD in economics from the Philipps University, Marburg. She worked on a university project on 'Structural Analysis of the Japanese Environmental Sector' in 1997–98, and since 2004 has been a Project Manager at KVB in Munich. She has spent two years living in Japan. Her major publications are *Interdependenz von Wirtschaft und Transportwesen – Visionen für das 21. Jahrhundert* (1997), *Die japanische Umweltindustrie – Anbieter, Nachfrager, Marktstrukturen* (1998) and *Steuerbarkeit gesamtwirtschaftlicher Entwicklung aus systemtheoretischer Sicht* (2004).

Mariusz K. Krawczyk obtained his PhD from Kōbe University, and is currently Professor in the Faculty of Economics at Fukuoka University. His research interests focus on the financial aspects of reform in transition economies, and he is the author of *Tōō no Shijō Keizaika* (*The Transition to the Market Economy in Eastern Europe*) (1999). His most recent publication is 'On the Perils of Adopting the Euro in the New Accession Countries' (*Homo Oeconomicus* 21, 3–4, December 2004).

Helen Macnaughtan is Lecturer in Japanese Business and Management at the School of Oriental and African Studies, London. She obtained her PhD from the London School of Economics, and is the author of *Women, Work and the Japanese Economic Miracle: The Case of the Cotton Textile Industry, 1945–1975* (Routledge, 2005). Her research interests focus on gender, employment, labour management and economic development in Japan.

Andreas Moerke is Senior Research Fellow at the German Institute for Japanese Studies (DIJ), Tokyo. He earned an MA degree in Japanese Studies and a PhD in Management Science, both from Humboldt University, Berlin, and as a company co-founder and business consultant for market entry strategies for Japan. His research focuses on industrial organization, corporate governance and international management. Recent publications include 'The Changing Trend in Links between Bureaucracy and the Private Sector in

Japan' (*Advances in International Management*, 2004), 'Mitsubishi Jidōsha e no Shien wo Kyohi shita Daimurākuraisurā Kansayakukai – sono Pawā to Yakuwari' (*Bijinesu Hōmu*, 2004) and is the joint editor with Gregory Jackson of a special edition of *Corporate Governance: An International Review*, 31, 3, May 2005, Blackwell.

Patricia Sippel is Associate Professor of Japan Studies at Toyo Eiwa University in Yokohama. She obtained her PhD from Harvard University. Her research focuses on Japan's economic and political history since the early modern era, and she is currently working on the history of copper mining in the Tōhoku region. Her publications include 'Abandoned Fields: Negotiating Taxes in the Tokugawa Domain' (*Monumenta Nipponica*, 1998) and '*Chisui*: Creating a Sacred Domain in Early Modern and Modern Japan' in C.L. Bernstein, A. Gordon and K. Wildman Nakai (eds), *Public Spheres, Private Lives in Modern Japan: Essays in Honor of Albert Craig* (2005).

Cornelia Storz has since 2001 been Professor of Japanese Economics at the Faculty of Economics and the Centre for Japanese Studies, University of Marburg. She took a PhD in economics at the University of Duisburg, and was previously Professor of Japanese Economics and Society at the University for Applied Sciences at Bremen. Her research focuses on the comparison of economic systems, genesis and change in institutions (especially institutional change in Japan), comparative institutional analysis and entrepreneurship. She is the author of *Der mittelständische Unternehmer in Japan* (1997), and recent publications include two articles in edited volumes, 'Standardization and Convergence of Production Systems' (2004) and 'Institutionen in der wirtschaftlichen Entwicklung Ostasiens' (2005).

Takaaki Suzuki received his PhD from Columbia University and is currently an Associate Professor and Graduate Chair in the Political Science Department at Ohio University. Professor Suzuki's research and teaching interests include East Asian politics, comparative political economy and international political economy. His articles have appeared in a variety of scholarly journals and he is the author of *Japan's Budget Politics: Balancing Domestic and International Interests* (Lynne Rienner, 2000).

Acknowledgements

The majority of the chapters contained in this volume were initially presented in the Economics and Economic History sessions of the conference of the European Association for Japanese Studies held in Warsaw in August 2003. The editors would like to thank not just the contributors to this volume, but all those who presented papers at these sessions and participated in the fruitful discussions that took place. It will be apparent that the chapters in this book are characterized by diversity of academic discipline, academic approach and national origin, and the editors have not attempted to limit this diversity, which only partly reflects the richness of the range of contributions offered at the conference. We would like to thank the European Association of Japanese Studies for giving us the opportunity of organising the Economics and Economic History panels in a revised form that allowed us to focus on specific issues of change. We would like particularly to thank the Japan Foundation for generously supporting our section through the attendance of our invited guest speaker, Professor Okazaki Tetsuji of the University of Tokyo. Thanks also go to those individuals who helped us in preparing both the conference sessions and this publication, especially Per Larsen, Alexander Müller and Aashish Velkar. Finally, we would like to express gratitude to Peter Sowden of Routledge, who supported the publication of this book at a very difficult time. His contribution to the publication of work on Japan has been enormous, and we hope that he feels that this volume helps to do it justice.

Janet Hunter and Cornelia Storz
April 2005

1 Introduction

Economic and institutional change in Japan

Janet Hunter and Cornelia Storz

The malaise that has afflicted the Japanese economy since the start of the 1990s has been attributed by many commentators to problems with institutions and organizational technologies in Japan, limiting an effective response to changed economic and social imperatives, and undermining the ability of different groups to take the necessary action to regain the economic and technological competitiveness that characterized the country up to the late 1980s. Recent Japanese governments, particularly that of Prime Minister Koizumi, have argued that some of the answers to this perceived stasis can be found in changing the role of the state, but it is clear that such moves have encountered considerable opposition from both within and without the government's political supporters. The possibility and viability of substantial change in Japan, in institutions, organizations and technologies, therefore, remains high on the agenda.

Our understanding of the process of change over time has been considerably enhanced by recent developments in institutional economics, in the economics of organizations and in the study of technology, and in the application of some of these ideas to historical evidence and to more contemporary empirical concerns. While the papers contained in this volume are mainly empirical in approach, many are also informed by our recent greater understanding of how to analyse the processes of change in institutions and organizations, and in the utilization of both practical and organizational technologies.

Some of the key developments in institutional economics that have influenced our analysis of the actual process of change are mentioned by Ilona Koester in her paper, but it is appropriate to make a number of points here, and to mention one or two of the scholars who have been particularly influential in work in this area. Probably most influential for both economists and economic historians has, of course, been the work of Douglass C. North.[1] North's definition of institutions as 'the rules of the game' offered historians as well as economists a tool for conceptualizing and theorizing about things that they had always known to be important, but which they had, from a social scientific perspective, found very hard to pin down. The distinction that North drew between 'formal' and 'informal' institutions, differentiating between formal laws and regulations and the often unspoken rules that govern everyday life, acknowledged that, particularly when it came to the latter, there were limits on the ability of economic rationality and profit maximization to explain completely the actions and decisions of groups and individuals. It also seemed to offer a way of avoiding the dangerous term 'culture', a term which historians had long used to try and explain the observable differences between behaviour in different countries and regions, but which was for many social science historians unsatisfactory, or even irrelevant. The distinction between institutions and organizations as the manifestation of those institutions also proved valuable. North's focus on property rights and on transactions costs (drawing on Coase)[2] was quickly taken up by economists and economic historians and applied to a range of empirical studies.

North's work has, of course, been considerably extended by other economists seeking to illuminate historical processes. The work of Avner Greif[3] is just one example of how the institutional approach has been utilized to shed light on historical economic activity that at first glance appears either irrational or non-profit-maximizing, or both. Work on 'embeddedness' has illuminated further the social or ideological context within which economic decisions are made.[4] However, since many economists and economic historians have tended to regard more detailed analysis of societal factors as beyond their expertise, lying more in the province of anthropologists or social historians, there remains the danger that institutions are left as something of a black box, used as a catch-all explanation for those things that cannot be explained by economic rationality or individual maximization, equivalent to the residual or error term in an equation. What is now almost universally accepted, though, is that it is not possible to understand the nature of economic change without considering the institutions within which it is embedded, and in this Japan is no exception.

The ideas contained in institutional economics have focused mainly on two questions, namely the impact of, and changes in, institutions. Institutions and their stability are in general considered helpful, since they offer relief to actors, enabling them to search for more profound solutions. The theory of transaction costs mentioned earlier, and the theory of property rights, are important approaches for analysing the impact of institutions, but even more important in the context of this volume is the concept of path dependence, the idea that even relatively small historical events can influence subsequent developments. Contributions in evolutionary economics also refer to this process using the terms 'routines' or 'trajectories'. A focal problem in institutional economics is the fact that demand for new institutions and certain incentive structures does not necessarily lead to institutional change. Uncertainty, vested interests, changing costs, complementarities and mental models often lead to unexpected rigidities, often defined as path dependence or, in the case of more technological or organizational issues, trajectories and routines, as mentioned.[5]

Uncertainty is always an element of institutional change. This means that actors do not know which, and which kinds of, alternatives exist, so they may prefer to maintain the established institution. One argument put forward in political science, but increasingly acknowledged in political economy studies, relates to the existence of different interests. Here again, every change in institutions may induce a shift in power, which may in turn lead to opposition by those actors who were hitherto in favour of change. Transaction theory has shed light on the fact that change does not come free of cost. It is associated with a range of costs, such as the costs of learning and unlearning, as well as search and other types of costs; this again leads to undesired rigidities. A central additional factor is the presence of complementarities. This concept stems from the economics of standardization, and refers to the fact that the operation of an institution will depend upon the way in which it functions in conjunction with other institutions and rules (including, in the case of standards, technical rules), and its own embeddedness in these rules. Every change in one rule, or in one institution, therefore necessitates a change in another rule or institution, making the whole process of change extremely complex. A further factor that evolutionary economics has introduced into the concept of path dependence is the role of cognitive models, that is, basic individual and collective patterns of how the world is perceived and constructed. Since these patterns are so fundamental, it is almost impossible to change them directly. One example of this might be how entrepreneurial failure is understood in a society. Depending on the prevailing (unconscious) concept of market operation, policy makers may either try to support failed entrepreneurs, through providing some kind of social safety net, for example, or try to encourage them to search for solutions by themselves, for example by offering them incentives to build up more efficient capital markets. The editors of this volume stress, as do the authors in their individual contributions, that the incrementality of change and the rationality behind it should be taken seriously, but they also stress that, depending on the area of focus, there may be sufficient and often overlooked options which can be used to escape from undesirable aspects of path dependence. We may summarise, therefore, by stating that the traditional focus of economics led to a playing down, and even a disregard, of institutions and the role of history; instead, 'pure markets' were the object of analysis.[6]

Another element previously considered as a 'black box' is technology, and some of the chapters in this volume deal with both scientific and organizational technologies. Traditional neo-classical economics saw technology as exogenous; knowledge (whether organizational or technological knowledge) was not seen as an important factor in production. From an institutional perspective, however, it is not sufficient merely to react to prices; there is a constant need for innovation. Moreover, concepts of innovation systems have stressed that the adaptation and development of existing (radical) innovations is a central part of the innovation process.[7] This is an issue of special importance for Japan, which has been criticized as unable to give birth to 'real' (i.e. 'radical') innovations. It may be suggested here, however, that some of the more evolutionary contributions in innovation economics have also tended to overstress the danger of lock-in caused by established routines. In this volume it will hopefully become obvious that there also exist methods for achieving change, such as the creation of new modularities, or changing cognitive frameworks on the part of entrepreneurs. From a longer-term perspective, the works of historians such as Joel Mokyr and Daniel Headrick have also had a significant influence on the way in which economic historians approach the issue of technological change in history. Headrick's work has been particularly focused on specific historical case studies,[8] but both authors have extended their consideration from practical technologies to organizational and information technologies. Following part of a tradition dating back to Josef Schumpeter, Mokyr has spelt out the conditions conducive for innovation and invention in history, along with a distinction between macro- and micro-inventions.[9] Given that critics of Japan, and Japanese themselves, have often argued in recent times that Japan has been good at the micro-inventions, but not the macro ones, this distinction raises fundamental questions about Japanese technology, past and present. Indeed, Japan lost markets in leading-edge technologies to the United States in the 1990s, such as those in biotechnology or information and communication technology. In the leading international rankings of the last few years Japan is placed low, compared with other OECD members. One report, which was especially sobering for Japan, was the Global Information Technology Report of the World Economic Forum of 2004, which placed Japan in twentieth place, far behind the leading OECD members.[10] Obviously, current estimation of the Japanese innovation system and its technological capabilities is not too high, and Kerstin Cuhls' analysis in the final chapter of this volume of the technologies of information flow at the start of the twenty-first century has to be considered in this context. We need to remember, however, that the evaluation of Japan's technological creativity as recently as twenty years ago was somewhat different, as some of the chapters in this volume can also testify.

The chapters in this volume, and the ideas noted earlier, all relate to change or rigidity towards change. In that sense they are all concerned with a dynamic process, whether over a lengthy period, as tends to be the case with historians, or with a shorter period focusing around the present, as is the case with economists. We are familiar with the complaints that there has been a lack of change in contemporary Japan in response to crisis, but we need to note, in line with seeing change as process rather than event, that most change tends to be incremental rather than dramatic. Path dependence influences the shape and pace of change, but does not completely impede it. It may be suggested, moreover, that the contributions of approaches to the analysis of institutional change are often limited in three respects. First, they tend to lack a reference point. Second, they are inclined to underestimate the rationality behind incremental change, and overall neglect the fact that incremental changes may lead to radical changes as well. Third, they too often neglect the role of entrepreneurship and the options to leave or re-interpret given paths. According to Hall these changes can be differentiated according to whether they relate only to the setting of instruments, to the instruments themselves or to cases where even the hierarchy of aims has been changed.[11] Only if the instruments themselves and the hierarchy of aims are changed can institutional change be termed 'paradigmatic' or 'radical', something that because of path dependence is a rare event, but which does nevertheless exist. The changes in the corporate governance of Japanese firms outlined by Andreas Moerke in this volume can be seen as an example of radical change generated through entrepreneurship. The changes in corporate governance have embodied not only a change of instruments and their settings, but also change in the hierarchy of aims relating to which enterprise should be invested in, and the role of stability in interfirm relations.

Thus, the history of the modern Japanese economy suggests an ongoing presence of a dynamic of change, and a consistent willingness to countenance and encourage change. In that context, the present perceived 'stagnation' becomes particularly prominent. However, the reality of change is that it is often time-consuming, and accompanied by mistakes, but that these mistakes tend to get overlooked and forgotten if the longer-term outcome is seen as delivering 'success' or 'progress'.[12] The chapters in this volume do not underestimate the difficulties of delivering change in the present, but they do point to the fact that change has been taking place, for better or for worse. Japan may well be no more static or sclerotic at the start of the twenty-first century than it has been at other times in the past.

Collectively the chapters here, which deal both with macro-level and specific institutional or technological issues, raise a number of points. One is the significance of human agents and their ideas and their cognitive models in the process of change. Patricia Sippel's chapter (Chapter 2) on the nineteenth-century development of the copper mining industry highlights this. Not only did a succession of individual mining engineers, both Western and Japanese, play key roles in the overall process of technology change, but there was also, Sippel argues, an overwhelming belief and confidence in the need for, and advantages of, such technological changes. A precondition for change is therefore not just the existence of 'fit' or 'suitable' complementary institutions, but a conviction that change is feasible and desirable, inducing a readiness to learn, to bear the costs, and to develop new concepts. Katalin Ferber's chapter (Chapter 3) focuses very specifically on one human agent in the process of institutional change, the economist Tajiri Inajirō, credited with being a major influence both in forming monetary policy in the Meiji period, and also in educating the next generation of experts. Individuals and groups of individuals play a key role in many of the other accounts in this volume, from the charismatic Carlos Ghosn of Nissan–Renault described in Sigrun Caspary's chapter (Chapter 9), to the members of the ever-present Japanese bureaucracy that has figured so prominently in recent criticisms. The 'institution' clearly frames the ways in which individuals and groups act, but that makes it no less important to consider the human agency that can in turn influence the development of those same institutions. Institutional and technological change can only be carried out by groups and individuals, something powerfully highlighted in Mokyr's observation that invention requires inventors with an incentive to invent.

Associated with this concern with human agency is consideration of the extent to which change overall can be influenced or imposed by changes from above, particularly changes in formal institutions, and the conflicts or dynamic learning processes that are induced by them. A number of the authors analyse the impact of attempts to impose change through, for example, legislation. Helen Macnaughtan's chapter (Chapter 5) on the management policies of textile works in the post-1945 period notes the significance of the imposed changes of the Occupation era in pushing managers towards modifying earlier labour management practices.

Caspary's chapter stresses the impact of formal changes in the law, and Sippel focuses on the actors at the centre, while Ilona Koester's chapter (Chapter 10) on environmental pollution policy considers in some detail the influence of imposed or formal changes from above. The implication of much of the work here is that while top-down, formal or imposed changes may often have a limited or slow impact, and their relationship with informal change is often unclear, there is no doubt that such imposed changes can be influential, and that they can have a profound impact on informal institutions and methods of organization. In turn, as both Sippel and Cuhls demonstrate for very different periods, they will also shape the approach to technological change, and the available information about it. Significantly, the authors in this volume for the most part come to more optimistic conclusions about the viability of change than those found in earlier applications of the same ideas to, for example, Eastern Europe or Latin America. The concept of path dependence has perhaps too often been interpreted purely as a constraint, rather than as a necessary reduction of complexity which offers individuals the freedom to search for new solutions.[13] These chapters may, therefore, have something to offer in terms of stimulating institutional economics to move in new directions.

By itself, however, a top-down change in formal institutions may be of limited effect. Equally, if not more, important is likely to be the pressure to adapt in the face of shifting economic, social and other pressures. Macnaughtan's chapter, while acknowledging the significance of changes in legislation, argues powerfully that it was the changing fortunes of the textile industry and demographic and educational changes that compelled managers to modify old policies and alter the composition of their workforce. Cuhls shows how the process of 'foresight' surveying undertaken by the government has evolved to address the increasing emphasis on the social implications of science and technology developments. Both Caspary and Andreas Moerke, in his study of *keiretsu* evolution (Chapter 6), emphasize the extent to which economic imperatives can engineer relatively rapid changes and responses.

This does not mean to say, however, that we should downplay completely the element of path dependence. Both Caspary and Moerke stress the continuities that persist even in the face of ongoing change. In Moerke's study of the *keiretsu* it is argued that *keiretsu* may have been weakened by the recent economic problems, but they are likely to continue to exist. Caspary indicates that Japanese companies merging with non-Japanese ones are unlikely to lose their identity overnight, even though over time a new organizational form may emerge. The ability and willingness of organizations to adapt is contingent on finding a new way forward that identifies necessary modifications to cope with changed external circumstances in a form compatible with what already exists, and particularly with what continues to be considered of value. For sure, there is a path – without such reductions of complexity we would not be able to structure reality – but both these authors stress that there are options for learning which can naturally take place within the constraints of given paths.

This in turn raises the issue of Japan in a comparative context. The extent to which modern Japanese institutions, organizations and technologies have indigenous roots, and how far they have been transferred from the West, has been a topic of ongoing debate, a debate that has too often been influenced by the swings in nationalist sentiment and the level of national self-confidence. For historians of Japan's economy, the issue of how far the Japanese experience replicated that of Western European economies, and how far Japan can be claimed to have gone through a distinct industrialization path, has been at the heart of discussions of Japan's economic development since the second half of the nineteenth century, and continues today.[14] For economists, Japan's position raises not only the applicability of economic theories initially articulated in Western Europe and the United States to a non-Western country such as Japan, but also the issue of how far common economic and technological imperatives may, or may not, produce the same institutions and organizational forms across countries, that is, does the case of Japan support or undermine any concept of technological and institutional convergence.

A number of chapters in this volume refer to the now somewhat less fashionable idea that Japan is distinct and different, or, to cite a formerly well used word, 'unique'. None of the chapters here disputes the fact that Japan is distinct in the same way that all other countries are distinct, but they do collectively argue that it is possible to apply particular conceptual frameworks and theories to understand Japan in a comparative context, and, in many cases, to identify similarities in the processes of change and evolution in Japan with those in other countries. A number of them also suggest that the distinction between what is 'Japanese' and 'non-Japanese' is often blurred, particularly as the ongoing process of globalization has increasingly facilitated cross-country transfers both of factors of production and of technological and other knowledge.

Harald Fuess's chapter (Chapter 4) on the development of beer producers since the ninteenth century explicitly applies to the Japanese case Alfred Chandler's model of the modern firm, concluding that, if anything, Japanese beer firms were much closer to the model than were, for example, the smaller beer producers of continental Europe, particularly Germany. Koester's chapter, by contrast, contends that the neo-classical approach to understanding environmental policy falls short of explaining the policy environment in Japan, showing not only that institutions matter, but that such institutions are far from being dictated by the profit-maximizing imperative. Ferber identifies the transfer of cameralist theories to Meiji Japan, arguing that it was both because of their inherent value and because of the extent to which they resonated with earlier ideas that they found fruition in the monetary policies of Matsukata Masayoshi. But how far do imported ideas and institutions remain distinct from indigenous Japanese ones? Sippel suggests that mines using imported technology could be termed 'Western', but that the process of indigenization of imported technology was often rapid. The same applies to institutions. Caspary's consideration of how far Japanese firms involved in international M&A will remain 'Japanese' is germane to this question.

This issue of the value and applicability of Western theories and models to Japan is, of course, of fundamental importance to current debates on institutional and organizational change in Japan's economy. Pressure to make major changes in both political and economic institutions has often been strengthened in recent years through resorting to the superior claims of certain Western institutions, particularly those embraced by neo-classical economists. While these observations indicate some caution is necessary about not only Japan's ability to change itself overnight, but also the extent to which imported Western institutions can be easily made to work in the Japanese context, it is apparent that this debate on Japan in international context is at the heart of the banking crisis discussed in the chapters by Takaaki Suzuki (Chapter 7) and Mariusz Krawczyk (Chapter 8). Suzuki, like some of the other authors, stresses the importance of human agency, arguing that many of Japan's problems were due more to bad economic decisions on the part of the ruling Liberal Democratic Party in the 1980s, and less to the constraints associated with globalization and its weakening of political agency. The answer is therefore to be found in political institutions, if not in politics, and the key to stability lies in finding the always elusive balance between the state and the market. While Krawczyk, writing from an economics rather than a political science perspective, exhibits a significant level of agreement with Suzuki regarding the institutional framework, his conclusions are, as might be expected, angled differently, and his optimism over the availability of an appropriate solution somewhat greater. While he agrees with the argument that Japan's financial institutions served the economy at an earlier stage but now impede its progress, he too looks to human agency for a solution, but in this case in the realm of good economic policy-making and a more economically literate bureaucracy. It may be, of course, that this view can be reconciled with Suzuki's if we accept that politicians are best advised to follow the advice of their officials and experts, but this again brings us back to the significance of human agency, in the form of both individuals and groups, in the process of institutional and technological change.

Overall, the contributions presented here show that we have to use the concept of path dependence in describing institutional and technological change with a considerable degree of both prudence and discrimination. Paths will vary greatly as to their degree of rigidity, depending on the one hand on criteria mentioned earlier such as perceived uncertainty and complementarities, and on the other on learning abilities and capabilities. The present volume offers comment, and not necessarily consensus. We hope, however, that it will at the very least help to stimulate discussion of the value of an institutional approach in understanding Japan's economy and its history.

Notes

1 See for example *Institutions, Institutional Change and Economic Performance* (Cambridge: Cambridge University Press, 1990); 'The New Institutional Economics and Third World Development', in John Harriss, Janet Hunter and C.M. Lewis (eds), *The New Institutional Economics and Third World Development* (London: Routledge, 1995).
2 Ronald H. Coase, 'The Nature of the Firm', *Economica* 4, 1937; 'The New Institutional Economics', *Zeitschrift für die gesamte Staatswissenschaft* 140, 1984.
3 For example, 'Reputation and Coalitions in Medieval Trade: Evidence on the Maghribi Traders', *Journal of Economic History* 49, 4, 1989; 'Contract Enforceability and

Economic Institutions in Early Trade: The Maghribi Traders' Coalition', *American Economic Review* 83, 3, 1993.

4 Mark Granovetter, 'Economic Action and Social Structure: The Problem of Embeddedness', *American Journal of Sociology* 91, 1985; 'The Impact of Social Structure on Economic Outcomes', *Journal of Economic Perspectives* 19, Winter 2005.

5 For an application of these ideas to European law, see for example Wolfgang Kerber and Klaus Heine, 'Institutional Evolution, Regulatory Competition and Path Dependence', *Marburger Volkswirtschaftliche Beiträge* 6–2002, Marburg, 2002. For an application to the issue of international standards see Cornelia Storz, 'Implementation of Standards: What about the Possibility of a Convergence Production System by International Rules?', in Werner Pascha (ed.), *Systemic Change in the Japanese and German Economies: Convergence and Differentiation as a Dual Challenge* (London: Institute of Asian Affairs Hamburg/RoutledgeCurzon, 2004).

6 For a more detailed comparison see Bengt-Åke Lundvall (ed.), *National Systems of Innovation* (London: Pinter, 1992).

7 See Richard Nelson and Sydney Winter, *An Evolutionary Theory of Economic Change* (Cambridge, MA: Harvard University Press, 1982); Jens Nyholm, Clause Frelle-Petersen, Mark Riis, and Peter Torstensen, 'Innovation Policy in the Knowledge-Based Economy', in Daniele Archibugi and Bengt-Åke Lundvall (eds), *The Globalizing Learning Economy* (Oxford: Oxford University Press, 2001).

8 Daniel Headrick, *The Tentacles of Progress: Technology Transfer in the Age of Imperialism* (New York: Oxford University Press, 1988); D. Headrick, *When Information Came of Age: Technologies of Knowledge in the Age of Reason and Revolution, 1700–1850* (Oxford: Oxford University Press, 2000).

9 Joel Mokyr, *The Lever of Riches: Technological Creativity and Economic Progress* (New York: Oxford University Press, 1992); Joel Mokyr, *The Gifts of Athena: Historical Origins of the Knowledge Economy* (Princeton, NJ: Princeton University Press, 2002).

10 For this kind of critical perspective see for example Marie Anchordoguy, 'Japan's Software Industry: A Failure of Institutions', *Research Policy* 29, 2000; Akira Goto, 'Japan's National Innovation System: Current Status and Problems', *Oxford Review of Economic Policy* 16, 2, 2000.

11 Peter A. Hall, 'Policy Paradigms, Social Learning and the State: The Case of Economic Policymaking in Britain', *Comparative Politics*, April 1993.

12 For a historical comparison of institutional change in Japan see Janet Hunter, 'Institutional Revolution: The Case of Meiji Japan', in Magnus Blomstrom and Sumner La Croix (eds), *Institutional Change in Japan* (Routledge, forthcoming).

13 See Cornelia Storz, 'Path Dependence, Change and Creativity: What Do They Teach Us about Japan's Competitiveness?', *Lund University Working Paper in Contemporary Asian Studies*, 2005.

14 In the twentieth century this was a key issue for the Marxist-influenced historians, and recent historiography has built on the work of Hayami Akira in arguing for an 'industrious' revolution, and hence a labour-intensive path of industrialization, in Japan. See for example, Akira Hayami, Osamu Saitō and Ronald P. Toby (eds), *The Emergence of Economic Society in Japan* (Oxford: Oxford University Press, 2004).

2 Technology and change in Japan's modern copper mining industry

Patricia Sippel

Introduction

Japan's mining industry does not receive a lot of attention from economic and social historians these days. True, mining has a secure place among the negatives of modern Japanese history. Labor conditions in Japanese mines, particularly the coal mines of Hashima and Miike in Kyūshū, were notorious for their squalor in the opening decades of the twentieth century. The need to secure mine labor was a major reason for the forced relocation of hundreds of thousands of workers from colonial Korea and occupied China to Japan through to the end of the Second World War.[1] Environmental damage, too, was egregious. As early as the 1880s, minerals washed out from the Ashio Copper Mine in Tochigi prefecture contaminated the nearby Watarase River, killing fish, sickening those who ate the fish, and ruining crops that came in contact with river water.[2] Caught up in the demands of rapid modernization, the Meiji government was not immediately willing to restrict mine activities. It took a decade of petitions, protests, and national publicity before a minimal settlement was reached regarding compensation and pollution control. The Ashio incident was Japan's first recorded major case of industrial water pollution in the modern era, the first in a series that continued well into the post-Second World War decades.

While labor abuse and industrial pollution form an important part of modern Japan's record on human rights and environmental policy, they also point to the crucial importance of mining in the economic history of modern Japan. From the opening years of the Meiji era (1868–1912), Japanese mines experienced a surge in productivity that lasted well into the second decade of the twentieth century. Between 1874 and 1908, output of copper, silver, gold, and coal increased by some 20, 45, 54, and 72 times respectively (see Table 2.1).[3] Not only did the mining industry offer material resources for domestic use but, led by copper and coal, it played a vital role in securing export income in a period of heavy import dependence. Copper accounted for 4 percent of total exports in 1871–75, rising to 5 percent in 1886–90 (see Table 2.2). It was Japan's sixth most valuable export item in 1898, rising to third in 1908, and fifth in 1913.[4] Coal accounted for 3 percent of total exports in 1871–75, rising to 6 percent in 1886–90. It was ranked third in export value in 1898, fourth in 1908, and sixth in 1913. Summarizing their findings, Yamamoto Yūzō and Oku Kazuyoshi note that as top earners until the First World War

Table 2.1 Mineral output in Japan, 1874–1908

Year	Gold (in troy oz)	Silver (in troy oz)	Copper (in long tons)	Coal (in long tons)
1874	3,129	87,890	2,078.5	204,864
1875	5,598	224,842	2,363.1	558,288
1876	7,147	280,892	3,135.3	537,011
1877	11,264	355,126	3,884.2	491,835
1878	3,764	318,017	4,194.1	669,866
1879	3,402	202,172	4,562.4	815,057
1880	9,925	332,406	4,600.8	865,201
1881	9,792	574,270	4,701.4	911,720
1882	8,736	558,783	5,533.4	915,676
1883	9,669	775,840	6,674.8	987,818
1884	8,630	736,321	8,758.3	1,123,330
1885	8,811	766,360	10,396.4	1,274,775
1886	14,937	1,083,057	9,630.9	1,354,190
1887	16,739	1,024,608	10,901.1	1,720,909
1888	20,230	1,374,113	13,179.3	1,893,970
1889	24,709	1,381,497	16,015.5	2,353,849
1890	23,362	1,699,029	17,849.5	2,580,997
1891	23,217	1,886,324	18,754.6	3,120,581
1892	22,523	1,936,753	20,423.5	3,129,409
1893	23,676	2,226,825	17,750.8	3,274,244
1894	25,260	2,328,131	19,622.5	4,214,253
1895	40,808	2,323,673	18,834.4	4,718,914
1896	30,928	2,068,864	19,784.8	4,946,568
1897	33,617	1,745,657	20,091.5	5,131,628
1898	39,303	1,943,362	20,715.9	6,640,469
1899	58,654	1,805,879	23,920.6	6,653,476
1900	80,596	1,890,716	24,938.9	7,362,801
1901	101,683	1,760,158	26,990.0	8,879,511
1902	143,993	1,852,067	29,144.0	9,656,295
1903	139,623	1,884,162	32,111.0	10,021,893
1904	132,814	1,977,756	31,653.0	10,619,026
1905	148,645	2,678,511	34,975.0	11,467,845
1906	132,936	2,543,774	37,950.0	12,892,721
1907	134,153	3,091,022	39,556.0	13,736,182
1908	168,883	3,993,061	41,113.0	14,761,476

Source: Bureau of Mines, *Mining in Japan Past and Present* (Tokyo: Bureau of Mines, 1909), p. 54.

copper and coal improved the balance of international trade, while at the same time making possible the purchases of items necessary to promote industrial growth.[5]

That mining could impact so powerfully on economic growth and on the physical environment reflects in part its own rapid transformation through the application of advanced technology. As Japan entered the modern era, the remarkable expansion of mining that had begun in the mid-sixteenth century had faded, in part as a result of technological barriers.[6] Even in the areas of dressing and smelting, where Japanese methods were relatively sophisticated, innovation was hampered by a political system that restricted information transfer within Japan

Table 2.2 Exports of copper and coal, 1868–95
(in 1000s of yen and % of total exports)

Year	Copper	Coal
1868–70	119 (1)	188 (1)
1871–75	740 (4)	571 (3)
1876–80	615 (2)	852 (3)
1881–85	1,093 (3)	1,485 (4)
1886–90	3,218 (5)	3,375 (6)
1891–95	4,906 (5)	5,665 (6)

Source: Sugiyama, Shinya, "Kokusai Kankyō to Gaikoku Bōeki," in Umemura and Yamamoto (eds), *Kaikoku to Ishin*, pp. 196–97.

and access to new technologies developed abroad. By the end of the nineteenth century, however, the situation had changed dramatically. Supported by the pro-industrial policies of the Meiji government, mining was transformed by new technologies, many of them adopted from the West. Modern pumps, lighting, and ventilation systems, blasting equipment, and transportation devices allowed easier access to ores; new metallurgical processes significantly raised the level of extraction. Rapid, thoroughgoing technological change on Western lines thus powered the explosive development of mining in the first half-century of Japan's modern era.

If the fact of technological transformation in mining is uncontroversial, attempts to explain and characterize are part of a broader debate on the origins and uses of technological development in modern and contemporary Japan. Tessa Morris-Suzuki notes that explanations of Japan's technological dynamism commonly point to a range of factors, including cultural and institutional conditions, high educational standards, technical skill and adaptability, the strength of business organizations, and the power of the state.[7] Morris-Suzuki organizes her own analysis of Japanese technology around three main themes. First, in analyzing the relationship between imitation and innovation, she argues that even the importation of foreign technology was rarely a simple matter of copying and more often a matter of creative adaptation that fostered Japanese research capacity. Second, while recognizing the roles of government and big businesses at the political and economic center, she notes also the importance of small firms and local communities on the "periphery." Finally, she highlights the social context of innovation, in other words, the networks that linked research and production centers in Japanese society.

This chapter attempts to identify some characteristics of the uses of technology in modern Japan by examining the development of a modern copper mining industry. Relying especially on a series of official reports issued for international readers, it draws examples from present-day Akita prefecture in the Tōhoku region, where the mines of Osarizawa and Ani dominated copper production from the early modern era and where Kosaka grew from the 1860s to become, as a 1909 Bureau of Mines report declared, "the largest mine in the Far East." At least two phases can be identified. During the first phase, from the 1850s through to about 1885, the transformation of mining was powered by the direct importation of Western technology, particularly into government-owned mines. In the second phase, from the 1890s through to about 1915, a rising generation of private mine owners combined aggressive management techniques with persistent technological innovation to achieve continuously expanding production.

What does the history of copper mining suggest about technological change in modern Japan? This chapter makes three points, of which the first two relate to themes addressed by Morris-Suzuki. Concerning the issue of imitation and innovation, it argues that, although Western technology transformed mining in the second half of the nineteenth century, knowledge and practices developed in Japan before and during the modern era were also critically important. With regard to the relative contributions of center and periphery, it highlights the roles of actors at the political and economic center – first government and then mining companies – in making the huge investments in machinery, technical expertise, and infrastructure necessary for the rapid modernization of Japanese mines. The third point relates to the beliefs that underlay this effort. The history of mining suggests that a firm and widespread confidence in technology provided energy for its continuing application while at the same time diverting attention from negative social or environmental consequences. I will return to all three points in the conclusion.

Mining before the modern era

Although an aggressive mining industry played a crucial role in supporting economic growth in Japan's modern era, it was not for the first time. Japan's first mining boom was set in motion by warring *daimyō*, stimulated by the expansion in foreign trade that followed the arrival of European merchants in East Asia in the mid-sixteenth century. Between 1540 and 1600 at least 14 major gold, silver, and copper mines were opened on and around the island of Honshū.[8] Silver was mined at Ikuno and Iwami, both in western Honshū, silver and gold were extracted on Sadō off north-western Honshū, and there were gold mines in Izu and in the Tōhoku region. Japanese silver, in particular, supported a thriving silk import trade from the mid-sixteenth century.[9] The growth in mining was supported by the application of new technologies. In smelting, for example, the "Southern-barbarian squeezing" (*nanban shibori*), a liquation method[10] that was probably learned from the Europeans, improved the extraction of silver from copper ores.[11] By the end of the sixteenth century, Japan was the biggest exporter of silver in Asia. The boom continued into the opening decades of the early modern or Tokugawa era (1600–1867), with the Tokugawa Shogun and regional *daimyō* claiming much of the output. Even after Portuguese traders were expelled in the 1630s, a limited international trade was continued with Dutch, Chinese, and Korean merchants.

The boom in silver and gold peaked in the early seventeenth century, and then faded. By the mid-eighteenth century, domestic sources of both were mostly depleted – at the very time that precious metals were increasingly in demand for currency. The Tokugawa government responded by importing silver and gold for currency while boosting copper production at new and existing mines.[12] Copper was mined at Besshi, in Shikoku, in a modest way at Ashio, and most successfully in the Tōhoku sites of Ani and Osarizawa, in what is now Akita prefecture. Ani, for instance, started as a silver mine around 1575.[13] Soon afterwards, gold was discovered, and silver and gold alternated in importance in the seventeenth century. Meanwhile, copper production began in about 1622, expanded significantly from the 1660s, and by the turn of the eighteenth century dominated the regional economy. In 1702 the Satake *daimyō* of Akita domain took over the direct management of the Ani copper mine. By the 1730s Akita domain was the largest producer of copper in Japan, and Ani was Akita's richest source.

Ani's closest rival in the Tōhoku region was Osarizawa, across the mountains to the east in Morioka domain.[14] Osarizawa began as a gold mine around 1598 – one of a supposed total of 124 gold mines that was regarded as bringing prosperity to the Nanbu *daimyō* of Morioka in the first half of the seventeenth century. Drainage problems persisted from the late 1630s, and gold yields dropped. In 1672, however, a private contractor received permission to mine copper in the area and several gold mines switched to copper. Around 1710, the Nanbu government took nominal control of the Osarizawa mine, and from 1715 it sent copper to Nagasaki to meet Tokugawa-imposed quotas.

The examples of Ani and Osarizawa point to some of the strengths and weaknesses of mining technology in the Edo period. The weaknesses are most apparent in the extraction of ore, where technologies were crude – and well behind those currently available in Western Europe. Japanese mine operators made little use of mechanical devices even when (as in the case of pumps) they were available.[15] At Osarizawa, for instance, miners literally chiseled their way into the mountain, crushed the rock by hand, and carried it out in woven baskets. Above ground, women workers normally picked out the large bits of precious metal from the rock; the remainder was pounded to a grit of about 5 mm and then subjected to jigging in shallow willow or bamboo baskets (*zaruage*) that left the heavy (valuable) matter at the bottom for smelting.[16] Because the chiseling was done by hand, mine pits were narrow and barely timbered. Lighting and ventilation were poor. Nothing more complicated than the odd hole in a tunnel provided ventilation. As late as 1879 a German engineer Curt Netto, who had been stationed at Kosaka, a relatively new mine near Osarizawa, complained that the use of oil encased in bamboo to provide light had a "considerable effect in fouling the air."[17] The worst problems, however, were with water. Netto commented on the "miserable condition" of drainage, noting there was little deep mining because there was no machinery to put in shafts and nothing more than a crude wooden hand-pump to drain the bottom of the mine. If a mine was flooded, it was often simply abandoned.

The strengths of Japanese mining in the early modern era lay in the dressing and smelting processes. Sasaki Junnosuke estimated that, including the *nanban shibori*, some seven methods of metal refining were available in the sixteenth and seventeenth centuries.[18] But even here there were problems. The processes of roasting and smelting used massive amounts of fuel, contributing significantly to the problem of deforestation.[19] Moreover, since the actual operation of mines was left to contractors and subcontractors who worked under limited-term licenses and paid a percentage of their profits to *daimyō* or Shogun, there was no particular incentive to work a mine after the going became tough.[20] A flood or deforestation meant that a mine might be abandoned, perhaps to be started up again a generation or two later. By the end of the eighteenth century, output at both Ani and Osarizawa was in decline.

The transformation of mining in the modern era (to 1885)

When Japan embarked upon economic and military modernization in the second half of the nineteenth century, the strategic importance of mining had already marked it for special attention. In the final years of the Tokugawa regime, mining had been drawn into a newly pressing campaign to secure national defense.[21] Sensing the need to upgrade their military capacity to prepare for the inevitable encroachment of the Western powers, the Tokugawa and some *daimyō* governments ordered the construction of Western-style furnaces capable of casting iron for making cannon. In 1855, a group of samurai gathered in Saga domain in Kyūshū to build a reverberatory furnace based on a somewhat dated Dutch text. By 1868 there were at least 11 furnaces built or under construction in various parts of Japan. Even more impressively, in 1857, a samurai named Ōshima Takatō (1826–1901) built on his experience in the Saga project to construct a blast furnace at Kamaishi in his native Nanbu domain (present-day Iwate prefecture). These and similar events – part of the first officially sponsored comprehensive effort to introduce Western "hard" technology – mark the starting-point of the modern era in Japanese mining.

More striking progress came after the establishment of the Meiji government in 1868. Ownership of several established mines passed easily from the Tokugawa Shogun and *daimyō* to the Meiji government, whose approach to mining in the 1870s paralleled its policies in other targeted sectors such as communications. For around a decade, it managed the mines directly from the Bureau of Mines in the Ministry of Industry (Kōbushō), using its limited capital resources to introduce foreign technology, improve management, and stimulate production during the precarious early years of industrialization.[22] Initially, government efforts focused on the large gold, silver, and iron mines from the early modern era: Sado gold mine, silver-producing Ikuno and Innai in present-day Hyōgo and Akita prefectures respectively, and the Kamaishi ironworks. In 1870 it took control of the Kosaka silver mine, newly opened up by Nanbu domain just four years earlier. In 1873 government ownership extended to the newly developing coal industry, beginning with the Miike Coal Mine in Kyūshū; 11 sites in all were taken over that year. The impetus came in part from a January 1873 petition from Finance Minister Inoue Kowashi, who argued that, because of the urgent need for currency, mines were the "most important resource of the empire."[23] The Mining Law issued in 1873 stipulated that all new mine discoveries would become government property. In 1875 the government moved into copper, with the purchase of Ani mine in Akita prefecture.

Government ownership did not extend to the entire mining industry; nor did the expenditure of its capital resources result in an immediate jump in production. In the lifetime of the Ministry of Industry (1870–85), the government took over a total of 3 coal mines, 2 ironworks, and 6 gold, silver, and copper mines. Between 1877 and 1881, government-owned mines produced more than half of Japan's gold and silver but less than 10 percent of copper. Some of the richest holdings, such as the Takashima coal mine (which had been managed jointly by the Nabeshima family of Saga and the Scottish merchant Thomas Glover), were taken over in 1874, only to be sold off again within months. But developing even those holdings demanded – and received – a sizeable financial commitment. Figures published in 1879 showed that running costs through 1877, including purchases of equipment, far exceeded the value of mine output in all government-held mines, except for coal.[24] Between 1870 and 1885, some 31.5 percent of ordinary expenditures in the Ministry of Industry went to mining, second only to the 49.9 percent devoted to railways. In 1875 and 1876 payments to mining reached a peak at more than 1 million yen annually before dropping significantly as a result of competing fiscal pressures.[25] However, following administrative reform and the 1878 issue of government bonds as a separate source of funds for industrial promotion, payments to mining were set at 1.7 million yen, again second only to the almost 2.5 million yen for railways.[26] Of the mining budget, by far the largest amount was set aside for the Ani copper mine.

Government capital resources were spent heavily on the introduction of Western technology. Initially, this was accomplished through the hire of foreign engineers, who were invited to Japan on limited contracts to serve as advisors at specific mines.[27] Between 1870 and 1885, some 78 foreign engineers (including 35 British, 24 French, and 15 Germans) worked at Japanese mines.[28] For example, J.G.H. Godfrey was Mining Engineer in Chief from 1871 through 1877.[29] From 1873 to 1877, Curt Netto (1847–1909), a university-trained engineer from Freiburg, was stationed at Kosaka.[30] Alexis Janin, a German-born American, worked at Sado, also from 1873 to 1877. Another German, Adolf Mekkel, came to Ani as part of a team in 1879.[31] The distinguished mining expert Francisque Coignet (1835–1902) headed a group of French engineers at Ikuno. Although contracts with the foreigners did not usually include commitments to specific technology or equipment, their presence meant that in practice foreign methods were adopted and imported machines installed.

The Western-inspired improvements of these early years focused on modernizing mine structure and systematizing procedures. Uchida Hoshimi notes that the foreign advisers oversaw construction of comprehensive systems of mine passages with galleries wide enough to accommodate machines and dynamite.[32] They improved methods of ventilation and illumination and made it possible to dig deep by putting in vertical shafts using steam-powered machines for drainage. They reorganized the smelting operations, allowing customized treatment for different types of ores, and introduced power-driven machines for specific stages in the refining process. The foreigners also introduced some "new" smelting processes, such as the amalgamation method of separating silver and gold from other ores, known in the West since at least the sixteenth century and introduced at Sado by Janin. They encouraged the construction of better transportation systems for handling ores and timber, and they were able to use their geological knowledge for prospecting.

Uchida concludes, somewhat ironically, that since Japanese mining (and particularly metallurgy) was already at a fairly high level, it was possible to implement a new design, add in steam power and dynamite to old methods, and call the result a modern mine.[33] Yet the transformation of some mines was remarkable. Consider, for example, the Kosaka mine, which entered the modern era as a remote and barely exploited silver mine in a group of hills rising some 1,100–1,200 feet above sea level in Akita prefecture.[34] Taken over by Nanbu domain in 1866, it was managed briefly by the samurai Ōshima Takatō, who used his experience in furnace construction to build a mill and Western-style smelting and cupelling furnaces. The Meiji Restoration of 1868 halted operations, but modernization resumed after 1870 when Kosaka became a government mine (with Ōshima as manager), and especially after the 26-year-old Curt Netto was appointed as an advisor in 1873. Since silver could be extracted from the oxidized or "earthy" ore at shallow levels by a relatively simple, open-cut method, Netto did not need to work on deep excavation. Instead, his focus was metallurgy and overall plant modernization. Building on the reforms begun by Ōshima, he built new furnaces and introduced the latest European treatments, including the Ziervogel process (to extract silver from silver sulphate) and the Hunt and Douglas process (to extract copper from slag). In 1876 another German engineer brought 400 tons of equipment and firebricks by ship and overland from Yokohama. After the new plant began operation in 1877, Netto was able to extract as much as 75 percent of silver and 45 percent of the copper from the ore – three times higher than the level reached by Ōshima.

The rapid pace of change in government-owned mines fueled a sense of optimism about the future of Japanese mining. Especially among the early foreign engineers, there were hopes that the application of modern methods might produce vast riches in a land known to have yielded large amounts of gold and silver in the past. (Coignet wrote a booklet in 1874 entitled "Note sur la Richesse Minerale du Japon.") However, overall production figures were not dramatic, at least in the early years. Table 2.1 shows that neither gold nor silver made major gains in the 1870s. Copper production roughly doubled in the five years from 1874 but mostly in private mines that had not undergone major renovation. Only coal production, which grew about four times in the same five-year period, was impressive.

A sober estimate of the prospects of Japanese mining was offered by Curt Netto in a booklet *On Mining and Mines in Japan* written in 1879, just two years after he left his position at Kosaka. As professor of mining and metallurgy at the University of Tokyo, the former government mine advisor warned that Japan's mineral resources were not inexhaustible and that Edo period miners had been more thorough than the foreigners had expected. He pointed out that private mine owners had difficulty in raising capital for improvements, that use of foreign capital was severely restricted, and that the impact of the government's investment was limited by the fact that it had not necessarily chosen the best mines to revamp. Netto urged even more careful and "rational" exploitation. He argued that, in order to compete on international markets, Japan's mines needed more money, more modern technology, better transportation, and better organization, especially in the private sector. Ways had to be found to replace human labor with machines, use fuel more economically, train managers in modern methods, and instill discipline in workers. Finally, Netto concluded that Japan's mining potential lay not in gold and silver but in the newer areas of copper and coal.

Although Netto linked future advances in Japanese mining with its capacity to modernize on Western lines, he was aware – and his own experience confirmed – that the days of foreign consultants were over. Not only were the hiring costs expensive, but communication raised problems, and in some cases the foreign changes had less than optimal results. Moreover, although Netto argued vigorously in his book for the need to get more, cheaper, and more accessible fuel, he did not mention that his own modernization efforts at Kosaka proved so costly in fuel and wages that the national government had discharged him in 1877 and transferred the mine back to the former Nanbu *daimyō*. By the late 1870s, most foreign experts had been released. Their places were taken by Japanese engineers, who had to select and use the new technology and negotiate contracts for further purchases.[35] A few of these men had studied mining metallurgy abroad; most received their education in newly established engineering schools, such as the Imperial College of Engineering (Kōbu Daigakko) which had been set up in 1873 with active British participation and was later incorporated into Tokyo University. The level of their education explains the relative ease with which they were able to adopt and adapt mining technology.

The phasing out of direct foreign consultants was followed by the sale of government mines to private companies and the 1885 disbandment of the Ministry of Industry.[36] Driven by fiscal pressures, the Ministry had prepared for the sales from 1882. In 1884, Kosaka mine (which had been returned to the central government in 1880) was sold to Fujita-gumi, an Osaka-based company founded just three years earlier by three brothers of the Fujita (Kuhara) family. Natives of Yamaguchi prefecture, the Fujita brothers had personal connections with influential members of the government; Kuhara Shōzaburō negotiated the purchase of Kosaka and nearby Towada mines for 200,000 yen, to be repaid over 25 years.[37] The mines' 66 staff members and 710 miners became employees of Fujita-gumi. Returning as head of the mine was former samurai Ōshima Takatō who had spent some of the interim years in government service which had included inspecting refineries in Germany. Furukawa Ichibei (1832–1903), owner of Ashio mine since 1877, bought Ani (for 250,000 yen) and Innai in 1885.[38] Ikuno and Sado remained in government hands until 1896, when both were sold to Mitsubishi.

The shift from public to private ownership and from foreign to Japanese personnel coincided with a clear, across-the-board upturn in mine output. After purchasing Kosaka, Fujita-gumi increased its capital from 60,000 to 200,000 yen and invested heavily in skilled labor and related equipment. By 1888 Kosaka had overtaken the government-owned Ikuno mine to become Japan's top producer of silver; it remained among the top three positions through to 1897.[39] Table 2.1 shows that production increases in gold, silver, and copper accelerated, especially after about 1885. Coal showed steady increases throughout the decade of the 1880s. Both were important income earners. Sugiyama Shinya's analysis of foreign trade data for the period 1868–95 underscores the importance of coal and copper as sources of export income during the 1880s and 1890s. As shown in Table 2.2, coal exports, valued at 852,000 yen (or 3 percent of all exports) for the years 1876–80, reached 3,375,000 yen (or 6 percent of all exports) in 1886–90 and 5,665,000 yen in 1891–95. Copper increased from 615,000 yen (or 2 percent of all exports) in 1876–80 to 3,218,000 yen (or 5 percent of all exports) in 1886–90, and 4,906,000 yen in 1891–95. The chief markets for both were in Asia, notably China and Hong Kong. In the 1891–95 period, Japan's most important export industries, measured as a percentage of total value, were, in order, raw silk (36 percent), tea (8 percent), and silk, coal, and rice (6 percent each), copper (5 percent), and silk textiles (4 percent). Cotton textiles were still a mere 1 percent.

The golden years: mining and private enterprise (to the end of the Meiji era)

With the shift to private ownership in the mid-1880s, Japanese mining entered a period of sustained expansion that went well beyond Curt Netto's cautious optimism. Companies such as Fujita, Furukawa, Mitsubishi, and Mitsui competed to introduce new technologies and expand production. Table 2.1 shows that the gains in all four sectors – gold, silver, copper, and coal – continued through to 1908. Murakami Yasumasa and Hara Kazuhito have calculated that between 1880 and 1900 alone, output of gold increased 6.8 times, silver 5.7 times, copper 5.2 times, and coal by an astounding 8.5 times.[40]

Japan's progress in mining was reported in several English-language publications issued by the Bureau of Mines, which had been moved to the Ministry of Agriculture and Commerce in 1886, after the dissolution of the Ministry of Engineering. In 1893, for instance, a 25-year history of the mining industry since 1868 was published by the Bureau's director, Wada Tsunashiro (1856–1920). Further English-language reports issued by the Bureau included one in 1909 (perhaps in conjunction with the 1908 International Mining Exposition held in New York) and another for the World's Panama Pacific Exposition held in San Francisco in 1915. Each of these publications reflected pride in the achievements of Japan's mining industry and optimism about its future.

Wada Tsunashiro's own career reflected the new educational opportunities in mining available in Meiji Japan. Student, and then teacher, at government schools, he became professor of mining and geology at Tokyo University on its foundation in 1877, together with Curt Netto. Wada combined a long scholarly career with fieldwork and government service. His 1893 history of mining was published in Japanese and in English translation under the title *The Mining Industry of Japan during the Last Twenty Five Years 1867–1892*.

Unlike Netto, Wada saw few limitations on the future of Japan's mining. Recalling the writings of Marco Polo and Japan's historic association with mineral wealth, he declared contemporary resources to be "something enormous" and "almost inexhaustible."[41] He described the transformation from early government use of expensive foreign technology to the present-day competition among private companies for good mines, good engineers, and modern technology while at the same time generating profits. Wada especially commended Furukawa Ichibei, owner of Ashio copper mine since 1878, for his success in restoring an almost defunct mine to profitability and raising general interest in mining. Wada could not have been unaware of the water pollution at Ashio – in 1891 villagers had unsuccessfully petitioned the national government to close the mine temporarily and Tanaka Shōzō had made a speech on their behalf to the Diet – but he made no mention of such problems.[42] Among the main technological improvements of the era of privatization, Wada listed compressed-air rock drills and dynamite for blasting; wire-rope trams; Huntington mills for crushing ore; ore concentrators; magnetic separators for iron sand; new types of furnaces, boilers, engines, and turbines; and the use of hydro-electricity at Ashio since 1889.

Wada's evaluations were echoed in a 1909 report published by the Bureau of Mines under the title *Mining in Japan Past and Present*. The customary historical overview was followed by a discussion of new developments since the 1890s, mostly in smelting: the use of the Bessemer process in copper smelting, the construction of custom smelters, the use of cyaniding for leaching out gold in Kagoshima in 1897, the mechanical roasting introduced at Ashio copper mine in 1900, pyritic smelting adopted at Kosaka in 1901, and the adoption of pot-roasting at all of the major copper mines.[43] As a result of the new equipment and processes, mines became larger, power usage multiplied, and the total value of mineral products in Japan rose from 154,690 pounds sterling in 1874 to 11,638,667 pounds in 1908. As reasons for such rapid progress, the report cited: (1) the model works with foreign expertise established by the early Meiji government; (2) the education of Japanese experts; (3) privatization; (4) mining legislation; and (5) the use of hydro-electricity.

The Bureau of Mines report prepared for the 1915 Panama Pacific Exposition in San Francisco offers a snapshot view of Japanese mining at the end of the Meiji era. The report indicated that overall increases in mine output continued until the outbreak of First World War. Setting total value of mineral output at 100 for the years 1874–83, it calculated that for 1884–93 the comparable figure was 249, for 1894–1903 it was 893, and for 1904–13 the figure was 2,402 (see Table 2.3). Note that these figures covered the Japanese Empire and were therefore enhanced by the addition of output from Korean and Taiwanese mines. Total value of mineral production for 1913 was 172,108,829 yen, an increase of 109,550,408 over the previous ten years. Coal (72 million yen) and copper (43 million yen) were the most important followed by iron, petroleum, gold, and silver. While stressing the enormous growth of recent years, the report noted, however, that a shortage of investment capital was significantly limiting expansion.

Table 2.3 Value of output from Japanese mines

	Total output (in yen)	Index
1874–83	47,233,216	100
1884–93	117,584,292	249
1894–1903	421,979,213	893
1904–13	1,134,614,401	2,402

Source: The Imperial Bureau of Mines. *Mining Industry in Japan* (Tokyo, 1914). Prepared for the World Panama Pacific Exposition, San Francisco, CA, 1915, p. 3.

Table 2.4 Output and ownership of the main copper mines 1913

Name	Owner	Output (in thousand metric tons)
Ashio	Furukawa and Co.	10.4
Hitachi	Kuhara Mining Co.	9.8
Besshi	Baron Kichizaemon Sumitomo	7.6
Kosaka	Fujita and Co.	6.8
Osarizawa	Mitsubishi & Co.	2.1
Total of Top 5	36.7	
Ikuno	Mitsubishi & Co.	1.8

Source: The Imperial Bureau of Mines, *Mining Industry in Japan*, p. 25.

Of all mining sectors, developments in copper (and secondarily in coal) were introduced most enthusiastically in the official reports of the late Meiji era. The copper industry was dominated by aggressive, successful entrepreneurs; it attracted the most exciting new developments in the treatment of ores; and its expanded output had allowed it to remain profitable despite a significant price drop in the world market. Copper and coal were Japan's most valuable exports. As of 1913, there were 66 copper mines in the Japanese empire, of which the 6 largest are listed in Table 2.4. Ashio in Tochigi prefecture was the most productive, followed by Hitachi in nearby Hitachi, and Besshi in Ehime. Kosaka was in fourth place.

The output rankings point to some interesting shifts in relative prominence. Most obviously, they show that 50 years after the beginning of modernization the established copper mines of the Tōhoku region were no longer leading the industry. Despite early Westernization as a government model mine, and management by the energetic Furukawa Ichibei, copper output at Ani was growing only slowly at the end of the Meiji era.[44] Problems such as winter access for freight limited expansion, and Ani ranked only tenth in 1913. Osarizawa ranked fifth, but a considerable gap separated it from the top four producers.

By contrast, the appearance in fourth place of Osarizawa's near neighbor Kosaka points to an interesting episode in the development of a modern copper industry. It also suggests some of the challenges met and specific or local solutions found in the process of technological innovation. Kosaka had faced a series of challenges since its discovery as a silver mine in the 1860s. It had been thoroughly modernized by Curt Netto in the 1870s only to encounter a shortage of economically priced fuel necessary for firing the new, high-temperature furnaces. After Netto was discharged in 1877, the Japanese managers who replaced him had to find a more cost-efficient method of treating the ores. Success came in 1881 with the introduction of a chlorination process that used salt under lower temperatures thereby reducing the amount of smelting and fuel necessary for precipitating silver. Repeated improvements on this method reduced costs and raised efficiency. By 1891 Kosaka engineers had reached an extraction percentage that surpassed Netto's, of 78.59 percent for silver and 70.43 percent for copper.

In the 1890s, yet another challenge emerged. Silver supplies were running out from the layers of "earthy" ore and the Kosaka mine was facing closure. The solution, found in 1900, revolutionized mining operations at Kosaka.[45] For the first time in Japan, Takeda Kyosaku (1867–1945), an engineer who had studied German mines, succeeded in using the pyritic ore surrounding the deeper layers of *kuroko* ("black ore") to smelt the copper contained in the unoxidized, and hitherto unused, sections of the rock. With this success, a new series of open-cut mines was built to access the black *kuroko*, and Kosaka changed from being a primarily silver mine to becoming a major copper producer. In 1907 it became Japan's most productive copper mine; in 1908 it yielded 7,086 long tons of copper, more than Ashio's 6,972 long tons and more than any other Japanese competitor. In 1909 the Bureau of Mines declared Kosaka to be in its "golden age."[46]

Still, there were difficulties. As with Ani, access to fuel was a challenge. Wada Tsunashiro had written in 1893 that since coal was too expensive to transport, the mine depended on charcoal (brought in by horse) and wood – from nearby, but fast diminishing, forests.[47] In 1904, access was improved when a rail link to the mine was established, but there were more immediate environmental problems. The transformation of Kosaka into a modern productive mine had been accompanied by the release of increasing concentrations of sulphur into the atmosphere, stripping trees of their foliage, and compromising human health. The Bureau of Mines reports paid scant attention to the negative environmental consequences of the new mining methods: the 1909 report noted proudly that the Kosaka chimney was 200 feet high. It did not report that in the previous year residents of Kosaka and five neighboring communities had written to the governor of Akita prefecture to protest the pollution of their air by the mine.[48] That petition was neither the first nor the last in a series of public protests that continued into the 1920s.

The successes and problems of the Kosaka mine were paralleled, and even magnified, at Hitachi and Ashio, which surpassed Kosaka to become Japan's top-producing mines by the end of the Meiji era. Located in the northern Kantō region, both were old mines, but neither had seen significant exploitation until the Meiji era. Ashio was vast, consisting of more than 100 veins that were accessed with the help of three deep shafts. Under Furukawa Ichibei's management, it was the first Japanese mine to use hydro-electricity, and its advanced smelting processes allowed the highest levels of extraction. Hitachi, too, had developed fast, introducing pyritic smelting to replace the older style of roasting ore. At Hitachi and, even more, at Ashio, the environmental costs of development were apparent. Japan's most modern and productive copper mines were thus responsible for the country's first major encounter with industrial pollution.

Conclusion

What does the modern transformation of mining suggest about the history of technological change in Japan? As Uchida Hoshimi points out in his essay on technology transfers, the first important transfers – from the ancient world up to the Renaissance – were not from the West but from China, India, and the Mediterranean.[49] Much of Japan's very early mining technology originated in China. Technology transfers from Europe were set in motion in the sixteenth century, when the adoption of new technology in shipbuilding, firearms, and navigation made the voyages of exploration possible. The sixteenth-century boom in so-called "traditional" Japanese mining was part of this movement. Japan received Western techniques, such as the *nanban shibori* method of smelting, and incorporated them into an evolving body of knowledge and practices. By the end of the Tokugawa era, Japanese mining was highly sophisticated – a sophistication built, however, not on machines but on human capital.

The nineteenth-century transformation of Japanese mining was different. It was inspired by the political need to match Western military and economic might, and its first rule was to take advantage of Western, machine-based technology. Thus, in one sense, what occurred was the rapid and radical reinvention of mining based on the straightforward and highly successful incorporation of Western knowledge and practices. But the process was by no means simple. Let me conclude by returning to the three characteristics of the technological transformation of mining in modern Japan.

First, it is evident that the transformation of Japanese mining did not take place by simple substitution of new (Western) practices for old (Japanese) ones. Since the sixteenth century, Japan had participated in international markets for gold, silver, and copper. It entered the modern era with a substantial fund of knowledge about ores, techniques for treating them, and distinctive labor practices that had developed in mines such as Sado, Ikuno, Ani, and Osarizawa. The new information and techniques brought from the West after the mid-nineteenth century became part of this fund. The transformation was thus not a simple "transfer" but a more organic process by which new approaches were incorporated into an existing set of non-Western and non-modern but nevertheless sophisticated practices. Moreover, although the early period of technology transfer, through to the mid-1880s, came by way of foreign instructors, foreign textbooks, and foreign study, direct dependence on foreign technology was relatively short, and it was conditional. The history of Kosaka mine shows that even in this early period some of the most important breakthroughs were made by individual Japanese engineers responding to specific local conditions or attempting to fix new problems caused by the adoption of Western techniques. The transformation of Kosaka – in particular, the use of chlorination from 1881 to reduce the need for fuel and the invention of pyritic copper smelting from the 1890s – shows a pragmatic willingness and ability to adapt and reinvent and suggests that "Western" technology became "Japanese" technology within a single generation.

A second characteristic concerns the driving forces behind the transformation of Japanese mining in the modern era. Mining, like railways, shipping and other basic industries, required enormous quantities of new information, techniques, energy, and labor. Meeting these needs was, of course, expensive. Like its Tokugawa predecessor, the Meiji government was from the beginning convinced of the strategic and economic importance of mining. Unlike its predecessor, it was also committed to the rapid and radical transformation of mining through the application of the best technology. Until the early 1880s, this commitment was reflected in the purchase of model mines, the hiring of foreign advisors, the purchase of foreign equipment, and the setting up of educational institutions to train Japanese mining engineers. Fiscal pressures brought an early end to direct government management, but the new private owners of the mines – companies such as Furukawa and Co. and Kuhara Mining Co. – showed an equally strong commitment to increasing output through ongoing technological innovation.

This belief in modern technology shared across government and industry brings me to the final characteristic of technological change in modern Japanese mining: the destruction that was not creative. So focused were private mining companies on maximizing production that they paid little attention to the social and environmental consequences of the new methods they were using. And so convinced was the Japanese government of the importance of mining that it paid little heed to complaints. When the consequences became evident, as in Ashio and Kosaka, it took more than a decade for industry and government leaders to acknowledge the scale of the problem. In this, Japanese industry leaders and those who supported them were not necessarily different from their Western contemporaries.

Notes

1 Conrad Totman, *A History of Japan* (2nd edn, Malden, MA: Blackwell Publishing, 2005), pp. 342–45, 405–06.
2 There is much written about the Ashio pollution incident. See F.G. Notehelfer, "Japan's First Pollution Incident," *Journal of Japanese Studies* 1, 2, Spring 1975, pp. 351–83; Kazuo Niimura in Andrew Gordon (ed.), *The Ashio Riot of 1907: A Social History of Mining in Japan* (Durham, NC: Duke University Press, 1997); Julian Gresser, Koichiro Fujikura and Akio Morishima (eds), *Environmental Law in Japan* (Cambridge, MA: MIT Press, 1981); Kichiro Shoji and Masuro Sugai, "The Ashio Copper Mine Pollution Case: The Origins of Environmental Destruction," in Jun Ui (ed.), *Industrial Pollution in Japan* (Tokyo: United Nations University Press, 1992), pp. 18–63.
3 See also Totman, *History of Japan*, pp. 312–13.
4 Yamamoto, Yūzō and Oku, Kazuyoshi, "Bōeki," in Nishikawa, Shunsaku, and Yamamoto, Yūzō (eds), *Sangyōka no Jidai* 2, vol. 5 of *Nihon Keizaishi* (Tokyo: Iwanami Shoten, 1990), p. 103.

5 Ibid., p. 104.
6 See Tessa Morris-Suzuki, *The Technological Transformation of Japan from the Seventeenth to the Twenty-First Century* (Cambridge: Cambridge University Press, 1994), pp. 43–49; also notes 8–20.
7 Ibid., p. 4.
8 This overview of mining is derived from Sasaki, Junnosuke, "Kōgyō ni okeru Gijutsu no Hatten," in Sasaki (ed.), *Gijutsu no Shakaishi 2* (Tokyo: Yūhikaku, 1983), pp. 178–224; Kobata, Atsushi, *Nihon Kōzan Shi no Kenkyū* (Tokyo: Iwanami Shoten, 1968), pp. 3–44; Robert LeRoy Innes, *The Door Ajar: Japan's Foreign Trade in the Seventeenth Century*, PhD dissertation, University of Michigan (Ann Arbor, MI: University Microfilms International, 1980), pp. 532–72. See also Morris-Suzuki, *Technological Transformation of Japan*, pp. 43–49.
9 Tashiro, Kazui, "Tokugawa jidai no bōeki," in Hayami, Akira and Miyamoto, Matao (eds), *Keizai Shakai no Seiritsu 17–18 Seiki*, vol. 1 of *Nihon Keizaishi* (Tokyo: Iwanami Shoten, 1990), pp. 132–33, 137. See also Kazui Tashiro "Foreign Relations during the Edo Period: *Sakoku* Reexamined," *Journal of Japanese Studies* 8, Summer 1982, pp. 283–306; Innes, "The Door Ajar," pp. 21–76, 244–85.
10 The term "liquation" was commonly used in nineteenth-century texts, but is broadly equivalent to "liquefaction."
11 Sasaki, Junnosuke, "Zenkindai Kōgyō no Seiritsu," in Sasaki (ed.), *Zairai Gijutsu no Hatten to Kinsei Shakai*, vol. 2 of *Gijutsu no shakaishi* (Tokyo: Yūhikaku, 1983), pp. 178–224. The description of smelting is on pp. 192–95.
12 Tashiro, "Tokugawa Jidai no Bōeki," pp. 149–55.
13 Details of the Ani mine can be found in Ani-chō Shi Hensan Iinkai (ed.), *Ani-chō Shi* (Ani: Ani-chō, 1992), pp. 663–777.
14 Fumoto, Saburō, "Osarizawa to sono Shuhen," in Chihōshi Kenkyū Kyōgikai (ed.), *Nihon Sangyō Taikei*, vol. 3 (Tokyo: University of Tokyo Press, 1960), pp. 235–52.
15 Morris-Suzuki, *Technological Transformation of Japan*, p. 44.
16 Fumoto, "Osarizawa to sono Shuhen," pp. 245–49.
17 Curt Netto, *On Mining and Mines in Japan* (Tokio: The University, 1879), pp. 9–11.
18 Sasaki, "Zenkindai Kōgyō no seiritsu," pp. 192–95.
19 Totman, *History of Japan*, pp. 254–56. See also Conrad Totman, *The Origins of Japan's Modern Forests: The Case of Akita* (Honolulu, HI: University of Hawaii Press, 1985), esp. pp. 13–22, on deforestation in Akita. Mining, as Totman points out (p. 9), was part of the problem.
20 Kobata, Atsushi, *Kōzan no Rekishi* (Tokyo: Shibundō, 1956), pp. 132–77.
21 Uchida, Hoshimi, "Gijutsu Iten," in Nishikawa, Shunsaku and Abe, Takeshi (eds), *Sangyō no Jidai 1*, vol. 4 of *Nihon Keizaishi* (Tokyo: Iwanami Shoten, 1990), pp. 255–302; Morris-Suzuki, *Technological Transformation of Japan*, pp. 55–67; Iida, Ken'ichi, "Yoshiki koro no Ishoku to Kamaishi Tetsuzan," in Chihō Kenkyū Kyōgikai (ed.), *Nihon Sangyō Shi Taikei 3, Tōhoku Chihōhen* (Tokyo: Tōkyō Shuppankai, 1960), pp. 333–61.
22 Suzuki, Jun (ed.), *Kōbushō to sono Jidai* (Tokyo: Yamakawa Shuppansha, 2000), and especially Suzuki's chapter "Kōbushō no Jūgonen," pp. 3–22. On government mine purchases see Furushima, Toshio, *Sangyōshi III*, in vol. 12 of *Taikei Nihonshi Sōsho* (Tokyo: Yamakawa Shuppansha, 1966), pp. 202–09; Takamura, Naosuke, "Kan'ei Kōzan to Kahei Genryō," in Suzuki, *Kōbushō to sono jidai*, pp. 177–86; Takamura Naosuke, "Kōzan Kan'ei Seisaku to Oyatoi Gaikokujin – Gottofurei-ra no Yakuwari," in Takamura (ed.), *Meiji Zenki no Nihon Keizai – Shihonshugi e no Michi* (Tokyo: Nihon Keizai Hyōronsha, 2004), pp. 105–19.
23 Takamura, "Kan'ei Kōzan to Kahei Genryō," p. 177.
24 Netto, *On Mining and Mines in Japan*, pp. 31–37.
25 Takamura, "Kōzan Kan'ei Seisaku," pp. 119–29. For details of the Ministry budget, see Kamiyama, Tsuneo, "Kan'ei Jigyō no Zaigen Kakuho," in Suzuki, *Kōbushō to sono Jidai*, pp. 23–56.

26 Takamura, "Kōzan Kan'ei Seisaku," p. 123. Actual disbursements to mining were somewhat lower, at almost 1.7 million yen for mining, and considerably higher, at almost 4.4 million yen, for railways. Umemura, Mataji and Yamamoto, Yūzō, "Gaisetsu 1860–85 nen," in Umemura and Yamamoto (eds), *Kaikoku to Ishin*, vol. 3 of *Nihon Keizai Shi* (Tokyo: Iwanami Shoten, 1989), p. 32, give slightly different figures.

27 Uchida, "Gijutsu Iten," pp. 265–72.

28 Koichi Ueda, "J.G.H. Godfrey and his Colleagues – Their Contribution to the Modernization of Japanese Non-ferrous Mining Industry in Early Meiji Era," paper presented at the International Mining History Association, Sapporo, Japan 2003.

29 Takamura, "Kōzan Kan'ei Seisaku," pp. 105–33.

30 Kosaka-chō Chō-shi Hensan Iinkai (ed.), *Kosaka-chō Shi* (Kosaka: Kosaka-chō, 1975), pp. 421–22.

31 Ani-chō Shi Hensan Iinkai (ed.), *Ani-chō Shi*, pp. 723–36.

32 Uchida, "Gijutsu Iten," pp. 292–93. See also Murakami, Yasumasa and Hara, Kazuhito, "Sangyō Kakumei no Nihonteki Tenkai," in Iida, Ken'ichi (ed.), *Gijutsu no Shakaishi* vol. 4, *Junkōgyōka no Tenkai to Mujun* (Tokyo:Yūhikaku, 1982), pp. 22–23; Tsunashiro Wada, *The Mining Industry of Japan During the Last Twenty Five Years 1867–1892* (Tokyo: Tokyo Tsukiji Type Foundry, 1893), pp. 4–7.

33 Uchida, "Gijutsu Iten," p. 293.

34 Overviews of mining at Kosaka can be found in *Kosaka-chō Shi*, pp. 389–549; Dōwa Kōgyō Kabushiki Gaisha (ed.), *Shichijūnen no Kaiko* (Tokyo: Dōwa Kōgyō Kabushiki Gaisha, 1955); Wada, *Mining Industry of Japan*, pp. 90–102.

35 Uchida, "Gijutsu Iten," pp. 272–82. See also Kakihara, Yasushi, "Kōbushō no Gijutsusha Yōsei," in Suzuki, *Kōbushō to sono Jidai*, pp. 77–82; Takamura, "Kōzan Kan'ei Seisaku," pp. 119–21.

36 Nishikawa, Makoto, "Sasaki Takayuki to Kōbushō," in Suzuki (ed.), *Kōbushō to sono Jidai*, pp. 229–60.

37 Dōwa Kōgyō KK, *Shichijūnen no Kaiko*, p. 22.

38 Ani-chō Shi Hensan Iinkai (ed.), *Ani-chō Shi*, pp. 736–40.

39 Dōwa Kōgyō KK, *Shichijūnen no Kaiko*, pp. 29–32.

40 "Sangyō Kakumei no Nihon-teki Tenkai," p. 21.

41 Wada Tsunashiro, *The Mining Industry of Japan during the Last Twenty Five Years 1867–1892* (Tokyo: Tokyo Tsukiji Type Foundry, 1893), p. 1.

42 For Furukawa's strategies and the pollution problem see Notehelfer, "Japan's First Pollution Incident," esp. pp. 365–83.

43 Bureau of Mines, Department of Agriculture and Commerce in Japan, *Mining in Japan Past and Present* (Tokyo: Bureau of Mines, Dept. of Agriculture and Commerce of Japan, 1909), pp. 31–35.

44 Ibid.

45 Ibid., pp. 172–78; Dōwa Kōgyō KK, *Shichijūnen no Kaiko*, pp. 32–35; *Kosaka-chō Shi*, pp. 424–45.

46 Bureau of Mines, *Mining in Japan Past and Present*, p. 173.

47 Wada, *Mining Industry of Japan*, pp. 99–100.

48 Kosaka-chō Cho-Shi Hensan Iinkai (ed.), *Kosaka-chō Shi*, p. 198ff.

49 Uchida, "Gijutsu Iten," pp. 255–302.

3 Professionalism as power

Tajiri Inajirō and the modernisation of Meiji finance

Katalin Ferber

The financial institutions of Meiji Japan – both the financial structures that emerged during this period and the assumptions behind them – were shaped by the professionalism and power of a newly educated generation, not encumbered by pre-Meiji institutional experience but equipped with an international outlook. Members of this generation enjoyed a special opportunity. By working for the state they were able to exercise power and help to modernise the financial institutions of Meiji Japan. By educating successive generations of leaders they were able to influence their thinking and shape the nation's future financial development.

These 'public men' were able to shape early modern Japan's financial institutions both in the short-term during their bureaucratic roles and in the long-term through their educational roles. To paraphrase the title of Andrew Barshay's book, *State and Intellectual in Imperial Japan*, they were both bureaucrats and teachers.[1] As one student of Tokyo Imperial University reminisced, 'professors were usually involved in work of one sort or another for the government, either officially or behind the scenes. We were often left gazing enviously at a professor's back as he went flying out to the rickshaw that had come to fetch him halfway through the lecture because, as he would say, "There's a cabinet meeting today" '.[2]

Scholars have largely overlooked the role of this generation, focusing instead on the 'great men' of the Meiji Restoration, financial leaders such as Matsukata Masayoshi (1835–1924), Ōkubo Toshimichi (1830–78) and Ōkuma Shigenobu (1838–1922). By contrast, in this chapter, I focus on a key example of how one person from this new generation, Tajiri Inajirō, used his knowledge – in this case of European financial theories of cameralism – to establish himself in the national government and thus shape, but also reconfirm, many of modern Japan's financial institutions.

Tajiri Inajirō (1850–1923) was a foreign-trained financial bureaucrat and scholar. He was an archetypal 'public man' of the Meiji era. Intensely honest and hard-working, he believed strongly in the need to develop the nation so that it could stand proudly amongst the great powers of the world.[3] Tajiri taught at two universities in Tokyo and also worked as a bureaucrat in the Ministry of Finance. He used his knowledge instrumentally to secure a piece of political power, which in turn allowed him to imprint that knowledge on the financial heart of the state's governmental and educational systems. For Japan, Tajiri's knowledge was dynamic, sophisticated and, most importantly, new. Unlike the 'great men', Tajiri was only 18 at the time of the restoration and had no significant experience of either the restoration itself or the pre-Meiji period. Moreover, while the Meiji government fought to achieve financial liquidity and pacify the political enemies of the restoration, Tajiri was in fact busy overseas acquiring his new knowledge. It is important to recognise, however, that Tajiri did not return to Japan and suddenly transform Japan's pre-Meiji institutions. In this chapter, I argue that Tajiri's role in modernising Japanese assumptions and ideas about finance was not revolutionary but evolutionary. Tajiri benefited from the fact that Meiji leaders had followed a kind of proto-cameralism when managing the finances of their domains before the Restoration. They had themselves emerged from an institutional context not dissimilar to Tajiri's. His ideas, therefore, though more sophisticated than those of his superiors, shared many common traits with those familiar to them from their pre-Meiji experiences. This meant that upon his return to Japan, Tajiri's thinking was welcomed rather than shunned, and his international knowledge soon allowed him entry into the elite circle of Meiji government. However, the fact that both leaders and ideas were already well-established imposed limitations on his political role. Though well-known academically, in the political world Tajiri had to keep in the shadows of the 'great men'. He had to work through others – to be a lieutenant to the generals of the Restoration – to introduce his ideas incrementally. In other words, Tajiri had to become one of Japan's earliest 'faceless bureaucrats'.

Tajiri's early life: from Kyoto to Hartford

Tajiri was born in Kyoto in 1850, the third child of a samurai family. When he was 6 years old his father died, and his family moved to Kagoshima in Satsuma, his father's home domain. This return to Satsuma was to help Tajiri later in life, because his first professional mentor, Yoshida Kiyonari (1845–92), whom he met when studying in the United States, was also from Satsuma.[4] Soon after starting private education and bushidō training, Tajiri witnessed his brother fighting against the British when they bombarded Kagoshima in 1863. He attended one of the Satsuma schools and then, in 1869, went to Tokyo and attended Fukuzawa Yukichi's school, the Keiō Gijuku.[5] Fukuzawa believed that without foreign knowledge and individual motivation modernisation would be impossible, and his privately established school was one of the few educational institutions of the time to offer English language courses as well as various other western subjects. Fukuzawa advocated the philosophy of 'learn to earn, earn to learn'.[6]

Tajiri's family had insufficient wealth to finance his studies, but as a talented student he was fortunate in being selected as one of three pupils from Satsuma to receive a scholarship. After the Restoration, the Ministry of Education regularly sent Japanese students abroad, especially to America and Britain, and between 1868 and 1870, 130 students received government funds to study overseas.[7] Students who were financed by the government could not stay abroad longer than 10 years, and there was an informal agreement that after returning to Japan they would work wherever the government thought their knowledge and experience were needed. Although the new government offered scholarships to the domains in 1870, Tajiri in fact left Japan as a student of the Satsuma navy, but his scholarship fund was soon changed into a government one, and the young Tajiri suddenly found himself on a special 'mission' to study in America.[8]

Tajiri's mission did not, however, last long. He began studying at a high school in Hartford, Connecticut, from 1871, but in December 1873, financial constraints led to the Japanese government's stopping financing students abroad and ordering all students to return to Japan. Tajiri was preparing to enter university and without funds would have been unable to continue his studies. Fortunately, his schoolmaster and the local church offered additional money so that he could stay in Connecticut, and at the age of 24 years he entered Yale College, the predecessor to Yale University.[9] He later recalled that as his peers studying on America's east coast (e.g. at Harvard and Rutgers) had selected law-related majors, he wanted to study something different, so he chose economics and finance.[10]

Initially, Tajiri studied in the Department of Liberal Arts, but he later entered the graduate school where he had the opportunity to learn specific topics such as monetary and fiscal policy. He finished his dissertation in 1877 and returned to Japan in 1879. Among his classmates was Howard William Taft who later became the twenty-seventh president of the United States.[11] In his graduation year, Tajiri wrote his first proposal on financial and monetary affairs (*Zaisei Ikensho*) and submitted it to Yoshida Kiyonari, who was then extraordinary envoy and minister plenipotentiary in the United States.[12] Yoshida had a vigorous interest in financial and monetary problems and helped Tajiri submit the proposal to the Japanese government in 1878.[13] If we ask what economic and financial theories Tajiri learned in the United States, it seems that he returned to Japan as an advocator of cameralism. Certainly, Ōuchi Hyōe, one of Tajiri's students, argued that his professor's economic thinking 'could not be anything else but *cameralistic*'.[14] Before answering the question as to how Tajiri came to be a cameralist, however, we need to examine the nature of cameralist theory and its relationship to Japan.

The European concept of cameralism

The science of cameralist studies (*Kameralwissenschaft* in German) has its origin in the Latin word, *camera*, which was originally the name of the room where the king or ruler stored valuable items.[15] Cameralism (a fiscal term) and mercantilism, its foreign economic policy counterpart, were for a long time the dominant terms used in various European countries to describe how rulers and the state might attain wealth. The terms emerged in the sixteenth century and remained influential until the nineteenth century. Adam Smith used the expression 'mercantile system' to describe a policy whereby state authorities could restrict imports and encourage exports.[16] The goal of such a policy was to achieve a favourable balance of trade, thus bringing gold and silver into the country. By comparison, cameralism grew out of the authorities' efforts to increase the wealth of the central administration by setting up monopolies and establishing state-owned enterprises.[17] Put simply, mercantilism focused on external sources of wealth for a country, such as the generation of income from foreign trade, whereas cameralism elaborated on internal sources of state wealth other than taxes.

Cameralism was also at the root of the so-called state sciences (*Staatswissenschaft*), including the sciences of accounting and economic administration, which gained acceptance in the curricula of various German universities from the eighteenth century. By the beginning of the nineteenth century, cameralism was gradually being replaced by more diversified social sciences such as accounting, statistics, finance and political economy. However, the science of rational state administration had influenced successive generations of scholars, especially in the German states.

Proto-cameralism and pre-Meiji Japan

Historians writing on pre-Meiji Japanese financial institutions have rarely conducted comparative analyses of Japanese and European experiences and have thus overlooked the obvious presence of cameralist-like, or proto-cameralist, policies in pre-Meiji administrations.[18] One exception is Luke S. Roberts, but Roberts' monograph on the Tosa domain and its mercantilist-like practices refers only once to the concept of cameralism, with no elaboration.[19] Yet, Craig, Hall and Sagers describe in detail several examples of proto-cameralist policies being carried out in the most powerful feudal domains, Satsuma and Chōshū, from the early eighteenth century.

The Japanese word for cameralism, *kanbōgaku* (from *Kameralwissenschaft*), probably emerged only after the Meiji Restoration,[20] yet, remarkably, proto-cameralist concepts and practices had already emerged in the largest and most powerful Japanese domains (*han*). One of the earliest attempts to create wealth for domains came from two scholarly groups during the seventeenth and eighteenth centuries. The first group advocated policies of 'state' enterprises (*kokka keiei ron*), while the other argued for anti-exclusion, pro-trade policies (*kaikoku bōeki ron*).[21] The first group recommended that domain administrations establish enterprises and monopolies in order to increase the wealth of the central authorities, while the second group stressed the importance of foreign trade. The Satsuma administration, for example, used this foreign trade policy to increase revenues. Among scholars who advocated mercantilist or proto-cameralist policies were Dazai Shundai (1680–1747), Tanuma Okitsugu (1719–88), Zushō Hirosato (1776–1848) and Shimazu Nariakira (1809–58). They argued that wealth would come from the establishment of monopolies and 'state' enterprises, from the promotion of technological imports and from the rationalisation of central government revenues.[22]

Most members of the Meiji government had some Western knowledge, although levels differed greatly,[23] but the 'great men' who played decisive roles in the restoration and its aftermath had developed their knowledge in the pre-Meiji environment. Economics was therefore understood by most of these leaders as a state-led activity intended to create wealth for the nation.[24] Unfortunately, opinion on what policies would be most effective was extremely divided. These leaders considered the concepts of national wealth and state (government) wealth as interchangeable; they also believed that the state was limited in the financial and fiscal policies it could use to create wealth. The greatest limitation faced by the government, however, was the widespread disagreement between members of the administration concerning how to integrate new Western knowledge with their own experiences.

Maeda Masana (1850–1921), the author of the first comprehensive industrial policy (*Kōgyō Iken*),[25] Ōkubo Toshimichi, the first minister of home affairs, and Matsukata Masayoshi himself, were all followers and administrators of proto-cameralist policies in their domains before the Restoration. Ōkubo's ministerial approach until his assassination in 1878 is probably the best example of how proto-cameralism shaped the initial promotion of state-established industries in Meiji Japan. Ōkubo's first administrative experience had been under the Satsuma economic reformer, Shimazu Nariakira, who had appointed Ōkubo as a *kura yaku*, which in modern terms means treasury official.[26] Ōkubo, who believed that industrial promotion by the central administration would directly help strengthen military power, became from 1873 the equivalent of a prime minister in the Council of State (*Dajōkan*). Following Itō Hirobumi's suggestion that the government create a civilian economic policy-related ministry, Ōkubo became head of the newly established Ministry of Home Affairs (*Naimukyoku*), the most powerful post in the government. Although the equivalent of the Ministry of Finance (*Ōkurakyoku*) had already been established in 1869, the Home Ministry soon became the centre of state-led industrialisation. Ōkubo's successful centralisation of the decision-making process in economic and financial matters[27] meant that his ministry rapidly gained power and influence over the financing of industrial and military enterprises.

The establishment of the Home Affairs Ministry shows that the idea of *kokka keiei ron* deeply influenced early Meiji statesmen. Thus, state-promoted industrialisation between 1873 and 1880, led by the ministry, shared many similarities with cameralism; in particular, it focused on state enterprises and promoted military-related industrialisation. Nevertheless, it quickly became a very costly policy: the nature of the enterprises meant that expensive technologies and know-how had to be imported on a massive scale, and most of the state enterprises accumulated serious debts during the first years of their operation.[28]

A young man at Yale: Tajiri's neo-cameralism

Ōuchi Hyōe regarded Tajiri as a cameralist. Moreover, Tajiri had no pre-Meiji administrative experience, and though he hailed from Satsuma even his pre-Meiji education was quite limited. It therefore appears that his administrative and educational knowledge was based on his studies at Yale. Certainly, Tajiri was employed by the Meiji elders, such as Ōkuma and Matsukata, so that his Western knowledge could be properly utilised,[29] and this in itself is enough to suggest that he had adopted European cameralist or neo-cameralist thinking from the

United States rather than from the proto-cameralism of pre-Meiji Japan. However, it explains little about how Tajiri went about adopting and adapting European cameralist ideas, so to understand this it is necessary to look more closely at Tajiri's experience in the United States.

Tajiri spent four years at Yale. During this time, American higher education was becoming more professional, although the social sciences were still in their infancy, and colleges relied upon European countries for educational leadership.[30] In Tajiri's first two years as an undergraduate at Yale, the curriculum included Latin, Greek, rhetoric and European history. At the graduate level, economics and finance were also taught under the rubric of Political and Social Science. Tajiri's teacher at Yale, the man who shaped his views on social, economic and financial issues, was Professor William Graham Sumner (1840–1910), a sociologist.[31] When Tajiri first met Sumner, the American professor was at the beginning of his professional career. Sumner wrote on currency and banking issues and would have made his students read a wide range of publications. Thus, Tajiri would have had the opportunity to study the latest theories on state finance, monetary policy and currency stabilisation. In his early years as a scholar, Sumner attempted to popularise classic British economic theory rather than extend it. As Alfred Marshall, the British economist wrote, Sumner was a man of 'enormous ability', but lacking 'the nature fitted for epoch-making truths'.[32] Much the same could be said of Tajiri in later years.

Sumner believed strongly in a mono-metallic currency system and published a political pamphlet supporting it. His first book, entitled *A History of American Currency*,[33] also advocated a mono-metallic currency system. After Tajiri graduated from Yale, Sumner expanded his scientific interests into sociology and became well-known as a sociologist. His most famous sociological work, entitled *What Social Classes Owe to Each Other* (1883), caused him to be known as an apologist for social Darwinism.[34] Importantly, Sumner recommended to Tajiri the work of Paul Leroy-Beaulieu (1843–1916), especially his newly printed handbook on state finance, entitled *Traité de la Science des Finances*, which was published in two volumes in 1877.[35]

Later, in Japan, Tajiri recognised that his knowledge of Leroy-Beaulieu's book helped him find work with Matsukata, as the latter actually knew Leroy-Beaulieu personally. In fact, Matsukata had first met Leroy-Beaulieu in 1877 when he visited France to prepare for Japan's participation in the 1878 World Exhibition, and he and Leroy-Beaulieu regularly exchanged letters until the latter's death in 1916.[36] Since Leroy-Beaulieu argued that finance was a realm in which the state could act beneficially, both Matsukata and the young Tajiri were attracted to his writing and found his book extremely useful. The two volumes were published in Japanese well before they appeared in English.[37] Leroy-Beaulieu was also a remarkable personality and known as a great 'network-builder', even appearing in Marcel Proust's famous novel, *À La Recherche du Temps Perdu*, as the most important person in French academic circles. Leroy-Beaulieu had first studied in Paris, then in Bonn and later in Berlin. He returned to Paris in 1865, at age 22, and chose to become an economic journalist rather than a bureaucrat. Between 1867 and 1870 (a year before the Commune Revolution started in Paris), he won the French Academy Prize five times. He taught at various universities and, in 1877, was appointed professor of public finance at a relatively new school, the *École Liberté*. He was originally not an expert in public finance but as a pragmatic journalist utilised empirical methods for economic and financial research. His skills as a journalist allowed him to present complicated issues in a well-phrased and thus understandable way.[38]

One of Leroy-Beaulieu's most important ideas related to the quantity theory of money. He recognised that under inconvertible regimes the state could regulate the quantity of money without increasing taxes or printing additional money. Well before the gold standard system became the hegemonic currency system in most industrially advanced countries, he realised that a central bank, together with the Treasury, could control the value of domestic currency. Learning from his own country's inflationary history, he also warned that foreign borrowing in times of serious currency depreciation only helped temporarily; therefore the state should mobilise fiscal and monetary means to 'put a check' on the currency value.[39] Nothing could have been more useful for both Tajiri and Matsukata than Leroy-Beaulieu's concept of stabilisation, and Leroy-Beaulieu's views did much to shape the final stabilisation scheme of Matsukata's deflationary policy in 1882.

Leroy-Beaulieu's central arguments concerned how to increase revenues for the French state other than through import tariffs and, in this context, how to view state debt. These arguments recognised the actual *post-bellum* constraints on France. The country could not increase tariffs; however, it had had to pay a huge indemnity because it had lost the war against Prussia. Leroy-Beaulieu therefore focused on state-generated revenues, criticising other economists who believed that domestic (state) debts (i.e. borrowing from the populace) would cause serious long-term problems. He also argued that for the state to play an active role in productive investment was not in itself economically dangerous. Instead, if more productive investments, such as railways, harbours and canals, were built with public funds, more income and taxes would be generated. As such, state borrowing should be considered a positive part of the economy.[40]

Another work that strongly influenced Tajiri was a book by Wilhelm Roscher, a German scholar. This book, entitled *Principles of Political Economy*, was a bestseller and one of the most important *conceptual* books of the period.[41] Tajiri translated several parts of *Political Economy* into Japanese and taught it to his students. The work offered a comprehensive summary on historical method, its development and application. The major new concept contained in *Political Economy* was the idea that the public economy played an important role in the creation of national wealth. Roscher's argument was new compared to the arguments of Adam Smith (whom he criticised) and Friedrich List (with whom he agreed). He argued that society (the 'public') and the state were deeply interdependent and thus constituted an 'organic' unit. He also stressed the importance of 'public goods', such as infrastructure investments and compensatory state assistance to the poor, as key elements of national wealth.[42]

The influence on Tajiri of the ideas of Sumner, Leroy-Beaulieu and Roscher was more instrumental than conceptual, as he tailored their arguments to the needs of the Japanese state. For instance, he found that Roscher's concept of the organic links between state and society helped him to understand the dynamics of social and economic development. The organic state concept offered a means whereby the state financial network could be linked to the wider society, thereby allowing state or quasi-state organisations to access the larger pool of capital held by the population. Leroy-Beaulieu's assessment of state debt highlighted for Tajiri the benefits of state borrowing. Finally, thanks to Sumner's teachings, Tajiri developed his knowledge of banking and fiscal techniques. It was Leroy-Beaulieu's assessment of the simultaneous consolidation of state finances and the currency exchange rate that helped to reinforce Japan's proto-cameralist view that the central monetary authorities could withdraw notes from circulation and, at the same time, restore the 'old' parity of their currency. The Meiji government implemented both policies, leading to the Matsukata deflationary crisis.[43]

By the time he returned to Japan, Tajiri had thus become a firm believer in the state's special role in national finance. In accordance with the cameralism he adopted while in the United States, however, this view of the state was tempered by the realisation that its 'special role' should be to massage economic growth and development indirectly, that is to bend the market to the needs of the state, rather than to run the market directly. By adapting European financial ideas to the concepts that he had learnt in the United States, Tajiri developed a kind of neo-cameralist approach to state finance.

The return to Japan: Tajiri's academic legacy

Upon returning to Tokyo, Tajiri quickly re-entered Japan's rapidly developing, if chaotic, academic world, and it is here that his first great contribution as a 'public man' of the Meiji era can be seen, as he immediately became involved in the creation of Japan's modern education system and the education of Japan's new economic and political elite. First, he helped to establish a new faculty (a night school, *yagaku*) together with his peers at Keiō Gijuku.[44] Tajiri met Fukuzawa again, who had become, during Tajiri's sojourn in the United States, a prominent author, representative of economic liberalism and friend of many prominent businessmen and politicians, including Ōkuma. Fukuzawa's school had already become a large educational institution, and Fukuzawa was himself too busy to take on the extra work of managing a new faculty; Keiō needed a greater number of professional managers and teachers.[45] Fukuzawa therefore supported Tajiri and his friends in establishing an independent (private) school which was to become Senshū University. The word *senshū* means specialisation, and the new school, enjoying Fukuzawa's support, opened in 1880, offering courses in economics, finance and law. The founders of Senshū Senmon Gakkō had studied together in America and as well as Tajiri, included Komai Shigetada (1853–1901), Soma Nagatane (1850–1924) and Mekata Tanetarō (1853–1926).[46]

Unlike the Imperial University at this time, the new school had a Department of Political Economy. All the courses were taught in Japanese, including law, economics and statistics, and the first curriculum included history, principles of money, outlines of political economy and economic history. Less than two years after its establishment, the school was offering a three-year course that included courses on statistics, budgetary policy, government loans and commercial history.[47] Tajiri also became heavily involved in teaching and was thus able to shape the nature of the curricula then being established. Since Japanese education *in toto* was developing in conjunction with legal and political institutions, the Imperial University, the most important educational institution of Meiji Japan, adopted the European concept of state sciences (in German, *Staatwissenschaft*; in Japanese, *seijigaku* or *kokka gaku*). This concept embraced the legal and institutional frameworks of administrative and bureaucratic activities, as well as economics, finance and fiscal studies. In 1881 Tajiri was also asked to teach in the Department of Letters at the Imperial University, as an assistant teacher to Professor Ernest F. Fenollosa (1853–1903). As noted earlier, the university did not then have a faculty of economics or financial studies (the Faculty of Economics was not established until 1919).[48] Tajiri started teaching economics and finance there in 1882, and in 1888, the year the government completed the regulations for bureaucratic education, he also received a doctoral degree in legal studies.[49] He remained a part-time lecturer (*kōshi*) at the university until he retired in 1918.

The most impressive aspect of Tajiri's educational activities, which highlights his educational legacy most clearly, is the contribution made by his many students to the development of modern Japanese finance and social science. The cream of Tajiri's students included Kanai Noboru (1865–1933), a young political economist, Sakatani Yoshio (1863–1941), an influential financial bureaucrat, and the economist Ōuchi Hyōe (1888–1980). Kanai established with his colleagues the Association for the Study of Social Policy (*Shakai Seisaku Gakkai*), which is widely known thanks to Kenneth Pyle's seminal work.[50] Sakatani was the author of the first modern budget law (*kaikeihō*) in 1886 and was a leading expert behind the introduction of Matsukata's gold standard. Ōuchi Hyōe was one of Japan's most influential twentieth-century economists.

With Matsukata: bureaucrat in the shadows

Tajiri began seeking non-teaching work, as well, when he returned to Tokyo and again received help from Fukuzawa. Fukuzawa initially wrote a letter of recommendation to Ōkuma and later on actually introduced Tajiri to Ōkuma. Tajiri must have impressed the minister of finance, because Ōkuma introduced Tajiri to his wife's niece, whom Tajiri soon married.[51] Fukuzawa stressed in his recommendation that Tajiri's excellent command of English (and his financial expertise) would be crucial for achieving good results in any negotiations over Japanese state-issued bonds and ensuring that the Japanese government could continue to borrow. Tajiri was hired by Ōkuma and began working for him from 13 January 1880.[52]

The Meiji government was facing many challenges when Tajiri began work with the Finance Ministry in 1880. State finances were in urgent need of stabilisation, but it was unclear how this could be achieved, and much debate ensued throughout the bureaucratic and academic worlds. The government had had to increase military expenditure in order to put down the Satsuma rebellion, and this meant having to print additional money. The growing deficit in the balance of payments and the depreciation of the currency against silver exhausted the government's specie reserves, and rapid inflation endangered the process of economic modernisation.[53]

Different leaders had differing opinions on the causes behind the yen's depreciation and accordingly recommended different solutions. Ōkuma, for instance, argued that the depreciation of the currency was caused primarily by the rising price of silver. The government would therefore have to inject additional silver into circulation. However, when the government followed this approach, the silver rapidly disappeared due to excessive imports and because the public, suspicious of the government, tended to hoard precious metals. Ōkuma also suggested that the government borrow 50 million pounds from Britain in order to restore the original value of the yen and to stabilise the budget. However, Ōkuma's colleagues refused to accept this plan, fearing that the long-term burden of foreign debt would lead to Japan becoming dependent upon foreign lenders. As its previous experience of taking out foreign loans in the mid-1870s had shown, Japan's position in international capital markets was weak. Taking out loans in London or New York required personal negotiations, and interest rates at 6 per cent were high. Matsukata and Itō Hirobumi argued against Ōkuma and, in 1881, used his proposals to undermine his position and then remove him from government. Financial decisions, however, were not the only factor behind this move. What made Ōkuma particularly dangerous to the elder statesmen was his politics, for Ōkuma advocated a British-style constitutional monarchy instead of the German political system, a position which naturally threatened the power of the oligarchs.[54]

As monetary historians will well understand, Japan at this point faced the classic dilemma of simultaneously achieving currency and fiscal stabilisation, something which was also a common problem in Europe at that time. The challenge in the Japanese case, however, was to obtain funds for the restoration of the old yen parity. Since the country was largely unknown to Western financial and political leaders, and because the Japanese government worried about the dangers of long-term dependency resulting from overseas borrowing, it chose a policy almost identical to that analysed by Leroy-Beaulieu in his book. The result was that the old yen silver parity was restored without foreign loans. Instead, the newly created Yokohama Specie Bank managed to accumulate enough specie to restore the currency to its original rate, and the consolidation was realised via deflation. After the government had successfully restored the yen's original rate, the adjustment programme was completed through fiscal austerity and converting short-term government debt into long-term government liabilities.

Ōkuma's sacking led to the resignation of many of his protégés, but Tajiri's absence from Japan during the previous decade had allowed him to retain a neutral position at the Ministry of Finance and keep his position under the new minister, Matsukata. Tajiri freely provided the knowledge he had acquired at Yale, and it proved to be as indispensable to Matsukata as it had been to Ōkuma. Moreover,

Matsukata was also a believer in mercantilist and cameralist policies. He had first pursued naval studies in Nagasaki, then for a brief period was governor of Hida (now part of Ōita) before joining the new government. His thinking was influenced by the progressive *daimyō*, Nariakira, but his attitudes had also been shaped by Maeda Masana while the two men were in France in 1878.[55]

By the time Matsukata actually took up the tasks of currency stabilisation and fiscal consolidation, the administration already had in its possession several proposals for stabilisation, including those made by Godai Tomoatsu, later a businessman, in 1865, Itō in 1872, Inoue Kaoru in 1872, Matsukata in 1876 and Tajiri in 1878.[56] Matsukata believed that the main pillars of Japanese modernisation should be self-reliance and trade surpluses. He opposed both foreign loans (in contrast to Ōkuma) and Ōkubo's state-promoted and directly financed industrial policy. One of his earliest actions in this regard was to privatise all state-owned firms in order to decrease state expenditure. In the short term, this policy successfully reduced state expenditure and relatively quickly produced extra revenue through the sales. Nevertheless, in the long term, it proved less efficient, as Matsukata had been warned by Maeda.[57] Even though this privatisation helped strengthen Matsukata's political supporters, the wealthy business families, it also created many difficulties for the countryside and agriculturally based traditional industries. On the other hand, Matsukata was aware that, in the long term, industrial development could not be maintained without state help, because Japan had relatively few liquid capital sources and because the domestic capital market was still in its infancy. Accordingly, he proposed 'indirect' state support through the establishment of special quasi-governmental banks that could finance long-term investments too risky for private enterprise.

By the time Tajiri returned to Japan in 1879, Matsukata had gained enormous power within the government, and there is strong evidence that Matsukata, especially after he became minister of finance, sidelined anyone who even mildly criticised or doubted his concepts. As Richard Smethurst argues, Maeda Masana's fate was sealed by Matsukata when the latter recognised that Maeda's proposal on future economic development was exactly the opposite of his own ideas.[58] It is difficult to discern whether Matsukata (or other members of the Dajōkan) received Tajiri's suggestions via Yoshida Kiyonari, although it is highly likely that the proposal had reached the government before Tajiri returned to Tokyo. Certainly, Matsukata's final stabilisation proposal (he had already delivered two earlier versions) incorporated many elements of previous submissions, although Matsukata never explicitly referred to any of the earlier proposals, including Tajiri's.[59] The limited scope of this chapter does not allow for a systematic comparison of Matsukata's final proposal with Tajiri's 1878 proposal, but there are some strong indications that Tajiri's ideas played a key part in the final plan.[60] For instance, the consolidation plans of Tajiri and Matsukata were identical in two key areas. First Tajiri argued that restoring the currency's original parity was the most urgent task for the government. Second, he recommended a fiscal stabilisation scheme incorporating budget austerity together with new taxes and the conversion of government liabilities into long-term debts.

Matsukata's final proposal, submitted to the Emperor and approved, had three main objectives. First, it aimed to restore the original parity between the yen and silver. Second, it planned to reorganise ministerial budgets and enforce austerity on government spending. Third, it aimed to introduce a medium-range schedule for establishing non-private financial institutions in order to ensure the supply of long-term capital to weaker sectors of the economy, such as agriculture and small-scale industries. The idea of indirect state financial support was realised in the 1890s. Although this was originally one of Maeda's ideas, Maeda had by then been completely marginalised by Matsukata.[61] In contrast, Tajiri had become the most influential bureaucrat in the Ministry of Finance, and it is highly possible that Tajiri had used his 'neutrality' to persuade Matsukata of the idea's merits. The most obvious indication of Tajiri's influence is this movement towards the use of less direct means to finance state and pseudo-state enterprises. The idea of establishing non-private financial institutions linked to society and able to pro-vide capital for weaker sectors of the economy strongly mirrors the ideas of an organic state in Roscher's *Principles of Political Economy* and the beneficial uses of state debt in Leroy-Beaulieu's work. Both Matsukata and Tajiri were familiar with these works, but it was Tajiri who, due to his foreign studies, had the most comprehensive understanding of these concepts as well as the necessary professional training to implement them.

By 1885, the stabilisation scheme had restored yen and silver parity, the Bank of Japan had been established with Tajiri as its first auditor and state debts had been gradually converted so that their maturity dates and interest rates were uni-form. Tajiri played a fundamental role in executing the burdensome task of state debt consolidation. In addition, a systemic budget structure and a new state fund, known as the Deposit Fund (*Yokinbu*) which was intended to raise capital for state-backed enterprises, had also been created. The head of the preparatory committee to establish the Deposit Fund was Tajiri.[62]

In the three subsequent decades, Tajiri worked in all the important Finance Ministry departments, including the tax office, the state debts section and the bank-ing bureau. In fact, his Finance Ministry career covered almost all the major policy changes of the period, from the preparation of the deflationary policy until Japan's 1905 victory in the Russo-Japanese war. Between 1892 (just before the Sino-Japanese war) and 1898 Tajiri was vice minister (*sōmu chōkan*), the highest execu-tive position in the ministry. He also had a leading role in establishing a state examination committee for future bureaucrats. In short, no major financial or fiscal policy was implemented during this period without Tajiri's close involvement.

Conclusion

Tajiri represented a new kind of figure in the financial world of Meiji Japan. As his early life shows, he did not have any experience of pre-Meiji financial insti-tutions and did not participate in the Restoration or its aftermath. Although he studied in Satsuma and at Keiō in Tokyo before leaving Japan, his formative educational experience was at Yale. He was thus among the first foreign-trained professionals to return to Japan and begin working towards the nationalist objectives of the Restoration. Moreover, he brought with him a new and vastly more professional approach to both administration and education.

A key part of Tajiri's contribution to the institutional development of modern Japanese finance was his involvement in shaping long-term intellectual context for future administrators. Tajiri's involvement in establishing Senshū University and its curriculum, as well as his subsequent role as a professor both at Senshū and at Teidai, which included the publication of numerous textbooks and the mentoring of many students, illustrate his significant role in modernising Japan's early, chaotic education system. The next generation (educated mainly by Tajiri) by and large adopted the assumptions and ways of thinking that their professor had taught through his many years in academia.

Tajiri's second significant contribution to the financial institutions of modern Japan was more direct, even though it is harder for historians to identify. Unlike his peers who also studied abroad, Tajiri chose to study finance rather than law, and this meant that, when he eventually returned to Tokyo in 1879, he enjoyed the great advantage of having a virtual monopoly on the latest European financial thinking. Thus he had barely stepped off the boat, so to speak, when he was offered employment at the Ministry of Finance. In this context he was able to use the professional knowledge he had developed, directly under the influence of Sumner and indirectly from Leroy-Beaulieu and Roscher, to shape the development of Meiji financial institutions through his relationships with such notable figures as Ōkuma and Matsukata. Tajiri's neo-cameralist ideas in a way confirmed many of the key assumptions of the Meiji elders, whose thinking in turn had been deeply influenced by the cameralist-like ideas, or *kokka keiei ron*, of pre-Meiji financial institutions.

This was important in view of the timing of Tajiri's return from the United States. When Tajiri entered the government in 1880, the Japanese economy and the state's finances were both doing poorly. Ōkubo's proto-cameralist policies had done little to solve Japan's financial problems, and Ōkuma's more liberal financial and political ideas threatened the power of the Meiji elders. Tajiri's neo-cameralism, by providing more workable solutions to Japan's many financial problems, helped reinforce the central beliefs behind Japan's financial institutions as they were transformed by Japan's difficult modernisation process. Equally, Tajiri's commitment to the state – his willingness to accept the limitations of power based upon knowledge and to remain in the shadows of the bureaucratic world – was just as important to the Meiji leaders. In this light, his life was an early Japanese example of a professional elite being used to bolster the power of established institutions.

Acknowledgements

The librarians in the archive at Senshū University offered their time and assistance to complete this work. In particular, I would like to thank Mr Uchiyama Hiroshi who, though enjoying his retirement, graciously provided me with many excellent references and a great deal of extremely useful advice. I would also like to express my appreciation to my friend and colleague, Mark Metzler, whose ideas and concepts have greatly shaped my own thinking. Finally, I would like to thank Minato Teruo and David Envall for their comments and professional advice.

Notes

1 Andrew E. Barshay, *State and Intellectual in Imperial Japan: The Public Man in Crisis* (Berkeley, CA: University of California Press, 1988).
2 Byron K. Marshall, *Academic Freedom and the Japanese Imperial University 1868–1939* (Berkeley, CA: University of California Press, 1992), p. 48.
3 Kenneth B. Pyle, *The New Generation in Meiji Japan: The Problems of Cultural Identity* (Stanford, CA: Stanford University Press, 1969), chs. 2, 7.
4 Andrew Cobbing, *The Satsuma Students in Britain: Japan's Early Search for the 'Essence of the West'* (Richmond, VA, Surrey: Curzon Press–Japan Library, 2000), pp. 110–11.
5 Uchiyama, Hiroshi, *Tajiri Inajirō Nenpō* (Tokyo: Senshū Daigaku Shi Shiryōshitsu, 1923), pp. 2–12.
6 Norio Tamaki, *Yukichi Fukuzawa, 1835–1901: The Spirit of Enterprise in Modern Japan* (London: Palgrave, 2001), p. 97.
7 Minoru, Ishizuki, 'Overseas Study by Japanese in the Early Meiji Period', in Ardath W. Burks (ed.), *The Modernizers: Overseas Students, Foreign Employees and Meiji Japan* (Boulder, CO and London: Westview Press, 1985), pp. 161–86.
8 Tsuruoka, Isaku, *Kitanari Tajiri Sensei Den* (Tokyo: Iwanami Shoten, 1933), p. 32.
9 Ibid., p. 36.
10 *Yale Centenary Quarter Record (1905)*, Senshū Daigaku Shi Shiryōshitsu.
11 Ibid.
12 Tsuruoka, *Kitanari Tajiri Sensei Den*, pp. 387–402. The full text of the proposal is printed in this volume.
13 Cobbing, *Satsuma Students in Britain*, p. 110.
14 Ōuchi, Hyōe, 'Zaisei Gakusha toshite no Tajiri Inajirō', in Ōuchi (ed.), *Kyūshi Kyūyū* (Tokyo: Iwanami Shoten, 1948), p. 68. The original reads '*sensei ni yotte daihyō sareta gakumon wa dōshite mo kamerarisutikku narazaru o enakatta no de aru*').
15 The science of 'state administration' has a rich literature. Comprehensive summaries of the history of cameralism can be found in Keith Tribe, *Strategies of Economic Order: German Economic Discourse 1750–1950* (Cambridge: Cambridge University Press, 1995); David F. Lindenfeld, *The Practical Imagination: The German Sciences of State in the Nineteenth Century* (London: University of Chicago Press, 1997).
16 Charles Gide and Charles Rist, 'History of Economic Doctrines', in Roger E. Backhouse (ed.), *Early Histories of Economic Thought 1824–1914*, vol. VIII (London: Routledge, 2000), p. 83.
17 Katalin Ferber, ' "Run the State Like a Business": The Origin of the Deposit Fund in Meiji Japan', *Japanese Studies*, 22, 2, 2002, pp. 131–53.
18 Historical analysis of the pre-Meiji economic and financial experience from the post-Restoration perspective is rare. The outstanding example is John H. Sagers, *Intellectual Roots of Japanese Capitalism: Economic Thought and Policy 1835–1885*, unpublished PhD dissertation (University of Washington, 2001). Two English-language monographs that deal with economic and financial administration in the pre-Meiji period are John Whitney Hall, *Tanuma Okitsugu, 1719–1788: Forerunner of Modern Japan* (Cambridge, MA: Harvard University Press, 1955), especially ch. 4; and Albert M. Craig, *Choshu in the Meiji Restoration* (Cambridge, MA: Harvard University Press, 1961).

19 Luke S. Roberts, *Mercantilism in a Japanese Domain: The Merchant Origins of Economic Nationalism in Eighteenth Century Tosa* (Cambridge: Cambridge University Press, 1998), p. 24.

20 Unfortunately, I have been unable to identify the exact time of translation.

21 Hall, *Tanuma Okitsugu*, pp. 61–62.

22 Sagers, *Intellectual Roots of Japanese Capitalism*, ch. 2.

23 See Bernard S. Silberman, 'Bureaucratic Development and the Structure of Decision-making in Japan, 1868–1925', *Journal of Asian Studies*, 29, 2, February 1970, pp. 347–62, especially p. 354 concerning Western-educated bureaucratic appointees.

24 Tessa Morris-Suzuki, *A History of Japanese Economic Thought* (London: Routledge, 1990), pp. 13–14.

25 Sydney Crawcour, '*Kōgyō Iken*: Maeda Masana and His View on Meiji Economic Development', *Journal of Japanese Studies*, 23, 1, 1997, pp. 69–104.

26 Masakazu Iwata, *Ōkubo Toshimichi: The Bismarck of Japan* (Berkeley, CA: University of California Press, 1964), p. 35.

27 Sydney DeVere Brown, 'Ōkubo Toshimichi and the First Home Ministry Bureaucracy 1873–1878', in Bernard S. Silberman and Harry D. Harootunian (eds), *Modern Japanese Leadership: Transition and Change* (Tucson, AZ: University of Arizona Press, 1966).

28 Thomas C. Smith, *Political Change and Industrial Development in Japan: Government Enterprise, 1868–1880* (Stanford, CA: Stanford University Press, 1955).

29 Uchiyama, Hiroshi, *Tajiri Inajirō Nenpō* (Tokyo: Senshū Daigaku Shi Shiryōshitsu, 2002), pp. 5–8.

30 Keith Tribe, 'Historical Schools of Economics: German and English', *Keele Economics Research Papers* (February 2002), p. 2, http://www.keele.ac.uk/depts/ec/kerp, accessed Nov. 2003.

31 The curriculum of Yale College can be found in George Wilson Pierson, *Yale College: An Educational History, 1871–1921* (New Haven, CT: Yale University Press, 1955). On Tajiri and Sumner, see Komine, Yasue, 'Nihon Saishō no Zaisei Gakusha Tajiri Inajirō', *Senshū Daigaku Shi Shiryōshitsu*, 6, 1976, pp. 106–10.

32 On Sumner's educational and academic activities, see Robert C.Bannister, 'Foreword', in Bannister (ed.), *On Liberty, Society, and Politics: The Essential Essays of William Graham Sumner* (Indianapolis, IN: Liberty Fund, 1992), pp. ix–xxxvi.

33 William G. Sumner, *A History of American Currency* (New York: Henry Holt & Company, 1874).

34 Bannister, 'Foreword', p. xxiv.

35 The book was to become one of the earliest manuals for financial bureaucrats in Japan. See Dan Warshaw, *Paul Leroy-Beaulieu and Established Liberalism in France* (DeKalb, IL: Illinois University Press, 1991), pp. 50–53. Mr Uchiyama Hiroshi, retired librarian and archivist, brought this monograph to my attention.

36 On Matsukata's visit to France, see Crawcour, '*Kōgyō Iken*'. For the first encounter and subsequent friendship between Matsukata and Leroy-Beaulieu, see Komine, 'Nihon Saishō no Zaisei Gakusha Tajiri Inajirō'.

37 Buchanan's work seems to be the only partial translation of Leroy-Beaulieu's work into English.

38 Warshaw, *Paul Leroy-Beaulieu and Established Liberalism in France*, chs 3–4.

39 Marc Flandreau, 'Crises and Punishment: Moral Hazard and the pre-1914 International Financial Architecture', in Flandreau (ed.), *Money Doctors: The Experience of International Financial Advising, 1850–2000* (London: Routledge, 2003), pp. 13–49, especially pp. 19–21.

40 Paul Leroy-Beaulieu, *Traite de la Science des Finances* (2 vols, 7th edn, Paris: Alcan, 1908). James M. Buchanan's translation is *Public Principles of Public Debt: A Defense and a Restatement* (Liberty Fund, Inc., 1999), Library of Economics and Liberty, http://www.econlib.org/library/Buchanan/buchcvc8.html, accessed Nov. 2003.

41 William Roscher, *Principles of Political Economy*, vol. 2, (New York: Henry Holt and Co., 1878). For a recent full-length analysis of Roscher's concept of public economy, see Jeffrey E. Hanes, *The City as Subject: Seki Hajime and the Reinvention of Modern Osaka* (Berkeley, CA: University of California Press, 2002).

42 Roscher's work was part of Tajiri's curriculum at both Senshū and the Imperial University. See Komine, 'Nihon Saishō no Zaisei Gakusha Tajiri Inajirō', pp. 119–21.

43 See Marc Flandreau's excellent analysis of the deflationary crisis after the simultaneous stabilisation policy. Flandreau, 'Crisis and Punishment', pp. 23–24. In this context 'starving' means a drastic decline of high powered money and a serious decrease in prices.

44 Ueda, Toshio, *Yagaku* (Tokyo: Ningen no Kagakusha, 1998), pp. 9–16 (Senshū Daigaku Shi Shiryōshitsu).

45 Tamaki, *Yukichi Fukuzawa*, p. 163.

46 Chūhei Sugiyama, 'Pioneer Economics Department: Senshū School', in Chūhei Sugiyama and Hiroshi Mizuta (eds), *Enlightenment and Beyond: Political Economy Comes to Japan* (Tokyo: Tokyo University Press, 1988), pp. 128–29. Komai was also a bureaucrat in the tax office of the Finance Ministry, while Soma was president of the newly established Yokohama Specie Bank 1882–1924. Mekata, after holding various positions in the Finance Ministry, was appointed as a financial expert to Korea. See Senshū Daigaku, http://www.acc.senshu-u.ac.jp/koho/, accessed Nov. 2003.

47 Sugiyama, 'Pioneer Economics Department', pp. 130–31.

48 *Tōkyō Daigaku Keizai Gakubu 50 nen shi* (Tokyo: University of Tokyo Press, 1976), p. 294.

49 Robert M. Spaulding, Jr, *Imperial Japan's Higher Civil Service Examinations* (Princeton, NJ: Princeton University Press, 1967), p. 101; *Tōkyō Daigaku Keizai Gakubu 50 nen shi*, pp. 4–6.

50 Kenneth B. Pyle, 'Advantages of Followership: German Economics and Japanese Bureaucrats 1890–1915', *Journal of Japanese Studies*, 1, 1 (Autumn 1974).

51 Senshū Daigaku Shi Shiryōshitsu, personal files of Tajiri Inajirō.

52 Tsuruoka, *Kitanari Tajiri Sensei Den*, p. 30. The recommendation is reproduced in this volume.

53 Hugh T. Patrick, 'External Equilibrium and Internal Convertibility: Financial Policy in Meiji Japan', *Journal of Economic History*, 25, 2 (June 1965).

54 Andrew Fraser, 'The Expulsion of Ōkuma from the Government in 1881', *Journal of Asian Studies*, 26, 2 (February 1967).

55 Sagers, *Intellectual Roots of Japanese Capitalism*, ch. 6.

56 Nakamura, Takafusa (ed.), *Matsukata Zaisei to Sangyō Kangyō Seisaku* (Tokyo: University of Tokyo Press, 1983), especially chs 2, 5.

57 Crawcour, '*Kōgyō Iken*'.

58 Richard J. Smethurst, 'Takahashi Korekiyo's Economic Policies in the Great Depression and their Meiji Roots', in R.J. Smethurst and Masataka Matsuura, *Politics and the Economy in Pre-war Japan* (London: Suntory and Toyota International Centres for Economics and Related Disciplines Discussion Paper, 2000).

59 Matsukata's final proposal was published in its entirety in Masayoshi Matsukata, *Report on the Adoption of the Gold Standard in Japan* (Tokyo: Government Press, 1899).

60 Tsuruoka, *Kitanari Tajiri Sensei Den*, pp. 387–403. This is the full text of Tajiri's proposal. According to Tsuruoka, the proposal was sent to Yoshida Kiyonari in Hartford, Connecticut.

61 Smethurst, 'Takahashi Korekiyo's Economic Policies in the Great Depression'.

62 Tajiri, *Zaisei to Kin'yū* (2 vols, 1st edn, Tokyo: Dōbunka, 1901), vol. 2, p. 24.

4   Investment, importation and innovation
Genesis and growth of beer corporations in pre-war Japan

Harald Fuess

The industrial firm

Industrial firms played a key role in the rapid industrialization that transformed economies and societies across the world from the nineteenth century. In contrast to earlier business organizations, industrial firms grew to enormous size and complexity. What is especially noteworthy about this new institution is that it appeared in several countries within a relatively short period of time and then developed along parallel lines suggesting similar factors at work in its creation and continuity. This happened against the background of the nineteenth-century revolution in transportation and communication which went hand in hand with a revolution in the processes of production and distribution in capitalist economies.

One of the key institutional innovations of the modern firm was that it employed hierarchies of salaried managers holding little equity in the firm to run these large multiunit managerial enterprises, because individual owner-managers could no longer personally supervise organizations of such growing size and complexity. Alfred Chandler, the eminent business historian, argues for the superior capability of the industrial firm to effectively exploit the unprecedented cost advantages that were generated by the development of new technologies and the opening of new markets. Whereas the older labour-intensive type of manufacturers relied on the addition of workers and machines to increase output, the new more capital-intensive firm changed the capital–labour ratios through rearranged inputs, improved equipment, reoriented production processes or the application of new energy resources. Costs per unit dropped more quickly as the volume of materials increased. The Standard Oil Trust is one of the most striking examples of the effective uses of such cost advantages, since it concentrated close to a quarter of the world's production of kerosene in three refineries following its establishment in 1882, and its successor company, Exxon Mobil, was the largest oil company at the end of the twentieth century.[1] Chandler describes the emergence and development of the industrial firm in general terms:

> In the 1880s and 1890s, new mass-production technologies...brought a sharp reduction in costs as plants reached minimum efficient scale. In many industries the throughput of plants was so high that a small number of them could meet the existing national and even global demand. The structure of

these industries quickly became oligopolistic.... In many instances the first company to build a plant of minimum efficient scale and to recruit the essential management team remained the leader in its industry for decades.[2]

Although Chandler's theory of institutional change was originally meant as an explanation of an American phenomenon, the apparent universality of the cost paradigm makes it an intriguing tool of analysis for business history in other countries. Anywhere in the world managers in certain industries, given the right technology and market demand, should have striven to exploit the existing cost advantages of the economies of scale.[3] The non-emergence of large industrial enterprises in certain fields could then be explained in terms of the factors restricting expected growth. Moreover, not only does Chandler provide a template for the origin of industrial enterprises, he also suggests an explanation for why they continued to develop in the same manner and why the first movers to produce these cost advantages remained in a dominant market position when applying their experience towards further business growth.

Japan, an economic late developer compared to the pioneering Anglo-Saxon countries did also see large firms emerge after the 1880s, which later were called *zaibatsu* (financial clique). Mitsui, Mitsubishi, Sumitomo and Yasuda, the big four *zaibatsu*, initially engaged in non-industrial activities such as shipping, mining, banking and foreign trade. In these fields they often acquired a dominant position in oligopolistic markets. Mitsui alone handled one-third of Japan's foreign trade by 1900.[4] Later *zaibatsu* moved into the fields of heavy industry, especially in shipyards, steel and chemicals. The *zaibatsu* share of the Japanese economy was around one-third in 1930.[5] The economic influence of the *zaibatsu* and other large companies often exceeded their size. Productivity and wages were much higher at larger companies, whereas the more numerous smaller companies used conspicuously less capital and technology. These differences in the economy are so striking that they are commonly referred to as 'dual structure'.[6]

One suspects that the higher productivity of larger companies and a tendency towards concentrated market structures are at least partly influenced by what Chandler referred to as the cost advantages of the large multiunit industrial enterprise in mass production and distribution, one of his more recent ideas that has not yet received much attention in Japanese business studies.[7] An application of his concept to explain the origins and development of industrial capitalism in Japan seem promising. This study will examine the suitability of his ideas to the beer industry, an industry virtually neglected by historians probably due to the fact that its products were mostly meant for individual consumption in the domestic market. However, this industry nevertheless saw the emergence of several capital-intensive firms as early as during the Meiji period (1868–1912). After a background discussion on the international beer industry and the slow diffusion of beer drinking habits to Japan, the study will argue that several variables defined the modern beer firm in Japan from its inception, namely investment in joint-stock capitalization, the import of German technology and material and innovation as a continuous process fuelling further growth.

Background of the beer industry

The beer industry was one of the most important consumer goods industries worldwide around the turn of the twentieth century and an industry that was substantially transformed during the second industrial revolution. In the international context, the production and distribution of beer was an important economic activity, increasingly undertaken by larger plants in consolidating markets. In the 1860s the largest American breweries averaged an output of 1,090 kilolitres (8,000 barrels) per year, and by 1895 they produced 100 times that much.[8] In the British Isles, Guinness became the largest food and beverage business and the seventh biggest company by 1919. The German brewing industry was by far the country's largest consumer-goods industry, and in 1926 its capital assets were approximating those of the giant electrical machinery industry. Already by 1911 less than 10 per cent of the German breweries produced 37 per cent of the total beer output. Berlin's Schultheiss brewery led the market for about fifty years until the Second World War.[9] In all three countries breweries were well represented among the largest 200 industrial enterprises in the 1910s. Some entrepreneurs in what was a traditional craft had effectively exploited the cost advantages inherent in new technological innovations in the late 1870s and 1880s and formed large industrial enterprises.

By contrast, Japan initially lacked even a culture of beer consumption. Sake was the main alcoholic beverage, probably since the introduction of wet rice agriculture from China and Korea in the third century BC.[10] While often translated as 'rice wine' for its clear appearance and high alcoholic content, technically speaking sake is a 'beer', if beer is defined as an alcoholic beverage made from the fermentation of starchy material.[11] Sake was not only an ordinary alcoholic drink, its production and consumption was loaded with cultural, social and religious taboos or meanings.[12] The traditional homebound wedding ritual, for instance, had as its core ceremony an exchange of sake cups, as foreign visitors noticed with bemusement. It was usually wealthier peasants who engaged in sake brewing by processing surplus rice. Sake brewers as local men of influence and large taxpayers played a disproportionate role in Meiji politics, since many were elected to the national Diet established in 1890. Sake, with about a third of the total, was the biggest source of government domestic revenue after the land tax during the Meiji period.[13] In 1914 the sake industry was one of Japan's largest industries by output value, overshadowed only by textiles, railroads, military manufacturing and coal.[14] Based on such well-entrenched habits of consumption and the economic, political and social position of the sake brewers, the introduction of the new alcoholic beverage of beer was bound to be an uphill battle.

The beginnings of beer consumption in Japan were indeed far from auspicious. Japanese who had the opportunity to drink beer with Dutch traders in the eighteenth century described the beverage as rather tasteless. When the American Commodore Perry offered several barrels on the occasion of celebrating the treaty that opened Japan in 1854, the Japanese reaction ranged from 'bitter', through 'magic water' to 'horsepiss'.[15] It is no great surprise, therefore, that beer drinking for about a quarter of a century remained centred on the foreign community that clustered in the treaty ports such as Yokohama after 1859. Imports could easily meet the initial demand. As the number of residents from Western nations grew, however, there was an increasing incentive to establish local sources of supply, especially when considering that an average of 10,000 seamen were passing through on British ships alone.[16]

Around 1870, when Yokohama's Western population numbered about 600 people, mainly French and British troops, several foreigners began to make beer. William Copeland (1834–1902), a naturalized American who was trained in his native Norway by a German brew master, founded and managed Spring Valley Brewery, the first and largest foreign brewery. The main sales outlet was the beer garden in the grounds of the brewery, but the local market could not absorb the entire production so Copeland established sales offices in Tokyo and Shanghai during the 1870s. The still growing foreign population, the steady stream of beer imports and the foreign models induced Japanese entrepreneurs to follow this lead; some came from sake brewing families and worked at Spring Valley, which served as a kind of training ground for the first generation of Japanese brewers. Noguchi Masaaki was one of these disciples, and his family firm made beer from 1874 to 1901 in the town of Kōfu. Most Japanese breweries, however, clustered in the environment of urban Tokyo, even though a few sprang up in the cities of Ōsaka and Kyoto. Despite the fact that they produced a modern Western product, the methods and organizational forms of the early Japanese breweries remained rather traditional. Small-scale businesses owned and managed by the founder and members of his family were predominant. Some sake makers simply included beer as a new good manufactured through their existing facilities. No producer incorporated itself as a joint-stock company.[17] Employment figures remained relatively small, ranging from 8 to 40 people in the Tokyo breweries as late as 1888. The average annual production of 30 breweries in the country was 6,934 litres (39 *koku*), ranging from as little as 90 litres to a more respectable 44,100 litres (245 *koku*) in 1883.[18] Nevertheless, the total Japanese output in that year of 208 kilolitres (1,155 *koku*) was still less than half of the import volume of 450 kilolitres (2,500 *koku*) or less than half the production figures for a single large-scale American brewery in the 1860s.[19]

One early Japanese brewery stands out for its support by a government institution, namely Hokkaidō's Development Agency. In order to provide a viable economic basis for Japanese settlers in Hokkaidō, the agency promoted agricultural and industrial advancements. Beer seemed the ideal end product for the processing of hops already growing wild on the island, but for which Japanese had previously seen no use. Moreover, the northern location assured the supply of sufficient natural ice important to the brewing process. In 1876 the agency started the enterprise, which hired as its technical director Nakagawa Seibei (1848–1916), who had trained at the great Tivoli Brewery in Berlin. Despite its official backing and despite being one of the breweries with the highest output, the brewery in Sapporo only turned a profit in the year before it was privatized in 1886. The key problems were high transportation costs to Tokyo, its main market, technical problems with sterilization, and the high price of its product, equivalent to that of imports, but without providing the same quality.[20]

Therefore, although beer had been introduced to Japan, no modern industrial enterprise had yet sprung-up as a result by the mid-1880s. Imports easily supplied the still rather confined market of foreign residents and visitors, and urbane and wealthy Japanese adapting Western habits. Japanese consumers continued to prefer indigenous sake to Western alcoholic beverages. They did not like the bitter taste, poor quality and high price of beer. However, when change finally occurred it was rapid, big and lasting.

Japan's modern beer industry

The 1880s were a turning point in Japanese business history. The infrastructural reforms promoted by the government showed signs of the revolution in transportation and communication seen earlier in Europe and the United States. The first railway linked Tokyo to Yokohama in 1872, the telegraph connected all major cities by 1880, steamships regularly travelled between major ports, the Bank of Japan stabilized the currency and credit system after its establishment in 1882 and the Western concept of joint-stock companies found wider acceptance as a means to pool capital necessary for large industrial projects. The passing of the Commercial Code in 1893 provided a reliable legal basis for firm business growth. The 1880s started with high inflation, partly induced by the costs of the 1877 Satsuma rebellion, followed by budget retrenchment and recession, but finally the numbers and sizes of new enterprises exploded, especially in railways and textiles.

Economic historians in recent years have stopped invoking the vocabulary of rocket science in order to stress sudden departures, but the popular term 'take-off' still seems an apt characterization of the first beer boom in Japanese history. Japanese began drinking beer, and thus the total value of beer imports jumped from 99,243 yen (1884) to 450,915 yen (1888). With the increase in demand, it emerged that Japanese liked a different kind of beer from the one drunk by the British majority in the foreign settlements. Whereas English beer imports declined from 56,919 yen (1884) to 44,234 yen (1888), the value of beers imported from Germany increased precipitously by about ten times during the same five years, from 25,756 yen to 297,224 yen.[21] This overall rise in demand and shift in the national origin of imports showed the direction of the potential beer market in Japan. Japanese consumers were rejecting the dark ales, porters and stouts but enjoyed the so-called lager, a lighter, foamier and more durable new variety pioneered in Germany. Had there been no change in Japan, imports could have continued to remain the primary source of supply, but businessmen in Japan reacted swiftly and as early as 1890 exhibited 60 beers at the third national industrial exhibition.[22] Many of the new breweries only existed for a short time. For example, in 1887 the fifteenth head of the Ishikawa family, a sake-maker in the Tama region close to both the Tokyo and the Yokohama markets, hired a worker trained in the brewery of a relative and purchased a large iron vat.

The average beer output amounted to about a tenth of his sake production, but problems with fermentation could not be resolved and two years later he terminated the experiment, selling the equipment and trademark.[23]

Most new brewing establishments in Japan were of this kind of traditional small-scale variety, but these years also saw an organizational and technological breakthrough towards the large-scale industrial beer enterprise and the creation of a highly concentrated market. Today's dominant big three beer companies, Kirin, Sapporo and Asahi, were all established or substantially transformed during this initial beer boom. The Japan Brewery, now Kirin, began in 1885 on the grounds of the former Spring Valley Brewery. In 1887 investors reorganized and enlarged the privatized brewery in Hokkaidō, renaming it Sapporo Biiru Gaisha, and another group started the Nihon Biiru Jōzō Gaisha (not to be confused with its English competitor) with the Ebisu brand. In 1889 the Ōsaka Biiru Gaisha was incorporated to make Asahi beer. These new corporations posed a real threat to imports. In 1886, even before new-type breweries were fully operating, Japanese production had surpassed imports for the first time, but once large facilities began production in earnest the new-type breweries drove foreign beer imports out of the market. By 1893 beer imports accounted for merely 10 per cent of Japanese consumption, and three years later Japan exported twice as much as it brought in.[24]

All successful new-type companies shared three critical elements: the organizational form of the joint-stock company, the adaptation of leading-edge technology and the brewing of German lager beer. The combination of all three elements was essential. A joint-stock company brewing dark-type beer was bound for marginality and extinction as well as lager breweries too financially feeble to invest heavily in German technology. The joint-stock company's ability to raise large amounts of capital was a precondition for the acquisition of the expensive foreign know-how crucial for survival as a brewer. The effective use of technology enabled the breweries to become more cost effective, and by decreasing the initially high retail price transformed beer from an expensive luxury to more of a commodity product. Foreign technology also resolved the recurrent quality problems that had so much plagued earlier producers. Finally, the brewer's choice of lager beer was a significant factor in the expansion of the market in line with the tastes of a Japanese (male) urban drinking public.

Groups of investors pooled their resources to establish or acquire breweries, since these initially required a very large investment by contemporary standards. The first new-type brewery was unusual, since its main stockholders were British and German until it was sold in January 1907 to investors, which included the Iwasaki family, owner of the Mitsubishi *zaibatsu*. It is an indication of the lingering doubts among foreign investors about the protection offered to them by the Japanese legal system that they initially chose to incorporate the Japan Brewery in Hong Kong and to denominate the capital in Hong Kong dollars. Japanese founders of breweries in subsequent years did not follow that path. By the 1890s all had incorporated their business as joint-stock companies (*kabushiki gaisha*), fully authorized and with paid-up capital in yen. Capital increases became a matter of routine every several years in line with the expansion of production. Nihon

Beer, around 1900 the market leader in terms of sales, raised its capital from 150,000 yen (1890) to 800,000 yen (1905). In 1906 it merged with two other large breweries to form Dai Nihon Beer. The expanded enterprise continued to augment its paid-up capital by a factor of more than 23, from an initial 4,185,000 yen in 1906 to 97,750,000 yen in 1938, the year of the last capital increase.[25]

Major breweries were among the most capitalized and asset-rich Japanese industrial corporations during the 1910s and 1930s. Dai Nihon's paid-up capital placed it thirty-sixth in 1918 (8,800,000 yen) and seventh in 1930 (50,000,000 yen). The need for capital is also reflected in the fact that several breweries made the list of the largest 200 Japanese companies by asset size, which incidentally included not a single sake manufacturer (Table 4.1). However, their asset size ranking was usually slightly lower than their relative position as measured by the amount of paid-up capital, suggesting they needed more capital than assets to run their operations compared to other firms in the pre-war period.

Compared to firms in other industries with a similar size in terms of paid-up capital, Dai Nihon Beer generated the highest profits (9,153,000 yen) in 1930, with far fewer employees (3,022). Labour-intensive textile firms like Dai Nihon Spinning needed 27,913 workers to yield 4,721,000 yen, but even firms in more capital-intensive industries such as Fuji Paper employed 8,270 workers for 5,010,000 yen profit or Japan Oil 5,309 workers for 3,479, 000 yen. Firms in the emerging heavy and chemical industries, except Kawasaki Shipyards, had a lower level of capitalization and still often made losses, although some employed more workers.[26]

In the beer industry in general profitability remained rather consistently high, despite fluctuations and periods of intensive competition. Market leader Dai Nihon in the late 1920s generated an annual average profit rate of over 40 per cent and paid dividends of 30 per cent; and even during a slump in 1930, when the company was reducing its workforce by about thousand workers, the rate was still a respectable 20 per cent and dividends 13 per cent. It was only after 1940, during wartime, that dividends dropped to 10 per cent or less.[27] The dividends Dai Nihon

Table 4.1 Breweries among the 200 largest Japanese industrial firms, 1918 and 1930

Breweries	1918				1930			
	Rank	Assets	Sales	Workers	Rank	Assets	Sales	Workers
Dai Nihon	39	17,194	30,798	1,628	15	82,660	46,500	3,022
Kirin	89	6,652	5,344	397	71	21,656	23,009	783
Teikoku/Sakura	108	5,548	645	255	117	11,228	1,450	—
Kabuto/NBK	131	4,303	141	141	58	27,614	15,226	700

Source: Mark Fruin, *The Japanese Enterprise System* (Oxford: Clarendon Press, 1992), pp. 329–41.

Notes

Asset and sales figures are in 1,000 yen. In 1921 Kabuto Beer merged with soft drink maker Teikoku Kōsen to form Nihon Beer Kōsen (NBK), which Dai Nihon Beer bought in 1933. Teikoku Beer changed its name to Sakura in 1929, and was bought by Dai Nihon Beer in 1943.

Table 4.2 Market share of major breweries in Japan, 1890–1949 (%)

	Name					
	Sapporo	*Japan*	*Nihon*	*Ōsaka*	*Dai Nihon Beer*	*Top two*
Brand	Sapporo	Kirin	Ebisu	Asahi	Sapporo/Ebisu/Asahi	
First brew	1876	1887	1890	1892	1906	
1890	6.2	22.2	12.3			34.5
1900	11.9	15.3	31.1	23.6		54.7
1910		18.9			70.7	89.7
1920		18.9			64.1	83.0
1930		27.0			51.5	78.5
1940		26.5			66.0	92.5
1949		25.7			74.3	100.0

Source: Calculated from Sapporo Biiru KK, *Sapporo Biiru 120 nen Shi*, pp. 867–68.

Note
In 1906 Nihon, Ōsaka, and Sapporo merged to become Dai Nihon Beer. The Japan Brewery was renamed after its beer brand Kirin.

Beer paid out between 1906 and 1922 were almost every year twice as high as those of its smaller arch rival Kirin, suggesting higher profitability at the larger enterprise.[28] One of the outcomes of corporate development through capital increase and merger was to accelerate the trend towards a highly oligopolistic, almost duopolistic, market structure (Table 4.2), in which between 1906 and 1949 the market leader often had a market share of more than double that of its nearest competitor, and the top two companies accounted for between about 80–100 per cent of Japanese consumption.

The policies of the president of Nihon and later Dai Nihon Beer, 'King of Beer' Magoshi Kyōhei, who had previously worked for the Mitsui *zaibatsu*, speeded up the movement towards larger corporations. With the help of the Minister of Agriculture and Commerce he persuaded competitors, one of whom was rather reluctant, to merge into one huge enterprise in 1906. Over the following years he bought up smaller rivals whenever he had the opportunity. Although he failed to achieve his goal of a total market monopoly his company's dominance was overwhelming. Later market entrants, among others Hinode Beer, Sakura Beer, Nichi-Ei Brewing and Tōyō Brewing, failed to gain a significant market position. Dai Nihon and Kirin were the only two breweries to survive the Second World War.[29] Government policy supported the trend towards size. The revision of the unequal treaties permitted the Japanese government to raise tariffs on imports, which in the case of beer was promptly set at 25 per cent of import value starting 1 January 1899, despite the fact that Japanese industry had outgrown the need for infant industry protection.[30] Fiscal policies encouraged larger domestic enterprises. When the government raised taxes on sake brewers in the aftermath of the Sino-Japanese war, the sake lobby complained about the injustice that beer remained tax-free. In anticipation of government action beer brewers formed the *Zenkoku Biiru Gyōsha Dōmei*, their first industry association, which, however, failed to prevent the first beer tax of 7 yen per *koku* (180 litres) in 1901.[31] Accompanying further raises in the beer tax, which by 1925 amounted to a significant 39.5 per cent of a bottle's sales price, the government established a minimum annual production volume requirement of 180,000 litres (1,000 *koku*) to obtain a brewing license, a move that closed down small breweries and further promoted the development of large-scale production.[32]

One of the advantages of a strong capital basis was the ability to set-up modern breweries with state-of-the art foreign brewing technology. More than any other country, Germany was the international beer trendsetter in terms of taste and technology during the nineteenth century, but the German lager beer, named after the German word for storage, was more expensive to produce because of the additional need for cooling equipment, such as the artificial ice-making machine commercialized by the German Carl Linde after 1879.[33] Japanese breweries spent large sums of money to purchase artificial ice-making machines, which amounted to up to a third of setting-up costs. It was for that purpose that the Japan Brewery needed to increase its capital base.[34] Other technological advances such as Louis Pasteur's findings on fermentation and the spread of mass bottling revolutionized the beer industry in general, regardless of beer type. Nevertheless, Japanese brewers' choice of lager meant a larger initial investment in technology, which raised the barrier to later entrants and smaller competitors who lacked the necessary funds and thus could not brew at the same level of quality and cost.

While Germans and their new brewing techniques became influential in many countries, especially in the United States where Germans managed several leading enterprises, it was in Japan that German-type beer together with German technology and German material totally swept the market. Only German brewing experts were hired by major breweries, with Moritz Hermann Heckert the first to arrive in 1887 and Erwin F. Eichelberg staying the longest, at 16 years.[35] Demand for German brewers at one point was so strong that a German resident complained about receiving employment offers just because of his German nationality despite knowing nothing about this kind of work.[36] In line with hiring German experts, breweries took over entire brewing systems from Germany, ranging from modern brick factory architecture to wooden beer barrels and cork for bottle closing.[37] German brewers influenced some of the purchasing decisions, and Japanese employees studying in Germany reinforced a preference for German equipment, which they purchased for their companies on the advice of their teachers. German trading houses in Japan, such as Rohde and Raspe, promoted and benefited from this 'buy German' approach as long-term suppliers. Numerous advertisements of German brewing machinery manufacturers testified to strong Japanese demand.[38] While German diplomatic reports in the 1880s had complained about the decline in beer imports due to the activities of German brewers in Japan, they rejoiced later that all tools and brewing ingredients came from Germany.[39] Around the turn of the twentieth century, the German brew master Wilhelm Coblitz praised Nihon Beer as 'equipped with the most modern German machines and devices'.[40]

Japanese breweries not only knew of the benefits of modern German technology in the fields of production but also emphasized it repeatedly in their advertisement campaigns to stress quality and taste. If they could afford a German brew master or to train Japanese in Germany they would duly stress these facts in their public relations campaigns. The recurrent theme in the advertising slogans was the high quality and authentic taste that adherence to the German model produced. To what extent consumers really cared about German authenticity is unclear, but to the breweries and their sales agents the image of German taste and quality was worth considerable effort. When Nihon Beer thought about extending the contract of its German brewer, it decided to do so despite the high costs, since the top Japanese manager stressed the importance of the existence of a German brewer 'as a figurehead', especially as long as competing breweries still retained their German experts.[41]

As a result of the application of new technology Japanese beer production soared, increasing by a factor of 122, from 2,566 kilolitres (14,253 *koku*) in 1890 to 312,198 kilolitres (1,734,435 *koku*) in 1939, before dropping off during the war.[42] With higher production volumes costs gradually declined, which despite higher taxes led to a drop in the price of beer compared to those for other food products. In 1880 a bottle of beer cost 25 times that of a portion of soba noodles, but 60 years later it could be bought at only three times the price of such noodles (Figure 4.1).

After the turn of the twentieth century, beer and sake reached price parity, and by 1938 the beer price had fallen to less than half the sake price for the same volume. In that year the market for alcoholic beverages was still dominated by sake (73 per cent), but beer had achieved a respectable second place (19 per cent), above distilled liquors. The key limiting factor in faster market expansion was the reluctance of consumers to drink more beer. Individual taste was as much an issue

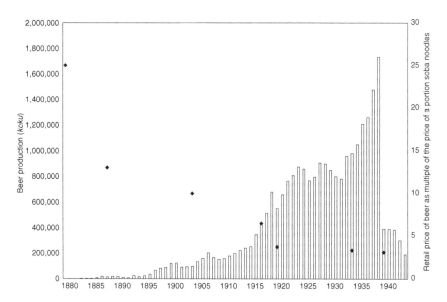

Figure 4.1 Beer production (*koku*) and beer price in Japan, 1880–1944.

Source: Sapporo Biiru KK, *Sapporo Biiru 120 nen Shi*, pp. 867–69.

as the still rather steep price with one *shō* (1.8 litres) of beer amounting to half a day's wage of a sake brewer.[43] Breweries at times overestimated demand growth and expanded their facilities too quickly, as in 1929 when the industry was only brewing at 53 per cent of capacity. However, the utilization rate among the two largest brewers was higher than among the smaller upstart competitors, showing the advantages of entrenched market dominance.[44]

Japan's modern beer enterprises were not only large players in an oligopolistic market, they also expanded in a way predicted by Alfred Chandler's model, namely by adding more specialized units to the enterprise. From brewing they integrated backwards to secure a predictable supply of water, barley and hops, the three main ingredients in the brewing process. Identifying water with the chemical properties best suited for beer was often one of the initial issues in determining the location of a brewery. The Ōsaka Beer Company even sent water samples to Germany for analysis before building its first brewing plant.[45] Nihon Beer had several fights and suits with the local establishment at its Meguro plant because of its growing thirst for water, which deprived farmers of their means of irrigation. Depending on the water, each plant produced a beer of distinctive flavour, so that Sapporo beer tasted different when made at the Sapporo or the Azumabashi breweries. From the 1930s the particular consistency of water was no longer an important issue due to the ability to add the desired properties through chemical treatment of the water.[46] During the early years, barley, in the roasted form of malt, was imported from Germany. Major breweries established their own malting facilities to process barley in the 1890s following the lead of Ōsaka Beer. Barley for malting, however, the breweries continued to purchase from abroad. Prior to the turn of the twentieth century several breweries began experimentation with domestic barley cultivation. To that end they imported barley seeds considered to be more suitable for beer than native varieties. These seeds they disseminated to newly formed farmers' associations, whose supply by the Taishō period covered most of the breweries' demand.[47] In contrast to barley, hops were more difficult to grow reliably at competitive cost and quality in Japan. This is ironic since the 1872 recommendation to establish a state-run brewery in Hokkaidō was mainly based on the observation that wild hops already existed on the island, and the brewery in Sapporo from its inception pioneered hop cultivation, partly with government support.[48] While hops could be grown climatically anywhere in Japan, strong winds, excessive rains and humidity, insects and disease repeatedly harmed the sensitive and labour-intensive crops. Despite decades of effort, Japan's breweries only achieved temporary self-sufficiency in hop procurement during the Second World War when production had declined. Breweries organized hop growers into associations just as they had done for barley farmers. As hop production was associated with both high cost and high risk, these associations attracted wealthier cultivators of mulberry trees and silkworms, so depending on the world prices their enthusiasm for the respective crops varied. In 1937 the government announced its intention to restrict hop imports, forcing the breweries to renew their efforts at domestic self-sufficiency. As a result Dai Nihon Beer hired a German hop expert and increased the acreage under cultivation tenfold within the next five years.[49] Self-sufficiency in procurement of barley and hops may have been driven as much by national pride as a desire for stability, security or economic necessity. Dai Nihon Beer in its initial advertisements justified its creation on the grounds of strengthening the domestic beer industry and ending foreign influence through the production of beer by Japanese experts with Japanese ingredients. Over the following years it remained one of the forerunners in indigenization drives.[50] Kirin, under foreign management and ownership until 1907, kept a German brewer until he was expelled during the First World War and continued to import all their hops until the embargo in 1937.[51] In fact, Kirin attributed its reputation for superior taste partly to its foreign image.

Almost all modern Japanese breweries added bottling capacities to their brewing operations. The move into glass manufacturing was an economic and technological necessity to overcome the reliance on the limited supply of recycled foreign imported bottles. Several independent Japanese glass manufacturers originally satisfied the demand from the brewers, but they did not expand their capacities and technology fast enough to keep pace. The two major problems the brewers needed to solve were how to devise ways of mass bottling production at low cost and how to close bottles effectively. New technical innovations coming from the United States around the turn of the century promised to solve these problems. The hand-blown glass bottles, whose shape turned out to be somewhat uneven, could be replaced by machine-manufactured standardized types. Instead of corks that easily popped these standardized bottles could be closed by the so-called crown cork, the metal caps found on most bottles today. Dai Nihon Beer led the drive to increasing and modernizing its bottle supply by integrating several independent glass companies into its business as subsidiaries.

In contrast to their active move into the sources of supply, especially malting and bottling, breweries did not expand much into distribution, remaining more manufacturing than sales companies. Their sales departments dealt with wholesalers, restaurants and liquor stores, but the breweries did not successfully establish franchise networks selling their particular brand exclusively to end users. Kirin left the exclusive sales and marketing, even branding, of its beer to Meidi-ya, a retail chain specializing in Western products. Originally this arrangement was a legal necessity, since the unequal treaties prevented foreigners from owning land and travelling outside the treaty ports without special government permission. One of the very reasons for the origins of Meidi-ya was Japan Brewery's desire to have a Japanese sales agent, since it was a foreign-owned corporation.[52] When the possibility emerged that the Japan Brewery was to be sold to a competitor, it was Meidi-ya's managers who organized the group of Japanese investors who acquired a major stake in the brewery in 1907.[53] One unusual development in the industry was the virtual end of sales competition through cartelization before the war. In 1933 the two dominant brewers joined forces by establishing a Joint Beer Sales Company for domestic sales and the Beer Export Union for overseas sales, even before the government actively promoted cartels. They kept the sales arrangement until 1945.

Other areas of expansion show that the initial one-plant breweries turned into large multi-unit enterprises by adding new product lines and venturing overseas.

Dai Nihon and its competitors moved into soft drinks after Magoshi Kyōhei noticed this practice on a visit to the Carlsberg Brewery in Denmark. By building up its own capabilities and acquiring beverage firms, Dai Nihon had taken a third of the emerging soft drink market by the 1930s, although this was less profitable than its established beer business. As mentioned earlier, Japan's breweries exported their products from the 1890s. With the expansion of the Japanese formal and informal empire they acquired or constructed breweries abroad. Dai Nihon's purchase of the Anglo-German Brewery in Tsingtao after the German defeat was the first overseas foray. In subsequent years, especially in the 1930s, breweries added several production facilities in Korea, Taiwan and Manchuria.

The large multi-unit beer corporation from the early stages needed a larger and better-trained labour force than the small-scale craft brewers preceding it. At Nihon Beer 36 managers and technicians were responsible for 235 workers in 1897.[54] Dai Nihon Beer began with 1,847 employees in 1906, growing rapidly to 5,196 in 1925 before a period of rationalization reduced the number again to 2,785 in 1933. Output and profits per worker continued to increase gradually in the prewar decades regardless of the size of the labour force. The output per employee rose from 61 *koku* per worker (1906) to 300 *koku* per worker (1939).[55] Unlike in other consumer industries such as textiles, the labour force consisted predominantly of men, with women mainly working in the bottling units.[56] Modern breweries hired university graduates of science departments for their technical positions, and many of these later took over high management responsibilities, especially those sent to Germany for further training. In 1888, Ikuta Hiizu was the first Japanese to study at the Weihenstephan academy, Germany's foremost centre of beer technology. Ikuta later became the managing director of Ōsaka Beer. Takahashi Ryūtarō, who also studied in Germany, not only followed Magoshi Kyōhei as president of Dai Nihon in 1937 but became a postwar cabinet minister, to name just two of the most successful.[57] After the turn of the century mostly salaried managers took key positions in the directorate of breweries instead of major stockholders.

Industrial capitalism between free-market models and protective practices

Alfred Chandler's theory of the rise of the modern industrial corporation goes a long way towards explaining the genesis and growth of the Japanese beer industry. Cost advantages of economies of scale determined by the rate of market growth and the adaptation of foreign technology shaped the nature of competition in the beer industry. In some ways, the Japanese beer industry conformed to a greater degree to Chandler's expectations than did breweries in the United States, or those in Great Britain and Germany, which he already calls 'a special case'.[58] Just as happened elsewhere, Japanese breweries integrated new technology effectively to expand the market and their role in it. Within their domestic markets, however, Japanese breweries appear even more capital-intensive, more dominant, more organizationally complex, more nationalistic and more internationally active than in the other three countries. Just like the large-scale American brewers, but unlike the more regionally minded smaller and traditional European brewers, Japanese brewers saw the entire nation as a potential consumer market. An additional feature is that they did not expand as much into distribution as the British brewers with their pub networks, nor did they become worldwide technological trendsetters like the Germans.

In all countries, the development towards an industrial beer enterprise was accelerated or slowed down by traditional customs of consumption and the regulatory attitude of national governments. The first mover in Japan, a relative latecomer to beer production, went more quickly through the structural transformation towards the modern industrial enterprise than the pioneers in countries with entrenched family-based craft beer customs. Once the modernization in Japan was underway, the state protected big Japanese firms from foreign threats and upstart local competition, whereas German legislation prevented large-scale national accumulations through the rule that regional specialists could only brew in their specific region.[59] As a result, two Japanese companies shared 100 per cent of the market in 1949 in contrast to about 100 breweries in Germany sharing 50 per cent of the market in 1930.[60]

In Japan it took the force of the United States Occupation's anti-monopoly policy to break-up the largest company, Dai Nihon Beer, into what today is Asahi and Sapporo, thereby perpetuating the older oligopoly with one more actor. Despite the entry of whisky maker Suntory into the field in 1964 and the proliferation of microbreweries (*jibiiru*) after the abolition of regulations preventing small-scale breweries in 1994, the market continues to be dominated by three companies established as modern industrial enterprises during the second half of the 1880s.

When it comes to the speed of separation of ownership and management in large corporations, the feature many scholars see as the crucial test of the applicability of Chandler's ideas, the Japanese beer businesses probably passes this test better than most Western breweries during the early twentieth century.[61] The greater difficulty in obtaining larger amounts of capital for faster expansion when capital was still scarce made domination by a single founder or his family less likely. From the beginning all modern Japanese breweries were incorporated as joint-stock companies with widely distributed ownership and increasingly guided by salaried managers and technicians, in contrast to the prevalence of owner-managers or descendants of the founding family in breweries elsewhere.

As predicted by theory, use of advanced technology and exploitation of market opportunities were key factors in shaping the beer industry in Japan as well, but it seems that if we apply Chandler's ideas to Japan, he is rather silent on one important feature in the establishment of the modern industrial Japanese corporation, namely the problem of overcoming the capital bottleneck in a developing economy. Even where entrepreneurs understood the cost advantages of scale production, German technology and market penetration, without the necessary funding, many of them not only had to give up any hope of becoming big but to stop competing at all. One of the important reasons why successful breweries were seeking *zaibatsu* affiliation from the early twentieth century was that they lacked the capacity and capital to go completely alone. The perennial rivalry between the Dai Nihon and Kirin breweries reflected the competition between the Mitsubishi and Mitsui *zaibatsu*, which supported them.

Notes

1 Alfred D. Chandler Jr, *Scale and Scope: The Dynamics of Industrial Capitalism* (Cambridge, MA: The Belknap Press of Harvard University Press, 1990), pp. 21–26.
2 Ibid., p. 26.
3 Although Chandler also discusses the cost advantages of economies of scope and transactions, these will be ignored here, since they are not relevant to the argument that follows.
4 Jeffrey Bernstein, 'Japanese Capitalism', in Thomas K. McCraw (ed.), *Creating Modern Capitalism: How Entrepreneurs, Companies, and Countries Triumphed in Three Industrial Revolutions* (Cambridge, MA: Harvard University Press, 1995), pp. 450–54.
5 Mark Fruin, *The Japanese Enterprise System* (Oxford: Clarendon Press, 1992), p. 62.
6 Takafusa Nakamura and Konosuke Odaka (eds), *Economic History of Japan 1914–1955: A Dual Structure*, vol. 3 of *The Economic History of Japan: 1600–1990* (Oxford: Oxford University Press, 2003).
7 William D. Wray, 'Afterword: The Writing of Japanese Business History', in Wray (ed.), *Managing Industrial Enterprise: Cases from Japan's Prewar Experience* (Cambridge, MA: Council on East Asian Studies, Harvard University, 1989), pp. 324–30.
8 Alfred D. Chandler Jr, *The Visible Hand: The Managerial Revolution in American Business* (Cambridge, MA: The Belknap Press of Harvard University Press, 1977), pp. 256–57. Barrel sizes for liquids in the US customary and British Imperial measure ranged from 31.5 to 42 gallons. Unless otherwise stated, this study will use the customary ale and beer barrel size of 136.27 litres (36 gallons/144 quarts) as a basis for conversion into the metric system.
9 Chandler, *Scale and Scope*, pp. 433–34.
10 Naomichi Ishige, *The History and Culture of Japanese Food* (London: Kegan Paul, 2001), pp. 22, 26, 34–35.
11 *Encyclopaedia Britannica 2003* (CD-Rom).
12 Klaus Antoni, *Miwa, der heilige Trank: Zur Geschichte und religiösen Bedeutung des alkoholischen Getränks in Japan* (Stuttgart: F. Steiner, 1988).
13 In 1902, 35.9 per cent; Sapporo Biiru Kabushiki Gaisha, Kōhōbu Shashi Hensanshitsu, *Sapporo Biiru 120 nen Shi* (Tokyo: Dai Nihon Insatsu, 1996), p. 866.
14 Jūrō Hashimoto, 'The Rise of Big Business', in Nakamura and Odaka, *Economic History of Japan 1914–1955: A Dual Structure*, vol. 3 of *Economic History of Japan: 1600–1990* (Oxford: Oxford University Press, 2003), p. 192.
15 Kirin Biiru Kabushiki Gaisha Gojūnenshi Henshū Iinkai, *Kirin Gojūnen Shi* (Tokyo: Kirin Biiru, 1957), p. 4; Miyake, Yūzō, *Biiru Kigyōshi* (Tokyo: Mitsutakisha, 1977), pp. 17–18.
16 J.E. Hoare, *Japan's Treaty Ports and Foreign Settlements: The Uninvited Guests, 1858–1899* (Richmond: Curzon, 1994), pp. 21, 23.
17 Harald Fuess, 'Der Aufbau der Bierindustrie in Japan während der Meiji-Zeit: Konsum, Kapital und Kompetenz', *Bochumer Jahrbuch zur Ostasienforschung* 27, 2003, pp. 232–41.
18 Ushigome, Tsutomu, *Meijiki no Tamagawa Ryūiki ni okeru Biirugyō no Kenkyū* (Tōkyū Kankyū Jōka Zaidan, 1997), p. 5. One *koku* is about 180 litres.

19 Asahina, Sadayoshi, *Dai Nihon Yōshu Kanzume Enkakushi* (Tokyo: Nihon Yōshu Kanzume Shinbunsha, 1915), p. 11.
20 Sapporo Biiru KK, *Sapporo Biiru 120 nen Shi*, pp. 24–80.
21 Ushigome, *Meijiki no Tamagawa Ryūiki*, p. 5.
22 Hamada, Tokutarō, *Dai Nihon Biiru Kabushiki Gaisha Sanjūnen Shi* (Tokyo: Dai Nihon Biiru, 1936), pp. 169–70.
23 Tani, Teruhiro (ed.), *Ishikawa Shuzō Bunsho*, vol. 6 (Tokyo: Kasumide, 1994), pp. 44–55.
24 Asahina, *Dai Nihon*, pp. 11–15.
25 Sapporo Biiru KK, *Sapporo Biiru 120 nen Shi*, pp. 176, 265, 852–53.
26 Fruin, *Japanese Enterprise System*, p. 336.
27 Sapporo Biiru KK, *Sapporo Biiru 120 nen Shi*, pp. 269, 852–53.
28 Kirin Biiru Kabushiki Gaisha Kōhōbu Shashi Hensanshitsu, *Kirin Biiru no Rekishi* (Tokyo: Kirin, 1999), p. 33.
29 Sapporo Biiru KK, *Sapporo Biiru 120 nen Shi*, p. 868.
30 'Bierbrauerei', *Deutsches Handelsarchiv. Zeitschrift für Handel und Gewerbe*, 1900, p. 485.
31 Kirin Biiru KK, *Kirin Gojūnen Shi*, p. 53.
32 Sapporo Biiru KK, *Sapporo Biiru 120 nen Shi*, p. 867.
33 Bob Skilnik, *The History of Beer and Brewing in Chicago, 1833–1973* (St Paul, MN: Pogo Press, 1999), pp. 25–27.
34 Endō, Kazuo, *Biiru no 100 nen*, vol. 10 of *Nihon no Gijutsu* (Tokyo: Daiichi Hōki Shuppan Kabushiki Gaisha, 1989), pp. 95–99.
35 Fuess, 'Aufbau der Bierindustrie in Japan', pp. 251–52.
36 *Frankfurter Zeitung. Abendblatt*, 30 January 1887. Reprinted in Kokusai Nyuusu Jiten Shuppan Iinkai Mainichi Komyunikeeshonzu (ed.), *Gaikoku Shinbun ni Miru Nihon* 2 (Tokyo: Mainichi Komyunikeeshonzu, 1990), p. 348.
37 Asahi Biiru Kabushiki Gaisha Shashi Shiryōshitsu, *Asahi 100 nen* (Tokyo: Asahi Biiru, 1990), pp. 122–25. Kirin Biiru KK, *Kirin Gojūnen Shi*, pp. 29–30, 34.
38 Fuess, 'Aufbau der Bierindustrie in Japan', p. 255.
39 'Bierbrauerei', *Deutsches Handels-Archiv*, 1900, p. 486.
40 Wilhelm Coblitz, *Die Pagode: Erinnerungen aus meinem Leben* (Berlin: Hermann Paetel Verlag, 1921), p. 149.
41 Naitō, Hiroshi, 'Meijiki Biiru Gyōkai ni okeru Gaikokujin Gijutsusha no Keifu – "Ebisu Biiru" no Baai o rei ni', *Keiei Shigaku* 29, 4, 1995, p. 67.
42 Sapporo Biiru KK, *Sapporo Biiru 120 nen Shi*, pp. 867–69.
43 Joseph Alphonse Laker, *Entrepreneurship and the Development of the Japanese Beer Industry*, PhD dissertation, Indiana University, 1975, p. 269.
44 Sapporo Biiru KK, *Sapporo Biiru 120 nen Shi*, p. 265.
45 Asahi Biiru KK, *Asahi 100*, p. 118.
46 Laker, *Entrepreneurship and the Development of the Japanese Beer Industry*, p. 229.
47 Sapporo Biiru KK, *Sapporo Biiru 120 nen Shi*, p. 231.
48 Ibid., pp. 32–33.
49 Ibid., p. 292; Laker, *Entrepreneurship and the Development of the Japanese Beer Industry*, pp. 235, 240–45.
50 Hamada, *Dai Nihon Biiru*, pp. 6–7. Asahina, *Dai Nihon Yōshu*, p. 2
51 Kirin Biiru KK, *Kirin Biiru no Rekishi*, p. 50.
52 Kirin Biiru KK, *Kirin Gojūnen Shi*, pp. 35–36.
53 Meijiya, *Meijiya 100 nen Shi* (Tokyo: Toppan Insatsu, 1988), pp. 87–95, 150–56.
54 Sapporo Biiru KK, *Sapporo Biiru 120 nen Shi*, p. 174.
55 Ibid., pp. 269, 852–53.
56 Employment records in Asahi Corporate Archives from around the turn of the century list no female staff ('Ōsaka Biiru Kabushiki Gaisha Shokuin Roku 1905'), but archival photos of the Taishō period show women on the bottling lines. In 1950 Nihon Beer listed 1,467 male and 461 female workers, with an average duration of employment in

1949 of 10.2 for men and 2.6 years for women (Sapporo Biiru KK, *Sapporo Biiru 120 nen Shi*, p. 912.

57 Asahi Biiru KK, *Asahi 100*, pp. 112–17.

58 Chandler, *Scale and Scope*, p. 433.

59 Ibid., p. 514.

60 Holger Starke, 'Ein bierseliges Land: Aus der Geschichte des Brauwesens von Dresden und Umgebung', in Stadtmuseum Dresden and Sächsischer Brauerbund (ed.), *Ein bierseliges Land: Aus der Geschichte des Brauwesens von Dresden und Umgebung* (Halle: Fliegenkopf Verlag, 1996), p. 77.

61 Hidemasa Morikawa, 'Prerequisites for the Development of Managerial Capitalism: Cases in Prewar Japan', in Kesaji Kobayashi and Hidemasa Morikawa (eds), *Development of Managerial Enterprise*, vol. 12 of *International Conference on Business History* (Tokyo: Tokyo University Press, 1986), pp. 1–30.

5   Managing female textile workers
An industry in transition, 1945–75

Helen Macnaughtan

Introduction

This chapter examines how employers in the Japanese cotton textile industry approached the employment and management of women workers during the early post-Second World War decades. The textile industry in Japan had long been a significant employer of female labour since its establishment in the early Meiji period and had built up a distinctive pattern in its employment of young females. However, the years after Japan's defeat in the Second World War brought a new and rapidly changing socio-economic environment, within which the industry was re-established and in many ways forced to reorganise its labour management strategies. This chapter examines why and how textile employers responded to these challenges.

The textile industry had a particular labour history. Its evolution in the pre-war period generated structural rigidities and a degree of path dependence, which challenged the post-war reconstruction of the industry within opposing forces of continuity and change. For post-war textile employers, the cost of change was often deemed to be greater than sticking to what the industry had already established. However, perceptions of pre-war labour conditions, as well as post-war reform, encouraged the industry to seek new ways forward and to endeavour to dispel the lingering criticism. As a traditional employer of large numbers of women and amongst the first industries to utilise females within the paid economy, the textile industry's response to challenges and change during these crucial years in Japan's history makes it a vital study of both labour market and institutional transition.

As an important industry designated for reconstruction during the allied occupation of Japan (1945–52), and as an industry that had earlier been on the receiving end of much international and domestic criticism of its employment structures, the textile industry was in many ways used as a key 'case study' of Japanese labour practice by the Supreme Commander for the Allied Powers (SCAP).[1] As such, the industry's pre-war use of large numbers of women workers, its recruitment strategies and its operation of factory dormitories came under the scrutiny of the occupation authorities and had a significant influence on subsequent labour reform and the establishment of labour legislation (including general labour laws as well as legislation specific to working women).

From the late 1950s and early 1960s, the industry faced new challenges in its continued employment of women workers. As Japan's economy began to take off, the labour market moved from a buyer's market to one with an increasing short-age of labour. Even the labour pool of young females witnessed a decline as ris-ing numbers of young women (and men) opted to remain in post-compulsory education for longer. Newer industries also began to compete for young labour, displacing the textile industry's previous 'stronghold' on the recruitment and employment of young female workers. From the mid-late 1960s textile employ-ers were forced to seek out alternative sources of workers in their efforts to meet the industry's labour requirements. Their key solution to this problem was to try and encourage 'older' Japanese women to enter the textile workforce, and this chapter will highlight the implications for textile employers in taking this path.

This chapter will examine key challenges facing the industry during these years in its employment and management of a largely female workforce and will discuss how textile employers responded to these challenges and how the situa-tion induced them to adjust their labour management strategies. In doing so, the chapter outlines the key management strategies used by the industry for its core workforce of young female workers (centring on their domicile in dormitories) and also alternative labour management approaches for the expanding group of older female workers. It will consider why certain management strategies were used, how they were implemented and what they were expected to achieve. The implications of socio-economic change and the response by industry managers during these years will be analysed, as will the various strategies for 'organising' females within the industry, particularly with regard to the crucial transition that took place in the demographic structure of the female labour force.

A new post-war environment for textile employers

In many ways, the early post-war years were for the Japanese textile industry a period characterised by a 'groping for a new direction' in labour management, often based on trial and error. Various factors were at play influencing the development of the industry's labour management strategies. These included ongoing historical issues, legal changes, new labour relations and recruitment foundations, new management theories from abroad and changing national social and economic circumstances. In some respects, early post-war textile managers were constrained both economically and psychologically by previous labour management institutions existing in the industry. At the same time, the changed post-war environment, as well as a desire to escape from the pre-war 'image' of the industry, brought pressure on employers to place renewed emphasis on the issue of labour management itself. This resulted in the industry probing for new ways forward, firmly based on existing structures, yet expanding its aims and operation to address the changing environment.

In general, the post-war period exposed the development of management strategies in the industry to broader trends. In the early post-war years, many management theories were brought in from the United States.[2] Textile managers researched and adapted these new systems to match industry circumstances, combining them with existing management methods developed by the industry in the pre-war period and compiling new labour management 'handbooks' for the industry. Two main factors were influencing employers as this process was carried out – the labour management history of the industry and the contemporary environment.

While more formal theories of labour management and their practical implementation had existed in the pre-war industry, there was a general view and feeling amongst textile management that the post-war years signified a very new period in labour management ideals and structure. The evolution of early labour management ideologies in the pre-war period had been to a large extent constructed around 'family' based relationships. The development of various forms of 'paternalistic' management, at least in rhetorical terms, can be said to have been strong in Japanese pre-war industry. The style of employment and composition of the labour force used by the pre-war textile industry certainly created a distinct pattern. Young women were relocated often far away from their family homes into factory–dormitory complexes, and because they were primarily young and unmarried, the industry immersed them in 'familistic management' from an early stage.[3] The enterprises took it upon themselves to 'train' and 'rear' workers from the time they were young, not only to secure skilled workers but also to create a labour force with a strong 'corporate consciousness'.[4] The textile industry also took it upon itself to 'train' female workers for their future married life by providing instruction in traditional female etiquette based arts, thereby promoting the 'cultivation of womanly virtues'.[5] This early establishment of significant company influence on an employee's life, both working and non-working, had a large impact on the development of later corporate styles in Japan.

The issue of the exploitative management of female labour in the pre-war years, known as *Jokō Aishi*,[6] was uppermost in the minds of managers as the industry's labour strategies were re-evaluated after the war. A focus of the industry's concern from the late 1940s onwards was how to overcome this 'inherited' view of working conditions for the core female labour force. Whether such conditions existed as harshly or not in the pre-war period as is often claimed is beyond the scope of this chapter, but the important point to be made is that the inheritance of the *Jokō Aishi* concept from the cotton industry's history did have a strong influence on the post-war image of the industry and became a basis for reforming ideas on the management of the female workforce.

Alongside these 'historical' considerations, there were contemporary socioeconomic factors influencing the development of labour management systems at this time. These included the establishment of new national labour laws in Japan in the late 1940s, high-speed economic growth after 1955, subsequent labour shortage problems, the rise in education, as well as technological advances and associated labour rationalisation policies. For example, new labour legislation required that employers now recruit young labour via nation-wide Public Employment Security Offices. This meant that textile employers could no longer directly canvas for labour or use agents as they had done in the pre-war decades. An expansion of the manufacturing sector to include new industries such as electronics increased the demand for labour and brought a much more competitive environment even for industries seeking to employ female workers. Advances in spinning and weaving technology meant some decline in workforce numbers but did not completely alleviate the industry's recruitment bids within an era of labour shortage. These years, therefore, represented a very new environment for the textile industry within which new labour legislation had to be adhered to and the industry's labour policies and management strategies had to be (re)defined.

A key principle of management that can be said to have been in operation in the industry was 'human relations' based labour management, which was management of workers through the implementation of an environment conducive to promoting the 'morale', 'fulfilment' and 'happiness' of workers. The dormitory and education systems[7] for young female workers formed a substantial component of this management approach. There were also 'organisation based' labour management strategies in use, which were more 'scientific' in approach and focused on the implementation of standards for job performance, the promotion of a suitable and safe workplace environment for labour and the creation of an 'efficient' workforce. However, at least for female employees, a concern for the 'welfare' and 'upbringing' of young girls as both workers and women remained paramount and formed a key basis for labour management strategies during these decades.

The 'gender factor' therefore played a large role in the process of managing and organising workers. The management of an industry where female workers dominated was felt to be very different from one where male workers predominated.[8] The cotton industry, particularly spinning, was still geared towards employing primarily young female labour, viewed as a workforce whose members would work for just a few years while they were 'post-schooling' and 'pre-marriage'.[9] They were not to be organised within a lifetime employment system as were males. Thus, the youth and the 'female' characteristics of the core workforce influenced the development of a labour management strategy based on three main components: (1) welfare facilities (centring around dormitories) for the 'enrichment' of workers' lives; (2) education to prepare workers for their future lives (not necessarily viewed as a 'working' lives) and (3) in-house training to develop their ability as workers.[10]

In essence, because women comprised the core labour force in the industry, the central labour management ideas that developed were aimed at managing female labour. In other words, what was essentially a system of 'female labour management' was developed. The transition encountered throughout the period, and discussed in the following sections, represented textile managers' response to the changed characteristics of the female workforce in terms of both composition and consciousness, as well as to changing socio-economic structures. It therefore offers a good case for highlighting the importance of institutional change during these years.

Managing young female workers – the role of dormitories

In the post-war years, young women were recruited into the industry in large numbers straight from school within a structured annual system known as 'group employment' (*shūdan shūgyō*). This group employment played a large role in the organisation of this young workforce into a working and living community. There is little doubt that in the textile industry the dormitory and education systems were a central focus of the labour management strategy for (young) female workers. A report by a labour manager in 1963 outlined how dormitory and education systems were not just to be seen as facilities (a non-working welfare benefit) but as an 'ideal' method of labour management.[11]

During these years, an overriding central desire and focus of employers was the creation of a 'stable' labour force in the industry, and within this a fundamental aim was to continue to use young females as the core workforce.[12] It was felt that a unified management system across the textile industry as a whole was needed nationally in order to ensure this stability. The dormitory and education systems for female workers became the focus of this unified system. During these years, therefore, the development of labour management ideas and strategies to organise labour took place in large-scale cotton spinning enterprises, in conjunction with industry associations and unions. Over the period it gradually saw a trickle-down effect to smaller-scale enterprises as well. The dormitory (and accompanying education) system in theory interacted as a 'complete management system' for young females in the textile industry. A key question is why the industry went to so much trouble to provide extensive dormitory and educational facilities, and how these labour management strategies, essentially providing for the 'non-working' life of employees, aimed not only to 'organise' workers but also to 'benefit' the company.

The dormitory system was felt to contribute directly to industry aims and to have practical application to the workplace. A 'stable' dormitory life had long been viewed as bringing stability to the production process. The textile industry, particularly spinning, was a processing industry highly dependent on overseas markets for raw materials as well as inevitably facing severe competition for export markets. This required a two-shift system of operation and a focus on high volume production. As long as factories continued with their present scale, location and operational structure, dormitories were felt to be inseparable from production. Further to this, it was felt that if dormitory management was carried out correctly, the industry could expect orderly and efficient labour operations as feedback. Moreover, textile jobs such as spinning and weaving belonged to the category of 'simple work', and while females were viewed as suited for such jobs, it was therefore recognised that these jobs could become monotonous. Providing young women with a full dormitory and school life would, it was hoped, contribute to relieving the monotony and boredom of work and encourage workers' individual development and growth.[13]

The central recruitment strategy during these post-war years continued to be aimed at young female school leavers. Therefore, despite some changes, not least the gradual increase in the number of older, female commuting workers during this period, the Japanese cotton industry still felt the need to maintain the dormitory system essentially in its 'traditional' operational form. This also meant that the dormitory (and education) systems continued to be prominently located within overall management strategy. Moreover, it is evident that dormitories were used as a means to integrate all young female employees into a specific management structure. Even young females recruited from local areas to factories were required to enter dormitory residence.

The operation of dormitories underwent a significant transition during these years, particularly with regard to the important improvement of dormitory standards. Two factors can be said to have played a role in this: national legislation and industry management strategies. The dormitory system was overhauled during an era when efforts for labour democratisation were being made under the influence of SCAP. The 1947 Labour Standards Law contained a section on dormitories. While the focus was mainly on physical standards for the operation of workplace dormitories, the legislation also required enterprises to draw up regulations governing the boarders' daily time schedules with the 'majority consent' of dormitory residents. This aspect of worker 'freedom' – or rather the lack of such freedom – had been heavily criticised in the pre-war years and was an issue that was particularly taken up by SCAP.[14]

The operation of the dormitory system came to be viewed by textile employers from two main perspectives. The first was the management of dormitories 'from above', identifying the structure and role of the company as financiers and administrators of dormitories. The second was the management of dormitories 'from within', which established the role of the so-called 'self-government system' in the daily operation of dormitories, whereby the boarders or workers themselves were given prime responsibility for the organisation and running of dormitories. As members of various self-government committees, female boarders had to conduct meetings, make administrative decisions and have contact with outside groups (e.g. unions) in the organisation of dormitory operations, activities and events. In addition to its practical operational role, the self-government system was viewed as a means of growth and development for young females. The aim was for this experience to enhance their qualities as both workers and 'social individuals'. The operation of dormitories for young female workers and boarders therefore became a significant area for textile employers in the post-war years both in terms of investment in facilities and in terms of strategic planning in the context of labour management policy.

Labour management practices in transition

Maintenance of the dormitory system naturally encountered the need for change during the period under study. The monitoring of dormitory operations and requirements was an ongoing part of discussions and reports by industry labour management committees, from which central themes and developments can be identified.[15] Textile managers were keen to recognise how management of the dormitories had progressed to date, to identify problems for attention and to focus on any implications and requirements for the future, particularly any need for adapting the strategy in light of any changes in the structure of the female workforce.

A crucial component of the management of young women living in the company dormitories was provision for their 'education' in the skills necessary for management of their private lives and promotion of their growth as 'individuals within a society'. To achieve this, it became common practice in many large-scale enterprises for female boarders to be no longer thought of in a uniform fashion as 'young', but to be classified according to age and length of service.[16] Various guidance and education policies were formulated to achieve differentiated management of different age levels. For example, at the entry-level age of 15 years, factory girls were characterised as 'socially undeveloped', with few opinions of their own and with a propensity to spend all their wages. They were deemed to require not only factory-floor training but also a range of instruction and teaching, from etiquette and manners to basic self-budgeting and guidance on recreational reading. At the age of 16, they were becoming used to factory life but were still considered to be 'young' and 'somewhat selfish', and thus required instruction on the importance of community, dormitory life, part-time schooling (provided for by textile companies) and various 'life topics'. It was noted that at 17–18 years old, they often became bored with factory and dormitory life and were prone to quit. Members of this group were therefore encouraged to further develop their lives as workplace 'seniors' and mentors to younger girls and were also encouraged to take up new hobbies and club activities. This is also recorded as being the age when employers took it upon themselves to begin some form of sex education within dormitory and/or educational institutions in the industry. At 19–20 years of age, female workers were encouraged to pursue part-time tertiary educational courses and were given guidance and practical instruction (e.g. home economics) with regard to their futures and to potential marriage.[17]

During this period, many large-scale textile companies also introduced a system whereby older or 'senior' girls lived in housing separated from the main dormitory complex. This was set up in the form of small apartments or dormitory units from which they could organise themselves within smaller living groups and have more freedom (e.g. freedom to entertain in the evenings).[18] The national textile union commented that, in general, there was a move towards making female dormitories more like 'apartments' in form during these years.[19] In many ways, this was to prepare older girls for running a household and for marriage within the wider context of the industry's responsibility for the 'socialisation' of young females.

As highlighted by these examples, a key issue that began to emerge for the industry was that there needed to be a more diversified approach to the organisation and management of young female workers. This was prompted in part by dormitory administrative problems that emerged during employer reviews of dormitory policy but was also the result of more general socio-economic changes taking place in Japan and a feeling that young women now demanded a more detailed and specialised management approach. Management records began to talk of what they identified as a move from 'heteronomy to autonomy', from 'singular management to pluralist management' and a movement from the 'convenience of management' to the 'convenience of the residents'.[20] A definite change was a shift from policymaking centred on employer requirements to one centred on employee needs and one which was driven by changes in the composition of the textile workforce. It was noted that the average age of dormitory boarders had risen and that more suitable management methods relative to the varying ages of boarders would have to be considered and included when making dormitory and other employment policy.

The effects of general socio-economic trends and change were also subjects for management discussion during this period. It was felt that there had been a change in the social consciousness of young females, to which the management of education and dormitory systems must adapt.[21] The rise in national education and living standards as well as the improved status of women as workers and members of society were considered. From the late 1960s and early 1970s, changes in the industrial environment such as technological progress, reductions in workforce numbers and moves away from the labour-intensive nature of textiles were also to be taken into account when considering future policy. Significantly, the cost of labour and the costs for management were changing, and young female workers were noted as no longer being the 'cheap' source of labour they had once been. Indeed, the constant need for monitoring of dormitory and other systems with reports and committees and the identification of ideas and devices to improve and make effective the process of labour management as an 'institution' were noted as significant postwar trends.

While management's response to these types of issues primarily centred upon adapting the dormitory system and existing employment practices to take into account the changed conditions, employers were further challenged as a key shift in the labour market took place. Textile employers found themselves increasingly unable to recruit sufficient numbers of young female school-leavers over this period and were forced to seek out and increase their employment of older women. Thus, it was gradually acknowledged that a new labour management approach was required that took into account both female dormitory boarders/workers and commuting permanent, temporary and part-time female workers – in other words, a widening range of female workers. Some form of new management system based on an individual's value and ability was deemed to be crucial, and in many ways this was contrary to the traditional employment and management of young females, which was based on values such as age (i.e. employment at school leaving age) and involved a strong company role in 'nurturing', 'guiding' and 'developing' young ability. This posed a key challenge for the industry in adapting its existing labour management strategies.

A push for change – managing older female workers

The dormitory-centred organisation of labour had long been established for the management of young females, but not for older females. Older women, at least in theory, were not felt to fit well into the industry's established mode of operations, which involved the relocation of workers into company dormitories. This was because older women were primarily married and, therefore, less flexible and less mobile, mainly desiring employment in close proximity to their permanent residence. In this respect, the textile industry initially took the view that it was difficult to incorporate older women into the current labour management structures and into shift-work operations. At the same time, because the dormitory system was already long 'entrenched' within the industry's mode of operations, companies made little attempt at first to employ commuting older women as a regular workforce.

The utilisation of older women in the industry during this period was primarily in the form of temporary or part-time production workers, although some were employed in more permanent non-productive roles such as dormitory matrons and school teachers. The industry itself commented that, in general, the textile industry, particularly the spinning sector, was 'late' in its utilisation of older women and part-timers compared with other industries, and that this was primarily due to the structure of the shift-system of employment in factories. Overall, it appears that the shift-system in textile production was seen as a 'barrier' to the employment of older women, rather than, for example, a system that allowed for flexibility in work hours. In many ways this view was taken because older women employed as temporary workers had initially emerged as an economic buffer force to counteract operational or labour fluctuations. By their very nature they were therefore seen as only 'temporary', and their integration into the management system established for regular workers was not seen as desirable or necessary.

However, despite the industry's long tradition as an employer of young females and a management and production style centred around their employment, there did occur a gradual and significant movement in the structural composition of the female labour force to include large numbers of older women as temporary, part-time and seasonal female workers.[22] While this did not significantly impact on the dormitory and education systems, which continued in operation for young females throughout the period, it did raise several issues, and the diversification of the female labour force had important consequences for management. Because the employment of young workers and older workers were essentially very different in nature and composition, they required different management styles and approaches. In many ways, the perception that older workers were not 'suitable' for the textiles mode of labour management and operations had to be reconciled with the reality that their actual employment within the workforce was increasing significantly, and that they would have to become a recognised focus of labour management strategy.

In some respects, the movement towards using older women could be encompassed within the new labour management strategy which was being generally employed in the management of young females – that is the movement from a 'unified' or 'singular' management approach to one of 'plural' management (by diverse age levels).[23] In other words, this strategy could be extended to include movement from an old unitary system of management based on young females living in dormitories as 'regular' employees to a new system comprising many layers: young females vs. middle-aged females, dormitory boarders vs. commuters and regular employees vs. temporary and part-time employees.

However, the positive utilisation of older women required not only the development of a further 'alternate' and 'new' labour management system but also required the creation of an environment within which older women could be incorporated into an essentially 'young' workplace and utilised effectively. There was a recognition that not only was the industry obliged to try and recruit and employ older female workers because of the decline in the availability of young workers, but that housewives in Japan at this time were being released from the home in increasing numbers with the aim of improving their standard of living and enriching their life and leisure time. However, the majority were not under formal labour contracts and only from the late 1960s did management policy towards this group of workers start to become a consideration for textile employers.

Temporary and part-time women workers were noted by the industry as being predominantly 'housewives', and it was therefore necessary for labour managers to understand their different characteristics relative to those of young female workers. One textile company identified several 'basic characteristics' of older female workers in a labour management report. Noting the 'strong' points of older women, the report recorded that they were emotionally stable, had a stable attitude to work and were quick to be assimilated into factory work. Noting their 'weak' points, it recorded that they were often absent due to housework responsibilities or child-related activities and absent for longer periods during school holidays and in the farming season.[24]

The identification of these characteristics highlights an important point. The ability to depend upon older women as regular workers appeared to be a significant matter of concern for the industry during this period. Doubts were primarily based upon the importance attached to these women's socio-economic role within the domestic sphere. In many ways the industry felt that married women could not be relied upon as a sole source of labour. In the 1960s, several prominent textile companies set up 'test factories' whereby they employed only older commuting women workers from the local area in an attempt to reduce the labour costs of employing young females (who required dormitory, welfare and educational facilities). These test factories were said to have failed because of the inability of employers to rely on older women who were often absent for domestic reasons.[25] In many ways, this image of older women may well have developed into something of a stereotype in the post-war period and created a kind of reinforcing cycle that permitted discrimination against female workers in the Japanese labour market. Indeed, the industry's very focus on dormitories and education as core management strategies, both containing a range of 'lifestyle' components that were far broader than the 'workplace skills' required from a labour force, systematically reinforced the view that the 'real' role of (even unmarried) women was not within the formal economy, except for temporary periods.

In many ways the commitment of older women to work could have been capitalised upon to a greater degree and at an earlier stage. In a 1972 Ministry of Labour survey, it was recorded that when workers were asked until when they wanted to continue working, fewer than 10 per cent of young females responded that they would like to work 'as long as possible', by comparison with 70–80 per cent of married women.[26] The national textile union certainly appeared keen to strengthen the position of older women as regular workers within the textile industry during the period and classified the integration of 'working mothers' into the textile workforce as a firm topic for union discussion and activities from the late 1960s onwards.[27]

In spite of these concerns, and notwithstanding a certain degree of 'reluctance' on the part of textile employers to employ older women in more permanent ways, it is evident that management strategies to deal with their integration into the textile labour force did evolve during the period, and that various labour management ideas and policies were drawn up in order to assist the integration of older women into textiles employment. These included the adaptation of factory training programmes, the provision of daytime shifts for women who had children and domestic responsibilities and in some cases the provision of nursery facilities. In addition to the problem of absenteeism associated with older workers, some employers noted the difficulty in having older women work directly with much younger women and the various 'generation gap' problems of incompatibility that arose. One company recorded that it had implemented a system whereby older and younger women did not always work directly together, with older women generally working in preparation and post-weaving divisions within the company. However, it also recorded that older women were often placed there as they were much more reliable in these jobs, as younger women were more liable to dislike or complain about these 'more messy' jobs.[28] Overall, however, general efforts were made to incorporate older women into the workplace so as not to discriminate between them and younger regular workers. Attempts to give older workers, particularly part-timers, a sense that they 'belonged' in the company and to integrate them (at least socially) with younger workers included encouraging them to take part in company trips and recreational events. Often, a 'contact committee' was established, and all workers were urged to meet periodically to discuss workplace issues and to discuss ways to improve human relations within the factory and boost morale. Employers often felt that the increased use of older women, whether one 'liked it or not', was necessary due to the decline in the availability of young workers, and that older female workers should be thought of as people who could bring knowledge and skills. In this respect, it was necessary to plan more positive ways of employing them and to 'modernise' workplace facilities to suit them.[29]

Overall, it does seem evident that, despite the overwhelming emphasis placed on the dormitory and education systems as the focus of labour management for the core (young) female workforce, a discrete labour management policy for older female workers did develop during these years. This was very much still in its primary stages and was often seen as problematic in nature, not least with regard to the industry's 'ability' to rely on older female workers and integrate them into established workplace structures, as well as reconciling this with their domestic roles. However, the features of the management of these workers highlighted in this chapter did go on to develop to a greater extent after the years under study, as the trends in the female labour market identified in this research took hold even further.

Conclusion

The Japanese cotton textile industry was greatly challenged in the early post-war decades by an increasingly limited supply of its 'traditional' key work force of young females, an increasingly competitive environment of demand for female workers in general, and the need to adapt its existing employment structures away from pre-war patterns and from young females alone to include older working women. Employers also felt the need to dispel the poor image of the industry's labour management history that they had inherited from the pre-war period. It is apparent from my research that the industry made substantial efforts to respond to all these challenges during these decades. It did this by improving and strengthening its existing employment practices, particularly the operation of dormitories. It also responded by devising varied and more focused approaches to managing its young female workforce, as well as coming up with strategies for managing its 'new' workforce of older women.

While improvements to labour conditions were prompted by the implementation of national legislative reform particularly during the occupation years, including regulation of work hours, controls on recruitment, standards for the workplace and dormitories and the specific protection of women workers,[30] it is also certain that the industry provided an improved environment for textile workers over and beyond that required by law. The provision of a full 'non-working' environment and opportunities for personal, social and educational development for young female workers was particularly notable and formed a fundamental element of labour management policy centring on the factory–dormitory mode of operations. Indeed, the attention given by textile employers to employment strategy and labour management policy in order to manage an increasingly diversified female workforce and provide an industry-level institutional response to significant challenges during these years was very evident.

The response of a key group of employers at this turning point in women's labour history in Japan can also be seen as a crucial factor in prescribing subsequent economic roles for women. The activities of the textile industry during these years were not only a response to a new socio-economic environment and legal framework but also a proactive approach to a continuing discourse on the role women were to play in the paid labour force. Female labour, particularly older females, were increasingly needed by Japanese industry during these years because rapid economic growth was placing pressure on the supply of regular, young workers. Moreover, females were a vital labour source during a period when a restructuring of the workforce and re-orientation of sectors of the economy was required. The early implementation of labour management strategies for female workers in the textile industry influenced not only how the employment of women would continue and take shape into the post-war years, as other industries looked to the textile industry's long history as a dominant employer of women workers, but also played a part in influencing how the employment of males would broadly be defined. In many ways, the male life time employment system that developed during the post-war period of economic growth in Japan depended on non-life time employment for women and the flexibility of older women. My research into the textile industry indicates that women were often employed as a 'temporary' or 'supplementary' or even 'hidden' workforce, which has had broader implications for the female labour market as a whole in contemporary Japan. However, their employment in large numbers and in important sectors of the economy, particularly in manufacturing, also showed them to be a dynamic force during the Japanese high-speed growth years, and a group of workers within the labour market that have consistently thrown up challenges and forced the implementation of change in Japanese institutions of employment.

Acknowledgement

This chapter is based on research conducted during 1997–2001 and published in Helen Macnaughtan, *Women, Work and the Japanese Economic Miracle: The Case of the Cotton Textile Industry, 1945–1975* (London: RoutledgeCurzon, 2005). All Tōyōbō materials are located in the Shashishitsu of Tōyōbō Head Office, Osaka.

Notes

1 SCAP, *Final Report of the Advisory Committee on Labour: Labour Policies and Programmes in Japan* (Tokyo: Supreme Commander for the Allied Powers, 1946); SCAP, *History of the Nonmilitary Activities of the Occupation of Japan, 1945–51: Textile Industries* (Tokyo: General Headquarters, Supreme Commander for the Allied Powers, 1951).
2 Tōyōbō, *Shokuba Rōmu Kanri no Jūjitsu Kyōka ni tsuite* (Osaka: Tōyōbō Shokuba Rōmu Kanri Senmon Iinkai, 1974) p. 1.
3 Hiroshi Hazama, *The History of Labour Management in Japan* (London: Macmillan Press Ltd., 1997); Janet Hunter, *Women and the Labour Market in Japan's Industrialising Economy: the Textile Industry before the Pacific War* (London: RoutledgeCurzon, 2003).
4 Hazama, *History of Labour Management in Japan*, pp. 92, 96.
5 Ibid., pp. 97, 107.
6 Translates as: 'Pitiful History of Factory Girls'. The phrase was the title of a book by Hosoi Wakizō (Tokyo: Kaizōsha, 1925) that became so famous that the phrase continues to encompass the historical image of the textile industry even today.
7 This paper is restricted to a discussion of the dormitory system only. The education system established by textile companies in these years was an opportunity for young female employees to further their formal education (on a part-time basis while working for factories) by undertaking senior high school and/or tertiary courses. Like dormitory residence, this was encouraged (and often 'compulsory') for young female operatives as part of the industry's policy of providing a full non-working life for workers and helping to 'guide' and 'rear' young persons in their employment. Macnaughtan, *Women, Work and the Economic Miracle*, chs 4, 5.
8 Nihon Bōseki Kyōkai, *Boshū Kankei Gyōmu Tantōsha: Gyōmu Techō* (Osaka: Nihon Bōseki Kyōkai, 1969) p. 27.
9 Ibid.
10 Of these three, dormitories were in many ways the pillar of the system. The domicile of workers in dormitories determined their daily working and non-working schedules; dictating their organisation into shop-floor teams and integration into the two-shift

system of factory production, their schedules for schooling and extra-curricular activities and even their daily sleep patterns.

11 Kobayashi, Sakaei, *Tōyōbō no Kishukusha Kanri* (1963) pp. 138–39 (located in Shashishitsu, Tōyōbō Head Office, Osaka).

12 The 'stabilisation' of labour (*rōdōryoku anteika*) is often mentioned in the primary industry documentation. It refers to the industry's aims and attempts to maintain a sufficient labour force, that is, one at required levels. In terms of recruitment, it refers to the industry's efforts to establish a unified system of recruitment which would effectively channel the required numbers of young female workers into textiles for a given period of time and reduce problems resulting from the imbalance in the supply of and demand for labour.

13 Kobayashi, *Tōyōbō no Kishukusha Kanri*, pp. 146–47.

14 Existing legislation, particularly the 'Regulations for Dormitories attached to Factories' (1927) resulting from the Factory Act, had dealt with various physical conditions and health and safety standards within dormitories but had not dealt with the 'human problems' of personal freedom for individual dormitory residents. The enforcement of regulations was also viewed as having left 'much to be desired' (SCAP, *Final Report of the Advisory Committee on Labour*, pp. 96–97).

15 Company reports used as sources include Kobayashi, *Tōyōbō no Kishukusha Kanri*; Tōyōbō, *Kongo no Joshi Kanri no Arikata* (Osaka: Tōyōbō Joshi Kanri Senmon Iinkai, 1969); and Tōyōbō, *Kongo no Joshi Ryō Gakuin Un'ei no Hōkō* (Osaka: Tōyōbō Rōmuka, 1977).

16 In the textile company Tōyōbō this operated as follows: 'Juniors' included two groups – 'first-term juniors' (1–2 years service) and 'second-term juniors' (3–4 years); 'Seniors' (5+ years service) were viewed as adults (*seijin*), being 20+ years of age. See Tōyōbō, *Kongo no Joshi Kanri no Arikata*, p. 14.

17 This breakdown of age-levels is based on entry after graduation from compulsory education (i.e. junior high school), which was standard at the beginning of the period under study, though saw some transition as increased entry after senior high school took place. All the information on analysis of age-levels and strategic response is taken from Nihon Bōseki Kyōkai, *Boshū Kankei Gyōmu Tantōsha*, pp. 38–40.

18 The term *seijin-ryō* (adult dorm) or *katei-ryō* (household dorm) is used in various industry sources, indicating the use of a similar system across medium-large-scale textile enterprises. See Kurabō, *Kurashiki Bōseki Hyakunen Shi* (Osaka: Kurashiki Bōseki Kabushiki Kaisha, 1988); Zensen, *Zensen Josei Undō Shi: Kishukusha Minshuka kara Danjo Byōdō Koyō e* (Tokyo: Zensen Dōmei, 1996).

19 Zensen, *Zensen Josei Undō Shi*, p. 48.

20 Tōyōbō, *Shokuba Rōmu Kanri no Jūjitsu Kyōka ni tsuite*, pp. 3, 5.

21 Tōyōbō, *Kongo no Joshi Ryō Gakuin Un'ei no Hōkō*, p. 1.

22 Data on the numbers of older 'non-regular' female workers is difficult to analyse as they were often unrecorded in official industry sources. However, one company noted that in 1969 the proportion of temporary and part-timer workers in the female labour force had reached 14 per cent on average and was as high as 30 per cent in some factories. Furthermore, on average, it had increased three-fold in the two years since 1967 (Tōyōbō, *Kongo no Joshi Kanri no Arikata*, p. 26). Another source indicated that the proportion of female workers who were 'non-regular' ranged from 30–40 per cent over the period 1969–75 (Nihon Bōseki Kyōkai, *Zoku Sengo Bōseki Shi* (Osaka: Nihon Bōseki Kyōkai, 1979), p. 796).

23 Tōyōbō, *Kongo no Joshi Kanri no Arikata*, p. 14.

24 Ibid., p. 27.

25 Original documentation on these 'test factories' no longer remains (because of their very 'failure'), but this information was gained from personal interviews during fieldwork 1997–98.

26 Ministry of Labour, *Sen'i Kōgyō ni okeru Fujin Rōdō Jittai Chōsa: Kekka Hōkokusho* (Tokyo: Rōdōshō Fujin Shōnen Kyoku, 1972), p. 84.
27 Zensen, *Danjokyō ni Shigoto to Katei ga Ryōritsu dekiru Kankyō Seibi e Mukete* (Okayama: Zensen Chūō Kyōiku Sentā, 1997), p. 48.
28 Ministry of Labour, *Chūkō Nenrei Fujin no Rōmu Kanri Jireishū.* (Tokyo: Rōdōshō Fujin Shōnen Kyoku, 1970), pp. 79–82.
29 Ibid., p. 83.
30 Including so-called 'motherhood protection' (*bosei hogo*), the idea of providing protection for all women workers with a firm regard for their female physiological and reproductive capabilities as (existing and potential) mothers.

6 Japanese inter-firm relations

On the way towards a market-oriented structure?

Andreas Moerke

Introduction

Few words are used to describe the Japanese economy in general, or inter-firm relations in particular, as often as the term '*keiretsu*'. Associated on the one hand with long-term relations, mutual assistance and stable transactions, and on the other with trade restrictions and closed markets, *keiretsu* have been at the centre of attention for years. However, the reason that the implications of *keiretsu* are so different is that the term *keiretsu* captures a number of different phenomena. The common theme that brings all these connotations together is that the term *keiretsu* can be understood to stand for an industrial group and the linkages of the firms belonging to that group.[1] We need, however, to distinguish between several kinds of *keiretsu*.

1 *Horizontal keiretsu* consist of enterprises from various industries that are linked through cross-shareholding, director dispatch (secondment), trading relations and regular meetings of their presidents. There have been 6 of these horizontal *keiretsu* (*kigyō shūdan*), each consisting of 20–30 companies, with a limited number of core firms as well as a bank and a trading company at the centre. The history of these groups often goes back to the Meiji period or before.[2]

2 *Vertical keiretsu* are groups with a huge manufacturer on top and a pyramid of first, second and third tier suppliers beneath. They are concentrated in one industry, and enterprises are linked through share holding, director dispatch and trading relations as well. In contrast to the horizontal *keiretsu*, these links are unidirectional.

3 *Distribution keiretsu* are involved – not surprisingly – with the sales and distribution network of a certain maker and have tended to be rather exclusive.

What makes *keiretsu* so important? First, their economic impact can be significant. According to a 2001 study by the Fair Trade Commission, 151 member companies of the 6 major groups (banks excluded) held about 13 per cent of the total capital of Japan's companies and realised almost 11 per cent of Japan's total sales.[3] A second reason is that these close linkages have often been said to be a main entry barrier to the Japanese market. In the 1980s, Japanese–US trade negotiations and the Structural Impediments Initiative talks explicitly made *keiretsu* a topic on the agenda. Finally, *keiretsu* are significant because of their long-term perspective and often-claimed stability.

In economic theory, *keiretsu* are an interesting topic in as far as they seem to ignore the classic split between the market and the hierarchy as alternatives for economic organisations.[4] Instead, *keiretsu* relations combine elements of both. While there is a lot of research dealing with *keiretsu* relations and analysing them for the 1980s and early 1990s, there is very little literature devoted to the implication for these relations of the crisis and the changes of the late 1990s or the new century. This contribution aims to fill this gap. It is concerned with where we can see changes in inter-firm relations over the last few years and how they can be characterised. Using the most recent data, it provides a thorough analysis of the changes that have taken place in Japanese *keiretsu* and clarifies the direction of those changes.

The chapter is organised as follows: in the following section, a set of definitions is given, enabling us to ask questions about the direction of change. The section on empirical investigation provides the empirical test of the hypotheses, while in the concluding section the findings are summarised.

Definition and data

All firms are characterised by a set of attributes, and the network with other enterprises and organisations is a part of those attributes. In terms of inter-firm relations, therefore, it is important to see whether a company is a member of a *keiretsu*. Equally important, but also difficult to investigate, are cases in which a company belongs to different kinds of *keiretsu*. To give two examples: Mitsubishi Motor Company (MMC) was – until DaimlerChrysler bought about one-third of its shares – on top of its own vertically oriented group and at the same time a member of the Mitsubishi group presidents' council. Daihatsu, on the other hand, has been an official member of the *Sansuikai*, the Sanwa group presidents' council, but is more than one-third owned by Toyota (itself a member of the Mitsui group), and seen as its subsidiary. In order to deal with this complexity, I will use here the definitions developed at the Science Centre Berlin for the analysis of Japanese enterprise data.[5] These definitions are as follows:

> *Horizontal (H):* A firm is regarded as horizontally integrated when it is a member of a presidents' council (*shachōkai*). The member firms are further-more interconnected by stable mutual shareholding and director dispatch (i.e. secondment) (e.g. Tanabe Seiyaku or Mitsubishi Electric).
> *Vertical (V):* A corporation is seen as vertically integrated if (a) another company owns more than 20 per cent of the shares, or (b) if the major share-holder owns more than 10 per cent and is at the same time the major cus-tomer (e.g. Daihatsu, Toshiba Tungaloy).
> *Independent (I):* A company is referred to as independent when it does not belong to a presidents' council, nor is it substantially owned by another firm (e.g. Omron).

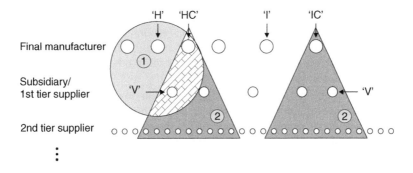

1 = Horizontal group
2 = Vertical group

Figure 6.1 Inter-firm networks in Japan.

Source: Andreas Moerke, *Organisationslernen über Netzwerke. Eine empirische Analyse der personellen Verflechtungen von Boards of Directors japanischer Industrieaktiengesellschaften* (Wiesbaden: Deutscher Universitätsverlag – Gabler, 2001), p. 33, based on Gerlach, *Alliance Capitalism*, p. 68.

Core firms (C): All companies at the top of one of the 20 largest industry groups (as identified by Tōyō Keizai) are regarded as core firms. Since all firms in the sample used here are listed on the Tokyo Stock Exchange, most of them have a number of subsidiaries. Therefore, in order to find the specific nature of core firms, size had to be taken into account, and the distinction was made according to the Tōyō Keizai definition. As already mentioned, core companies can be divided into two subgroups: (a) firms that are members of a horizontal *keiretsu* (referred to as 'HC', like NEC or Toshiba) and (b) firms that are independent (referred to as 'IC', for instance Sony or Matsushita).

Figure 6.1 attempts to visualise the definitions and the inter-firm relations with which this contribution deals.

Data set

The changes that have taken place in *keiretsu* over recent years will be analysed using three kinds of data. These data are:

1 Macro-data taken from macroeconomic statistics, mostly from the Tōyō Keizai database *Keizai Tōkei Nenkan* for 2004.
2 Financial data for the selected enterprises (all listed on the first section of the Tōkyō Stock Exchange)[6] derived from annual reports published in accordance with the Securities Trading Law (*yūka shōken hōkokusho*).

The CD-Rom version of Tōyō Keizai's *Kaisha Shikihō* (Quarterly Reports) and the *Kaisha Database*[7] were used for the purpose of this analysis.

3   Biographical data of executives derived from the hard copies of the annual reports which contain information on each board member's university degree, career to date, (including employment in other companies, financial or state institutions), areas of responsibility and level in the hierarchy achieved. For our analysis, data from the automotive, electrical engineering and machine tool industries were used due to these industries' high levels of export-orientation and globalisation. The Japanese pharmaceutical industry, which is far from internationally competitive, was taken as a control variable. The total number of firms analysed is 70, and the time period was limited to 1986–2001.

To discuss the findings and test against misinterpretations of the quantitative data, relevant people from research institutions and state institutions (related to the industries involved) were also consulted. Discussions on several specific issues were also held with Japanese managers wherever possible.

Empirical investigation

This section consists of an empirical investigation of the extent of stable (cross-) shareholding, changes in trading relations, the insurance function and the characteristics of the movement of directors (director dispatch) in relations between industrial firms in Japan.

Changes in stable (cross-)shareholding

Stable (cross-)shareholding in the present form was mainly established in the re-building phase of the Japanese economy in the 1950s and 1960s and was aimed at avoiding hostile takeovers, stabilising management and strengthening relations with other companies.[8] Such shareholding was accompanied by intensive trading relations as well as stable and preferential lending, in terms of bank–firm relationships. These stable shareholdings differ in terms of their direction (unilateral or bilateral) according to the nature of the relationship between the companies. In horizontal groups, shareholding tends to be bilateral (cross-shareholding), while in a vertical relationship shareholding is mostly unidirectional (top-down, the OEM (original equipment manufacturer) owns at least a large part of the supplier).[9] Stable (cross-)shareholding could have merits for the companies concerned, in that it enabled them to partially isolate themselves from the capital market and, therefore, allowed other stakeholders to participate in the distribution of income insofar as higher wages for employees or higher prices for favourite suppliers could be paid.[10] The system worked well in the beginning but reached its limits when the whole Japanese economy slid into crisis after the asset and stock price bubble burst, as Figure 6.2 shows.

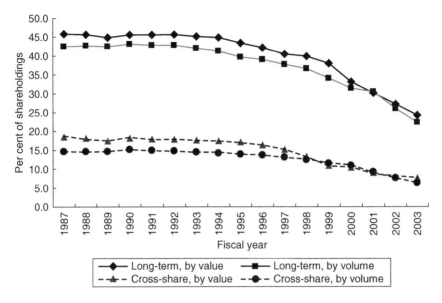

Figure 6.2 Stable shareholding and cross-shareholding.

Source: Nissei Kiso Kenkyūjo, *Kabushiki Mochiai Jōkyō Chōsa, 2003-nendo Han* (Tokyo: Nissei Kiso Kenkyūjo, 2004), pp. 4, 16.

Table 6.1 Unwinding cross-shareholding (% of all shares)

Year	Cross-shareholding in %		Difference between keiretsu *and others*
	Corporate groups	*Others*	
1987	28.0	12.1	15.9
2000	16.7	7.5	9.2
2004 (estimated)	13.2	6.1	7.1

Source: Fumiaki Kuroki, *The Present Status of Unwinding Cross-Shareholding – The Fiscal Year 2000 Survey of Cross-Shareholding* (Tokyo: NLI Research Institute, 2001), p. 30, and own estimations.

It comes as no surprise that cross-shareholding in horizontal groups should be more intense than in other kinds of relationships, but changes in the Japanese economy as a whole have forced *keiretsu* firms to change their shareholding behaviour as well. Table 6.1[11] exemplifies three facts: (a) the declining rate of cross-shareholding for *keiretsu* as well as for non-*keiretsu* firms (b) the existence of a remarkable gap between *keiretsu* and other firms but also (c) the narrowing of that gap.

A similar trend is seen within our sample. Since we do not have data on cross-shareholding, the ratio of 'stocks to total capital' was calculated using data from the balance sheet. Even allowing for the fact that the stock price will influence the

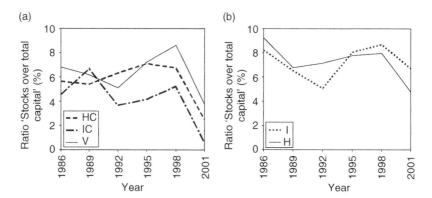

Figure 6.3 Ratio of stocks to total capital. (a) Core and vertical firms. (b) Independent and horizontal firms.

Source: Own calculations on the basis of annual reports.

value of the 'shares owned', and a declining share price naturally results in a lower value of the shares owned by a company, a look at Figure 6.3 immediately highlights the important finding that all firm types in our sample have experienced a decrease in the value of stocks owned; this is partly due to falling share prices and partly due to sales of stocks owned after 1998. We can therefore infer from this that, due to the relaxation of mutual shareholding, the *keiretsu* groups have been weakened.[12]

Changes in business relations

These changes in the shareholding structure have indeed been accompanied by changes in business relations, and this holds for the horizontal *keiretsu* (HC) as well as for the vertical ones. As an investigation of the horizontal groups (H) by the Fair Trade Commission pointed out, 'business transactions among affiliates have been decreasing in general'.[13] Using the ratio of purchases from firms inside the group in relation to overall purchases, the following table shows the decrease in in-group transactions as well as in transactions between *keiretsu* member firms and *keiretsu* trading houses. At one-digit ratios of in-group business, Table 6.2 shows furthermore that – at least in the case of horizontal relations – the relations are far from being 'closed'. The data thereby confirms the finding of previous research that in terms of trading relations horizontal *keiretsu* are no longer an entrance barrier for foreign companies.[14]

Vertical inter-firm relations are by their very nature different from those in horizontal groups, tending to be somewhat hierarchical in terms of ownership, governance structures and business relations. Although favouring the enterprise on the top of the pyramid,[15] this structure was not necessarily bad for the suppliers since relations were oriented towards the long-term and enterprises in one vertical

Table 6.2 Decreasing business transactions within *keiretsu* groups

Year	Ratio of purchase from	
	In-group companies (%)	*In-group trading houses (%)*
1996	7.47	6.31
2001	6.44	5.30

Source: Based on JFTC, *State of Corporate Groups in Japan*, p. 6.

group in large part shared the twin objectives of market share and growth.[16] One interviewee even stated, 'We felt ourselves as members of a large family.'[17] Of course, such personal judgements are hard to question, but there are figures, numbers and theory at hand to investigate these relations.

From a theoretical perspective, transaction cost theory allows us to explain the economic effect of these relationships. The more specific a transaction is, the more the commitment needed on both sides. Mutual dependence increases the likelihood of ongoing relations; in other words, the more specific a part or product, the more the involvement necessary and vice versa. Conversely, the more standardised the product is, the more the relationship between seller and buyer will be a market-based one. Of course, factor specificity differs across industries.[18] It is lower in the electronic industry, where components are relatively standardised, and higher in, for instance, the automotive industry, with its longer lifecycles. In the Japanese case, the relationship between buyer and supplier is said to have been very close. A Ministry of International Trade and Industry (MITI) investigation found that in 1987 about 40 per cent of suppliers had only one customer.[19] However, the globalisation of a number of industries (especially automotives, electrics/electronics and machine tools) has led to the globalisation of purchasing policy and changes in buyer–supplier relations in Japan as well. The re-shaping of the Nissan group by Carlos Ghosn is only one example of this, albeit a very famous one. It was Ghosn who, after taking over at Nissan, shook up the whole group. He cut the number of suppliers by about half, set targets for price-cuts for new products at about 30 per cent,[20] took steps to eliminate stable shareholding[21] and forced the suppliers to look for more customers. On the other hand, the suppliers have had to do their best to reduce their dependency on their previous customers. According to the Japan Auto Parts Industries Association (JAPIA), the average number of customers per supplier firm has risen to 5.8 in 2001, still low compared with European firms but higher than it had been in the 1980s.[22]

Within our sample, it was not possible to ascertain exact numbers of supplier or customer firms. However, it was possible to use information from balance sheets to analyse the pattern of business between suppliers and assemblers. The following analysis uses as a measure the ratio of trade receivables to trade notes payable plus trade accounts payable. While the first term (the numerator) gives information on the amount of products and services an enterprise has delivered and is waiting to be paid for, the second term (the denominator) provides

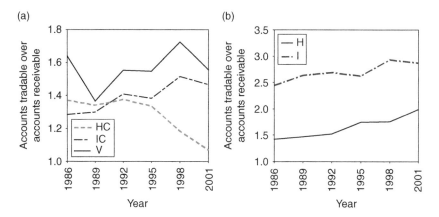

Figure 6.4 Ratio of trade receivables to trade notes and accounts payable. (a) Core and vertical firms. (b) Horizontal firms.

Source: Author's own calculations based on annual reports.

information on the extent of any material the same firm has received on credit. The implications of this ratio are easily assessed: the higher the ratio, the higher the debt obligations of the firm.

A look at Figure 6.4 on the left (the comparison of core and vertical firms) shows a substantial difference between vertically integrated firms (V) and core firms, especially those in the horizontal *keiretsu* (HC). This suggests that the former group was under considerably more pressure than the latter group. Comparison of the horizontal dimension ('pure' horizontal firms vs. 'pure' independent firms) reveals that *keiretsu* membership can still be an advantage, since the independent corporations are subject to greater pressure from their customer firms.

Insurance function

It has often been said that *keiretsu* affiliation can be seen as constituting a competitive advantage,[23] since firms inside a group can benefit from economies of scope.[24] Perhaps more importantly, it has been argued that member firms can also rely on support from other firms in the group and especially the *keiretsu* bank.[25] This 'mutual insurance scheme' is said to be the reason for the lower but more stable profitability of *keiretsu* firms.[26]

However, things have been changing over time, leading Lincoln, Gerlach and Ahmadjian to state that 'the combination of deregulation, structural change, and macroeconomic shocks explains the fast decay of the redistribution pattern among the big-six *keiretsu*'.[27] The sample here is, therefore, used to analyse whether or not the sub-sample of *keiretsu* firms indeed shows greater stability than other firms. In order to do this, sales figures and rates of

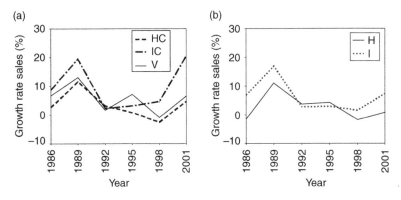

Figure 6.5 Growth rate of sales. (a) Core firms and vertical firms. (b) Horizontal and independent firms.

Source: Own calculation based on annual reports.

return are used. To exclude size effects,[28] the growth rate of sales is used. Figure 6.5 reflects the overall industrial downturn from 1989 until 1999, as well as the fact that differences between the sub-samples are not as high as one may expect.

Since average values are only a rough measure, and since our focus is on how inter-company relations have changed, dividing the time-span into two parts is potentially instructive. The first part, which we can call the 'bubble period', consists of data for 1986, 1989 and 1992. The second period, the 'crisis period', contains data from 1995, 1998 and 2001. The coefficient of variation for each of the sub-samples and each period was then calculated.[29] As the low coefficient of variation at the beginning of the time span investigated shows, the group of horizontal core firms (firms like Toyota or Mitsubishi Electric) was the most stable in terms of sales growth, followed by independent core companies (e.g. Matsushita, Sony or Honda). Interestingly enough, the sub-sample of independent corporations (firms like Dijet Industrial or Taishō Pharma) show less variation than the sub-sample of *keiretsu* firms (Mitsui Toatsu, Oki Electric and others). More interesting, however, is the way in which the variation develops. As is evident, the member firms of the horizontal *keiretsu* groups exhibit conspicuous diversification in their development. The coefficient of variation for these horizontal sub-samples has been increasing tremendously, indicating that dispersion among certain firms in the group is growing. In other words, the homogeneity of the horizontal *keiretsu* groups has been diminishing rapidly (Table 6.3).

As we have seen above, in-group trade counts for only a small portion of all sales. To check whether or not *keiretsu* membership still enables these firms to insulate themselves from capital markets and pay out income more in the form of wages and investment, thus having lower but more stable profitability,

Table 6.3 Coefficient of variation, growth rate of sales

Group	Coefficient of variation		Factor of increase
	1986–92	*1995–2001*	
Horizontal	2.02	8.27	4.09
Horizontal-core	0.98	5.53	5.64
Independent	1.67	3.02	1.80
Independent-core	1.10	1.72	1.57
Vertical	1.75	5.16	2.95

Source: Own calculation based on annual reports.

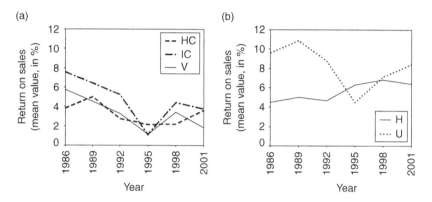

Figure 6.6 Comparative rates of return. (a) Core and vertical firms. (b) Independent and horizontal firms.

Source: Own calculations based on annual reports.

rates of return have been investigated. Return on sales (as per cent of ordinary income over sales) was calculated and compared for the different sub-samples. As can be seen from Figure 6.6, the group consisting of horizontal *keiretsu* firms could on average maintain their stability better than the other groups. Independent firms seem to have suffered more acutely in times of crisis but to have recovered more quickly. An investigation of returns on total capital showed the same tendency.

These figures indicate that the insurance function remained intact through the 1990s. To verify this, coefficients of variation in rates of return for the same two sub-periods were calculated. The picture is not very different from the sales growth ratio. Until 1992, core firms (including horizontal core firms) tended to have a rather similar performance, but this does not hold for other groups. Compared with the first half of the period, dispersion has been increasing among each sub-sample in the second period. The greatest increase in dispersion (nearly doubling in value) is found among horizontal core firms, followed by independent firms (1.86), followed by vertically integrated (1.57) and horizontal (1.22) firms.

Only independent core firms have somehow managed to remain homogeneous (an increase of 1.07).

To summarise the findings, we observe that the horizontal *keiretsu* firms seem to have lost a considerable amount of their power, but it is also clear that collusion between group members and mutual support functions to ensure stability have not disappeared, something that was also pointed out in an investigation by the Fair Trade Commission:

> As to corporate management, 19.1 percent of the surveyed said that they have received some sort of approach from their affiliates. [...] Offers of financial assistance at times of poor financial performance were the most common form of approach from affiliates; a total of 20 companies said that they have received it. Financial assistance included the acceptance of new shares and the extension of the payment due date. It indicates that corporate groups, particularly prewar zaibatsu-origined groups, still maintained the function of mutual support to affiliates facing a financial crisis. Other common supports included coordination and advice to joint projects (10 companies) and coordination and advice on business affiliation involving stock acquisition.[30]

Director dispatch

So-called 'director dispatch' is a further link between Japanese corporations. Directors are seconded from other corporations, from financial institutions or from the state bureaucracy. As in the case of shareholding, in horizontal groups director dispatch is multi-dimensional, while in vertical groups it is mostly unidirectional and top-down.[31] Dispatched directors account for most of the 'outsiders' in the boards of Japanese corporations.[32] In the horizontal dimension of inter-firm relations, these dispatched directors fulfil the task of securing information flow and strengthening business relations, while in the vertical dimension they are mainly seconded to monitor the subsidiary. Furthermore, due to the standard Japanese career path and the seniority-based system, subsidiaries quite often have to appoint as directors individuals from their parent company or OEM who do not have a chance to progress in their careers there.

The question we need to ask is whether, and how, the decrease in the long-term or cross-shareholding ratio that has been identified influenced the seconding of directors. The Fair Trade Commission's report provides an overview on this issue, stating 'Of the six major group companies, 37.17 per cent, down 11.43 percentage points, accepted board members sent by affiliates. As shown..., the ratio has been decreasing'.[33] To investigate this question using our sample, we used the index of director dispatch developed in the author's earlier work. This involved the development of two indices for looking at directorships, one to measure the intensity of relations within a corporate group, the other relations with enterprises outside the group, based on the compilation of a database of the ten largest shareholders in every firm compiled from shareholding reports (*yūka shōken hōkoku*).

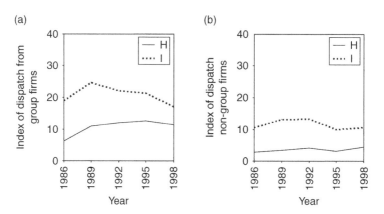

Figure 6.7 Network ratio of director dispatch (horizontal dimension). (a) Networks with group firms. (b) Networks with non-group firms.

Source: Own calculations based on annual reports.

Note
Due to data availability, biographical data from the 2001-year reports could not be used.

Through assigning points to the level of interlocking directorates, an index could be produced, and since this index takes current and previous secondments into account, a detailed picture can be shown of how the personal networks in Japanese companies' top management changed.[34] Figure 6.7 shows the difference between dispatch within the group and from firms outside the group. It becomes quite obvious that for *keiretsu* firms and for independent firms there is hardly any director dispatch from outside the group. It is important to point out that, contrary to expectation, firms in the latter half of the 1990s do not seem to have appointed more outsiders. It seems, therefore, that Japanese firms, and *keiretsu* firms in particular, still follow a 'closed-shop strategy'.

Even more obvious is the difference between in-group and out-group networks for the vertical dimension (core-firms vs. vertical firms, as shown in the comparison in Figure 6.8). The intensity of the personal networks through dispatched directors is quite high for corporations that are linked through capital (i.e. shares, in our context). In this regard, a well-known corporate governance scheme can be seen as the driving force. Major shareholding allows personnel to be sent to monitor the investment, strategic or other aspects of behaviour of the owned firm, something that has been observed even in Europe and the United States.[35] With non-related firms, the intensity of director dispatch decreases to about one-third, while it is extremely low, at one-sixth, for vertically integrated firms. This shows that Japanese firms are mostly connected through director dispatch when they are also connected through shareholdings, and that the concept did not change significantly in the 1990s.

Another remarkable finding is that in the case of linkages with firms outside the group, the ratios of director secondment in core firms (HC and IC) and

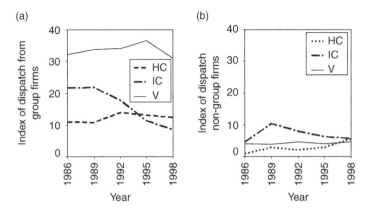

Figure 6.8 Network ratio of director dispatch (vertical dimension). (a) Networks with group firms. (b) Networks with non-group firms.

Source: Own calculations based on annual reports.

vertically integrated firms (V firm) do not differ at a statistically significant level, and these firms do not broaden their links to other companies outside the group (Figure 6.8b). The tendency to stick together and not to really open up the boards of directors seems obvious here as well.

One caveat should be added, however, to these observations. These data do not cover the period after 1998, a time during which a number of foreign firms entered the Japanese market via mergers and acquisitions and sent their personnel into the boards of their Japanese partners. Among the well-known examples are the alliances between Renault and Nissan, Roche and Chūgai, DaimlerChrysler and Mitsubishi, to name but a few.[36] Furthermore, the effects of a new piece of commercial legislation (*shōhō*) that gives companies a choice between the traditional board structure and a United States-like board have not been captured here either.

Conclusion

Japan's inter-firm relations have been experiencing a great deal of change. Long-term and cross-shareholding has been reduced since the mid-1990s, allowing for more mergers and acquisitions. With OEMs reducing the number of their suppliers, and suppliers increasing the number of their customers, as well as with declining intra-group trade inside the *keiretsu*, business relations were becoming increasingly more market-oriented. However, the impact of these changes on corporate groups seems to be limited. First, because these changes did not lead to changes in the management structure, Japanese firms are still insider-dominated and do not show much willingness to change in this regard. Second, the impact of these changes appears to be limited because the enterprises themselves do not see further change forthcoming: '34.4 percent of the surveyed (enterprises from the Fair Trade Commission survey) said that current corporate groups would be maintained'.[37] (FTC 2001: 9). It seems that *keiretsu* are here to stay – weakened, but existing.

Notes

1 The literature on the topic is too numerous to capture within one article. Among the most influential writings in the field are Michael L. Gerlach, *Alliance Capitalism: the Social Organization of Japanese Business* (Berkeley, CA: University of California Press, 1992); Takeo Hoshi, Anil Kashyap and David Scharfstein, 'Corporate Structure, Liquidity, and Investment: Evidence from Japanese Industrial Groups', *Quarterly Journal of Economics*, 106, 1, February 1991; and as standard reference the regularly published investigations by the Japanese Fair Trade Commission (Kōsei Torihiki Iinkai), to name but a few.

2 Pre-war conglomerates are known as *zaibatsu*; they were dissolved by the Allied Powers after the Second World War. Cf. Kikkawa, Takeo, *Nihon no Kigyō Shūdan – Zaibatsu to no Renzoku to Danzetsu* (Tokyo: Yūhikaku, 1996), Hidemasa Morikawa, *Zaibatsu: the Rise and Fall of Family Enterprise Groups in Japan* (Tokyo: University of Tokyo Press, 1992), or Shimotani, Masahiro, *Nihon no Keiretsu to Kigyō Gurūpu* (Tokyo: Yūhikaku, 1993) for explanations on the linkage between *zaibatsu* and *keiretsu*.

3 Japanese Fair Trade Commission (JFTC), *State of Corporate Groups in Japan: The 7th Survey Report* (Tokyo: JFTC, 2001), p. 2.

4 With respect to Coase, see Oliver E.Williamson, *Die ökonomischen Institutionen des Kapitalismus* (Tübingen: Mohr, 1990), p. 4.

5 For a detailed explanation and examples of application see Andreas Moerke, Ulrike Görtzen and Rita Zobel, *Grundleende methodische Überlegungen zur mikroökonomischen Forschung mit japanischen Unternehmensdaten* (Berlin: Wissenschaftszentrum Berlin für Sozialforschung, 2000); Ulrike Görtzen, *Wissensgenerierung und -verbreitung als Wettbewerbsfaktor. Eine empirische Analyse am Beispiel japanischer Industrieaktiengesellschaften* (Wiesbaden: Deutscher Universitätsverlag, 2001); or Rita Zobel, *Beschäftigungsveränderungen und organisationales Lernen in japanischen Industrieaktiengesellschaften – eine empirische Analyse anhand der Kaisha-Datenbank* (Berlin: PhD thesis, Humboldt University, 2000).

6 'Domestic stocks [in Japan] are assigned to either the First Section or the Second Section. In addition, some domestic stocks and foreign stocks of emerging companies are assigned to another section, called "Mothers." Newly listed domestic stocks are assigned to the Second Section except under certain conditions.' (*TSE Fact Book*, 2004, p. 26). Companies that are listed on the First Section tend to be larger than those on the Second Section (market capitalisation of 4 billion yen or more, as against 2 billion yen or more) and do have more shares to be listed (20,000, vs. 4,000).

7 The database was created at the Berlin Science Centre for Social Research on the basis of hard copies of the annual reports. It is now maintained at the Beisheim Graduate School of Management. The *Kaisha Database* contains balance sheet and profit-loss statement data from the unconsolidated accounts of 111 of the largest companies (in terms of sales, as of 1992) from 1970 in the following industries: chemicals, machine tools, electrical engineering and pharmaceuticals. The automotive industry is covered from 1985.

8 Jan O. Steinbrenner, *Japanische Unternehmensgruppen: Organisation, Koordination und Kooperation der Keiretsu* (Stuttgart: Schäffer-Poeschel, 1997).

9 James R. Lincoln, Michael L. Gerlach and Peggy Takahashi, 'Keiretsu Networks in the Japanese Economy: A Dyad Analysis of Intercorporate Ties', *American Sociological*

Review 57, 5, October 1992; Ulrike Schaede, 'Understanding Corporate Governance in Japan: Do Classical Concepts Apply?' *Industrial and Corporate Change* 3, 2, 1994.

10 Iwao Nakatani, 'The Economic Role of Financial Corporate Grouping', in Masahiko Aoki (ed.), *The Economic Analysis of the Japanese Firm* (Amsterdam: North Holland, Elsevier Science Publishers B.V., 1984).

11 The table refers to the overall economy and is based on NLI data, so the classification indicated above is not used here.

12 Japan's FTC report on corporate groups comes to the same conclusion, Japanese Fair Trade Commission, *State of Corporate Groups in Japan: The 7th Survey Report* (Tokyo: JFTC, 2001), p.11.

13 JFTC, *State of Corporate Groups in Japan*, p. 6.

14 Martin Hemmert, *Japanische Keiretsu – Legenden und Wirklichkeit* (Tokyo, Deutsches Institut für Japanstudien Working Paper 96/2, 1996); Fujio Uryu, Toru Sunada and Yasushi Nakahashi, *The Realities of Keiretsu Phenomena: A review of Research and Arguments on Keiretsu* (Tokyo: Research Institute of International Trade and Industry, 1993).

15 Harald Dolles, *Keiretsu: Emergenz, Struktur, Wettbewerbsstärke und Dynamik japanischer Verbundgruppen* (Frankfurt am Main: Peter Lang, 1997), p. 183; Kenichi Miyashita and David W. Russel, *Keiretsu: Inside the Hidden Japanese Conglomerates* (New York: McGraw-Hill, 1994), p. 161.

16 Masahiko Aoki, 'Aspects of the Japanese Firm', in Masahiko Aoki (ed.), *Economic Analysis of the Japanese Firm*; Banri Asanuma, 'Japanese Manufacturer-Supplier Relationships in International Perspective: the Automobile Case', in Paul Sheard (ed.), *International Adjustment and the Japanese Firm* (Sydney: Allen & Unwin, 1992); Hiroyuki Okamuro, *Risk-Sharing in the Supplier Relationship: New Evidence from the Japanese Automotive Industry* (Berlin: Wissenschaftszentrum Berlin, 1997).

17 Interview with Kasai Kōgyō, 22 April 2003.

18 Oliver Williamson, *Ökonomische Institutionen des Kapitalismus*.

19 Martin Hemmert, *Japanische Keiretsu*, p. 14.

20 This was stated in two different interviews with suppliers.

21 For instance, at that time Nissan owned a minor part of the shares of Fuji Heavy Industries Ltd., a competitor of Nissan's.

22 JAPIA, *Heisei 13-nendo Jidōsha Buhin Shukka Dōkō Chōsa* (Tokyo: JAPIA, 2001).

23 Max Eli, *Japans Wirtschaft im Griff der Konglomerate* (Frankfurt am Main: Frankfurter Allgemeine Zeitung, 1988); Max Eli, 'Netzwerkstruktur unter Keiretsu-Effect', in Joh Heinrich von Stein (ed.), *Banken in Japan heute* (Frankfurt am Main: Fritz Knapp Verlag, 1994); Nakatani, 'The Economic Role of Financial Corporate Grouping'; Jörg Sydow, 'Strategische Netzwerke in Japan', *Zeitschrift für die betriebswirtschafiliche Forschung* 43, 3, 1991.

24 Paul Sheard, 'Japanese Corporate Governance in Comparative Perspective', *Journal of Japanese Trade and Industry* 1, 1998, p. 9.

25 Nakatani, 'Economic Role of Financial Corporate Groupings', p. 229.

26 Itō, Takatoshi and Hoshi, Takeo, 'Kigyō gurūpu kessokudo no bunseki', in Horiuchi, Akiyoshi and Yoshino, Naoyuki (eds), *Gendai Nihon no kin'yū bunseki* (Tokyo: Tokyo University Press, 1992), p. 87.

27 James R. Lincoln, Michael L. Gerlach and Christina L. Ahmadjian, 'Keiretsu Networks and Corporate Performance in Japan', *American Sociological Review* 61, 1, 1996, pp. 67–81.

28 Core firms ('HC' and 'IC', horizontal and independent core) are much bigger than 'pure' horizontal ('H') and 'pure' independent ('I') or vertically integrated firms ('V'). Furthermore, firms of the big six *keiretsu* tend to be bigger than independent firms, and this holds true for core firms as well as for non-core firms. In mathematical terms, $H > I$, and $HC > IC$. For details, cf. Andreas Moerke *et al.*, *Grundlegende methodische Überlegungen*.

29 Calculated as the ratio of standard deviation over the mean value of a variable.
30 JFTC, *State of Corporate Groups in Japan*, p. 8.
31 James Lincoln *et al.*, 'Keiretsu Networks in the Japanese Economy'; Ulrike Schaede, 'Understanding Corporate Governance in Japan'.
32 Andreas Moerke, 'Rumble in the Boardroom? The Change of Japanese Corporate Governance Schemes', *Zeitschrift für Japanisches Recht* 8, 15, 2003.
33 JFTC, *State of Corporate Groups in Japan*, p. 5.
34 A detailed description of this exercise can be found in Andreas Moerke, *Organisationslernen über Netzwerke: eine empirische Analyse der personellen Verflechtungen von Boards of Directors japanischer Industriacktiengesellschaften* (Wiesbaden: Deutscher Universitätsverlag – Gabler, 2001). The sources were first used to compile a database of the ten largest shareholders of every firm. One index, GROUP, measured the intensity of the relations within a corporate group, and the second one, OUTSIDE, measured relations with enterprises outside the group. Companies were defined as belonging to the same group when they were connected through reciprocal shareholding. The method ensured that both direct and indirect ownership were taken into consideration (e.g. Toshiba Tungaloy and TEC were both connected via Toshiba Ltd). If no ownership could be found, the relation was seen as an outside link. The calculations can be summarised as follows: Index for 'Networks with Group Firms' – As a first step (=A), the (current and previous) posts for all directors were counted. For every current interlock, one point was given, for a previous mandate 0.5 points. These were added up. In the next step (=B), the rank of the director was included into the calculation. The higher the rank, the more information a director gets and the more influential he or she is likely to be. Certain groups of ranks were thus allotted certain points, which were multiplied with the above number of mandates (3 points for representative directors (*daihyō torishimariyaku*) and advisers (*sōdankyaku*); 2 points for senior managing directors (*senmu torishimariyaku*) and managing directors (*jōmu torishimariyaku*); 1 point for 'plain' directors and auditors (*kansayaku*)). This allowed us to identify the hierarchical structure of the board as a whole (=C). Finally the intensity of the network for the whole company was measured through totaling the values for all directors. The index for 'Networks with Non-Group Firms' was calculated the same way, the only difference being that posts in firms outside the corporate groups were taken into account.
35 Ulrike Schaede, 'Understanding Corporate Governance in Japan'.
36 A look at MMC reveals that the interest of Japan's firms in accepting foreign board members without pressure has been quite limited. After DaimlerChrysler refused to participate in the planned capital increase and was displaced as the major shareholder by Phoenix Capital in 2004, MMC dismissed almost all the personnel from DC and changed the enterprise structure back to the old one. See also Sigrun Caspary's (Chapter 9) in this volume.
37 JFTC, *State of Corporate Groups in Japan*, p. 9.

7 Global finance, democracy, and the State in Japan

Takaaki Suzuki

Introduction

Does the rise of global finance erode democratic choice and state authority? The ability to move large volumes of money swiftly across borders is seen by many scholars and policymakers as representing one of the most significant global transformations in the post-Cold War era. Whereas the architects of the Bretton Woods system explicitly rejected the principle of free capital movement in favor of free trade,[1] the collapse of the Bretton Woods system in the early 1970s has been followed by the dramatic rise of capital mobility that increasingly dwarfs the total volume of world trade. Foreign exchange transactions, which hovered between 10 billion dollars and 20 billion dollars per day in 1973, grew to 80 billion dollars in 1980 and to 1.2 trillion dollars by 1995, raising the ratio of foreign exchange trade to world trade from 2:1 in 1973 to 50:1 in 1980 and roughly 70:1 by 1995.[2] Signs of greater capital mobility can also be seen in other financial transactions. In the international bond and equity market, portfolio holdings of equity and long-term bonds reached an astonishing 5.2 trillion dollars in 1997. Moreover, the annual turnover in derivative contracts among the world's top 71 banks and securities, valued at 3.4 trillion dollars in 1990, skyrocketed to more than 130 trillion dollars by 1998.[3]

Understandably, these profound changes have drawn the attention of a wide range of scholars, journalists, and policymakers. Helen Milner and Robert Keohane, two leading scholars in the field of international political economy, suggest that given the rise of global finance, international capital should be treated as a "structural characteristic of the international system similar to anarchy," the key ordering principle in the study of international relations. Just as states can only ignore the anarchical international system at the risk of jeopardizing their own security, so too, argue Milner and Keohane "the international capitalist economy has become a fact that individual states confront and can only ignore or seek to change by paying such high costs that no state can afford it."[4] Their position is not a unique one; in fact it simply reinforces and formalizes what many others have stated elsewhere, including those who look specifically at the case of Japan.[5]

Curiously, many observers draw similar conclusions about the effects of global capital despite occupying different ends of the political spectrum.

Economic conservatives, who draw their inspiration from the anti-statist tenets of nineteenth-century liberalism, celebrate the spread of global capital because it allegedly enhances economic freedom and disciplines the state to adopt market friendly measures.[6] In contrast, many on the political left lament it precisely for these very reasons; greater economic freedom gives large asset holders of mobile capital greater voice and power in the political arena that will presumably erode democratic practices and weaken the state's ability to address the widening gap in democratic legitimization.[7] Hence, despite their clear normative differences, both sides seemingly take as a "matter of fact" the rise of global capital and its effects.

In this chapter, I challenge this "matter of fact" portrayal of globalization and its effects. To make explicit at the outset the normative position of this essay, I contend that this picture of globalization is a myth, in the sense of an "idée force," a powerful discourse that is capable of turning empirically and theoretically questionable assertions into unchallenged common sense.[8] As such, this discourse offers at best an incomplete picture of the relationship between politics and markets that serves to both occlude the states ongoing involvement in structuring the global economy, and unduly limit the range and realm of political agency in the face of globalization. There are a variety of ways in which the state is an active participant in the liberalization process. Moreover, after financial markets are liberalized, the state faces a new set of challenges that it must address, and it can do so with a varied range of options at its disposal.

I seek to demonstrate in the remaining portion of introduction both the theoretical and empirical fallacy of this assertion about the inevitability of financial globalization and its inexorably debilitating effects on the state by examining the politics of Japanese economic policymaking during the 1990s. Based on this critique, I then provide in the section on institutional analysis an alternative theoretical framework, grounded in the literature on historical institutionalism, which illustrates how and why the Japanese state actively intervenes in the economy despite, and to some extent because of, the rise of global finance. The two main issue-areas that I examine are the series of Keynesian stimulus measures that were adopted throughout this period and the succession of government responses to the financial crises, in particular the creation of new state-backed institutions that have been authorized with substantial financial resources and regulatory powers to recover bad loans and restore financial stability. These two issue-areas were selected because they represent two of the most important points of contention concerning the erosion of democratic choice and the role of the state in a post-Keynesian era marked by the globalization of the international capital market.

Fiscal policy

In the issue-area of fiscal policy, many have argued that the dramatic globalization of the international capital market will restrict the government's ability to adopt Keynesian fiscal policies because mobile asset holders at home are now more capable of exercising their "exit" threat on governments that fail to adopt more "market friendly" measures. Moreover, since international financial investors deem governments with large budget deficits to be less creditworthy than those that have their fiscal house in order, the competition to attract global capital encourages governments to retrench and adopt more stringent budgets. On a more formalized level, scholars have built on the Mundell–Flemming model to illustrate how fiscal policy loses its effectiveness under conditions of capital mobility and flexible exchange rates, as greater fiscal spending generates upward pressures on both interest rates and the exchange rate.[9]

The basic insight of the Mundell–Flemming model is that a country can simultaneously achieve only 2 out of the following 3 economic objectives: a fixed exchange rate, monetary autonomy, and international capital mobility. Hence, under a fixed exchange rate system, the tradeoff becomes one of either unrestricted capital mobility or monetary autonomy. If priority is given to capital mobility, then monetary autonomy will be sacrificed since domestic interest rates are committed to maintaining the fixed exchange rate. Any attempt to pursue independent monetary policy objectives will generally falter over time. For instance, efforts to stimulate the economy by lowering domestic interest rates will create a downward pressure on its currency as capital flows out of its economy to take advantage of higher returns abroad. Conversely, raising domestic interest rates to combat inflation will exert an upward pressure on the economy as more investors demand that currency, given the higher rate of return. In either scenario, the initial monetary policy decision must be countermanded in order to maintain the fixed level of exchange. In essence, under a fixed exchange rate system with unrestricted capital mobility, both interest rates and the level of inflation are determined in world markets, and monetary autonomy is sacrificed in order to preserve exchange rate stability. Accordingly, if monetary autonomy is sought under a fixed exchange rate system, then capital mobility must be restricted in order to prevent the disparity between domestic and international interest rates from disrupting the fixed level of exchange.

Under a flexible exchange rate system, it is possible to have both capital mobility and monetary autonomy simultaneously since monetary policy is no longer committed to maintaining a fixed level of exchange. But, according to this model, the effectiveness of monetary policy does not work its way through to changes in domestic interest rates; unrestricted capital mobility insures that domestic interest rates will remain tied to those set in world markets. Instead, the main effects of monetary policy take place through changes in capital flows, exchange rates, and trade balances.[10] For example, an expansionary monetary policy will induce a depreciation of that currency as capital flows out of the domestic economy to take advantage of higher interest rates abroad. In turn, a weaker currency will have the effect of stimulating exports and reducing imports as goods produced in the economy become relatively cheaper.[11]

When fiscal policy, the key instrument of Keynesian economic management that is associated with the modern welfare state, is brought into this framework, the bottom line conclusion under conditions of capital mobility is seemingly straightforward: "fiscal policy completely loses its force as a domestic stabilizer when the exchange rate is allowed to fluctuate and the money supply is held constant."[12] Fiscal expansion may initially create excess demand and higher income, but this creates higher demand for money and higher interest rates. Higher rates in turn lead to an inflow of capital and an appreciation of the currency, which produces a deflationary effect. These latter effects are seen to cancel out the initial effects of the fiscal stimulus. According to Mundell, the negative effect on income of exchange rate appreciation has to offset exactly the positive multiplier effect on income of the original increase in government spending. In the goods market, higher government spending is offset by higher imports while in the capital market, increase in government debt is equal to increases in capital inflow.[13] The bottom line conclusion, therefore, is that when exchange rates are flexible under conditions of increasingly mobile capital, such as in the case of the post-Bretton Woods era, fiscal policy loses its effectiveness, and monetary policy becomes the only effective tool for influencing national economic performance.

Consistent with this line of argument, others point to an accompanying ideational change, or "policy paradigm" shift, from Keynesianism to Monetarism that has become entrenched in key decision-making institutions since the early 1980s.[14] Although the first two decades of the postwar era have been hailed as "the golden age of capitalism,"[15] it was one that nonetheless represented a "class" or "embedded liberal" compromise in favor of Keynesian remedies that sought to mitigate the social costs of market adjustment through government spending.[16] By the 1970s, however, this consensus began to erode. In the wake of the stagflationary pressures that emerged after the oil crisis, the economic limitations of funding large sums of government spending through tax revenues, combined with the political pressure to expand government spending while keeping taxes down, created a common tendency among advanced industrial democracies to spend beyond their means, most noticeably through deficit-financing. In turn, the specter of large budget deficits and the resultant fear of "structural" inflation have sparked a counter-trend that seeks to repudiate Keynesianism in favor of Monetarist prescriptions.[17] Hence, while even a Republican President such as Richard Nixon could pronounce during the "golden age" that "we are all Keynesians now," the 1980s ushered in a "post-Keynesian" era marked not only by Thatcherism and Reaganomics, but one where a Socialist President such as François Mitterand would abandon after only a year in office many of his socialist oriented programs and adopt a policy of fiscal austerity in the face of a serious fiscal deficit.[18] Similarly, in Sweden, the Social Democrats in the 1976 elections were voted out of office for the first time since 1932, in large part due to their effort to promote the Meidner Plan, an ambitious socialist program designed to transfer company profits to a union-managed fund. Although the Social Democrats were able to regain power in 1982, they did so only after they watered down their original plan and adopted a more conservative framework.[19]

From a comparative standpoint, the Japanese case is critically important because those who have presented the most cogent arguments that refute the claim of a global convergence toward Monetarism and the demise of the modern welfare state have focused primarily on advanced industrial democracies that have strong left-wing governments backed by an encompassing and highly union-ized labor organization.[20] According to this view, left-wing parties in power are more apt to continue using the public purse string and expand the welfare state than conservative ones given the greater weight the former accords to full employment and income redistribution.[21] Moreover the presence of an encom-passing and highly unionized labor organization are seen to give left-wing governments the ability to pursue these objectives while keeping inflation down by mitigating the collective action dilemma associated with spiraling wage demands.[22]

These characteristics, however, are nowhere to be found in the case of Japan. In comparative terms, Japan is rightly viewed as the polar opposite of Sweden. Whereas Sweden historically represents the classic example of a one-party dominant social democratic regime, Japan has been ruled almost exclusively by the conservative Liberal Democratic Party (LDP) since its formation in 1955.[23] Moreover, as seen in Table 7.1, the organizational strength of Japan's labor union ranks among the lowest in the circle of advanced industrial democracies. Despite labor's mixed successes in industry-specific negotiations with business,[24] its com-paratively low level of unionization (left-hand column) and high level of internal fragmentation (right-hand column) have excluded labor from effective representation over an extended period of time in economic policy-making at the national level.[25]

Table 7.1 Comparative index of union strength

Country	Unionization rate[a]		Number of unions[b]	
	1970	1990	1970	1990
Sweden	66	83	29	23
Austria	61	46	16	14
France	19	10	—	—
Norway	56	54	35	29
Finland	52	72	31	24
Denmark	60	74	45	30
Italy	33	34	24	20
Germany	33	31	16	16
Belgium	41	55	19	18
Netherlands	38	23	20	17
UK	45	38	150	76
Japan	33	25	99	81
Canada	29	32	110	90
US	28	15	124	91

Source: Garrett, *Partisan Politics*, p. 14.

Notes
a Union membership as a percentage of total labor force.
b Number of unions affiliated with largest confederation.

Accordingly, this study represents a "crucial" case study; it empirically refutes the conventional claim of a global convergence towards economic conservatism under conditions where such outcomes are "least-likely" to occur.[26]

To be sure, the politics of macroeconomic policy-making in Japan throughout the 1980s at first glance appears to be consistent with both the general argument positing the shift from Keynesianism to Monetarism, as well as the specific argument concerning the macroeconomic policy preferences of conservative-led governments. The administrative and fiscal reform movement that was headed by Rinchō (short for *Dai Niji Rinji Gyōsei Chōsakai*, or the Second Provisional Commission on Administrative Reform) and launched in the early 1980s explicitly rejected the heavy use of Keynesian deficit spending that was the hallmark of the 1970s. Instead, its main objective was to pursue "fiscal reconstruction without tax increases" (*zōzei naki zaisei saiken*) and eliminate the issuance of deficit-financing bonds by 1990.

Upon close scrutiny, however, it is clearly evident that while the government was indeed able to meet its target by 1990, the measures that were adopted to achieve this goal strayed widely from Rinchō's basic tenet. Whereas Rinchō sought to eliminate deficit-financing through cuts in government expenditures, over 80 percent of the deficit reduction was in fact attributable to either higher than projected increases in tax revenues or shifting government expenditures out of the main budget (General Account Budget) to other government accounts.[27] Moreover, any pretense of repudiating Keynesian fiscal policy was abandoned throughout most of the 1990s, as the government adopted a series of pump-priming measures in the face of Japan's worst economic recession in decades.

As Table 7.2 illustrates, the Japanese government adopted nine sizeable economic stimulus packages between August 1992 and October 2000, totaling 129 trillion yen or 26.5 percent of GDP. To be sure, the actual fiscal impact of each stimulus package was smaller than the announced figures. The amount of fresh spending in these stimulus packages, or what the Japanese term *mamizu* (pure water), was invariably lower than the announced figures because a sizeable portion of these stimulus packages was simply a re-classification of existing spending or loans that presumably could have otherwise been raised in the private capital market. Moreover, once the economy began to show signs of a recovery, posting a real GDP growth of 1.5 percent in 1995 and 3.9 percent in 1996, the Hashimoto administration temporarily turned its attention to the task of reducing the sizeable deficit incurred in the first half of the decade. The government not only adopted a stringent budget for fiscal year 1997, but it also phased in as scheduled a consumption tax increase from 3 to 5 percent. Moreover, in November 1997 the Hashimoto administration enacted the Fiscal Reform Law, which called for the elimination of deficit-finance bonds by the end of fiscal year 2003, and the reduction of the combined budget deficit of national and local government to 3 percent of GDP or less.[28]

Within less than a year of the enactment of the Fiscal Reform Law, however, the government was forced to reverse course as the economy slid back into a serious recession. In April 1998, the Hashimoto administration unveiled a new

Table 7.2 Fiscal stimulus packages, 1992–2000

Date	Amount (in trillions of yen)	Percent of GDP
August 28, 1992	10.7	2.3
April 13, 1993	13.2	2.8
September 16, 1993	6.0	1.3
February 8, 1994	15.3	3.2
[April 14, 1995][a]	[7.0]	[1.4]
September 20, 1995	14.2	3.0
April 24, 1998	16.7	3.4
November 16, 1998	23.9	4.9
November 11, 1999	18.0	3.5
October 19, 2000	11.0	2.1
Total	129.0	26.5

Sources: OECD, *Economic Surveys: Japan* (Paris: OECD, 2000), p.53; Tamim Bayoumi and Charles Collyns (eds), *Post-Bubble Blues: How Japan Responded to Asset Price Collapse* (Washington, DC: IMF, 2000), p.108; IMF, *World Economic Outlook 1998*, p. 115.

Note
a The April 1995 package was excluded from the total figure because these allocations were primarily for the Kobe earthquake relief rather than for economic stimulus.

stimulus package worth over 16 trillion yen. Although the pure water content of this package was once again smaller than the government proclaimed package, the tax cuts and public works spending contained within it would enlarge the deficit and force the government to push back the target year of the Fiscal Reform Law to 2005.[29] Seven months later, with no recovery in sight, the government announced an even bigger stimulus package, worth 24 trillion yen. With this package, the government suspended the Fiscal Reform Law, as the bond dependence ratio soared to a record high 38.6 percent.[30] The following year, the Ōbuchi administration launched in November 1999 a new pump-priming package worth 18 trillion yen in the face of a 1 percent decline in the economy during the July–September period from the previous quarter.[31] By 1999, the cumulative effects of these economic packages, together with the decline in tax revenues caused by the poor performance of the economy, had raised the General Account Budget's dependence on debt to 43.4 percent of the total budget, a level even higher than that recorded during Japan's fiscal crisis of the late 1970s.[32]

In short, these trends in Japanese fiscal policy clearly refute both the general argument about the impact of capital mobility on fiscal policy as well as the more specific argument about the contrasting macroeconomic policy preferences between left-wing and conservative-led governments. Greater capital mobility in Japan during the 1990s did not force the government to adopt a policy of fiscal austerity. Instead, the government throughout most of this decade adopted a series of fiscal stimulus measures at a time when economic growth, and hence tax revenues, remained stagnant. These combined factors produced by the end of the

Table 7.3 General and Central government financial balances. Surplus or deficit (−) as a percentage of nominal GDP

	General government financial balance				Central government financial balance			
	1970	*1980*	*1990*	*2000*	*1970*	*1980*	*1990*	*2000*
United States	−1.0	−1.3	−2.7	1.4	n.a.	−2.6	−3.0	2.0
Japan	1.7	−4.4	2.9	−8.2	n.a.	−8.6	−0.5	−11.4
Germany	0.2	−1.8	−2.0	1.6	n.a.	−1.8	−2.0	1.4
France	0.5	−1.3	−1.4	−1.2	n.a.	−1.2	−1.4	−2.3
UK	2.9	−4.0	−1.1	3.6	n.a.	−4.0	−1.1	3.6

Sources: OECD, *OECD Economic Outlook*, various issues; IMF, *World Economic Outlook*, various issues. The central government figure for Japan in 1990 is not zero because it includes construction bonds. The figures for Germany are those for West Germany in 1970 and 1980, and the United German Republic for 1990 and 2000. The figures for 2000 are estimated figures from IMF, October 2000.

decade a gaping fiscal deficit higher than that of any other G-7 advanced industrial democracies (Table 7.3). Moreover, although party politics did undergo some notable changes during this period, they did not represent a shift toward a strong left-wing government backed by an encompassing and highly unionized labor organization. In fact, the 1990s witnessed a further decline in the unionization rate and the virtual vanquishing of the Social Democratic Party (SDP), Japan's main left-wing political party since the early postwar era.

Financial policy

The same discrepancy between theory and evidence can be found in the issue-area of financial markets and the role of the state. In both popular and scholarly accounts, many portray the dramatic globalization of the international financial market as a force that has eroded the authority and autonomy of sovereign states. According to this view, regulatory barriers to international capital are increasingly costly to erect, both politically and economically. Greater capital mobility, transnational linkages, and the growth of international market structures are seen to introduce a competitive system whereby transnational actors not only exercise more power over states by utilizing greater "exit" threats, but where states often undermine their own regulatory powers willingly in order to attract "footloose" capital flows.[33] Hence, even in the case of east Asia, where the developmental state model had posed a serious challenge to classical liberal orthodoxy, the financial crisis that has plagued this region in the 1990s is now seen as evidence of the need to withdraw the visible hand of the state and adopt greater free-market reforms.[34]

Although the theoretical model that supports this general claim is not as formalized as in the case of macroeconomic policy, the basic argument usually combines, either explicitly or implicitly, a mixture of rational choice models including collective action, game theory, and Hirschman's exit, voice, loyalty options. For example, Stigler and Peltzman's classic theory of regulation argues that in a closed economy, producers generally win out over consumers in securing favorable regulatory policies in the political marketplace because producers are more willing and able to organize and lobby effectively than consumers given their smaller numbers and higher stakes in the outcome.[35] However, under conditions of greater capital mobility, asset-holding consumers of financial commodities can more readily exit, or threaten to exit, one political marketplace and enter another where regulations are less burdensome, with presumably lower transaction costs and more diversified financial products.[36] Moreover, the competition among states, and the producers of financial commodities based therein, to attract mobile capital creates a situation much akin to the Prisoner's Dilemma model.[37] Although each state may benefit more if a collective agreement to regulate is achieved, the risk of other states defecting induces each state to defect in an effort to prevent capital flight and court mobile asset holders. The collective impact of each state competing in this manner is thus seen to produce a "race to the bottom" in regulatory laxity.[38]

Here again, as in the case of fiscal policy, there are elements of this argument that appear consistent with the Japanese case. Financial liberalization began in the early 1980s as Japanese corporate borrowers increasingly utilized the Euromarkets to raise funds and as Japanese banks grew weary of purchasing government bonds below market rates without the ability to sell them back in the secondary market. The former led to the gradual but significant liberalization of the domestic bond market, easing the ability of Japanese corporations to issue straight bonds and convertible bonds in the Japanese financial market without the heavy collateral restrictions that had been in place since the prewar period. In exchange, banks received greater entry into the private placement market. The latter led to the first major break in Article 65 of the Securities Exchange Act, the Japanese equivalent of the Glass–Steagall Act, enacted in 1948 under the US Occupation. With the passage of the 1982 Banking Law, banks were allowed to enter into the retailing and dealing of government bonds, thereby breaking the firewall that had hitherto separated the banking and securities industry.[39]

International political pressures also contributed to the liberalization process. Amid growing US concerns over its mounting bilateral trade imbalance with Japan, US government officials met with their Japanese counterparts in 1983–84 in an effort to raise the value of the yen against the dollar. The agreement that was struck in May 1984 helped liberalize the Euroyen market in several key areas: restrictions on Japanese corporate access to the Euroyen bond market was eased, foreign governments and non-Japanese private corporations were authorized to issue unsecured bonds in the Euroyen market, and the foreign exchange market in both forward transactions and currency swaps was liberalized for both residents and non-residents. US pressures also helped foreign firms gain entry into the Tokyo Stock Exchange (TSE) in 1985. In turn, the presence of foreign securities companies in the TSE allowed large Japanese institutional investors with foreign offices to circumvent the high and fixed commission rates charged in the TSE by placing their orders through their foreign offices.[40]

By the following decade, amid mounting concerns that the Tokyo financial market would increasingly lose market shares to other international financial centers, together with the growing recognition that the existing rate of return on savings would not sufficiently cover the growing costs of a rapidly aging society, the Hashimoto cabinet launched in November 1996 the "Japanese Big Bang." With the aim of making the Tokyo financial market comparable in scale to those of London and New York, the plan called for sweeping financial reforms that would transform Japan's financial market into one that was "free, fair, and global" by the year 2001. The targeted areas for reform covered the banking, securities, and insurance industries as well as accounting and foreign exchange. The key components of the "big bang" measures included liberalization of international capital transactions; product liberalization in securities, investment trust, derivatives, loan securitization; deregulation of cross-entry among financial industries; removal of the ban on financial holding companies; liberalization of fixed brokerage commissions; and stricter accounting standards and disclosure rules for banks and securities.[41]

Admittedly, these changes are consistent with the general claim that greater capital mobility prompts state regulators to embrace financial liberalization. However, these changes offer at best only an incomplete, if not distorted, picture of how the relationship between the state and the market has unfolded in Japan during the 1990s. From a comparative perspective, critics of those who see a growing convergence in the financial regulatory policies of advanced industrial democracies rightly note that states have not responded in a uniform manner to financial globalization.[42] For example, one insightful comparative study, which includes the case of Japan up to the mid-1990s, reveals how financial globalization has meant "freer markets" *and* "more rules": the Japanese state has opened the financial market to more competition by liberalizing interest rates and commercial activities across financial sectors, but it has also introduced new regulations and reorganized its control of private sector behavior.[43] Along similar lines, others have argued that financial liberalization does not lead to regulatory laxity but rather to the creation of more stringent prudential regulations, such as capital requirements and mandatory disclosure rules.[44]

The evidence has become more compelling in the second half of the 1990s; greater financial liberalization has been accompanied not simply by "more rules" but by the creation of several powerful state-backed institutions entrusted with substantial financial resources and a wide range of regulatory authority that go well beyond what is deemed "prudential regulatory" safeguards. In response to the collapse of the Housing Loan Companies (*jūsen*) and bank failures such as Hyōgo, Taiheiyō, and Hanwa, Diet deliberations were held in 1996 that authorized the creation of the Housing Loan Administration Corporation (HLAC) and the Resolution and Collection Bank (RCB). In turn, the political backlash over the use of taxpayer money to liquidate the *jūsen* led the Diet to approve in June 1997 the creation of a new government organization – the Financial Supervisory Agency (FSA, *Kinyū Kantoku-chō*) – authorized with the power to supervise and inspect private financial institutions.[45] The following year, as banks and other financial institutions continued to record staggering levels of non-performing loans, the Diet passed a package of bills that provided roughly 60 trillion yen [12 percent of nominal GDP] of public funds, to be supervised by a newly created Financial Reconstruction Commission (FRC, *Kinyū Saisei Iinkai*). The new law gave the FRC the mandate to protect depositors of failed banks, recover bad loans, liquidate and temporarily nationalize failed banks, and strengthen the capital-adequacy ratio of solvent banks.[46]

With these new laws in place, the government took immediate action. Two major banks, the Long-Term Credit Bank (LTCB) and Nippon Credit Bank (NCB), were nationalized within three months of these bills being passed. Moreover, before the fiscal year had ended (March 31, 1999), the FRC had injected 7.7 trillion yen of public funds into the banking system in an effort to strengthen the capital-adequacy ratio of solvent banks. Roughly 80 percent of this sum was in the form of preferred stock or bonds, with the right to convert the pre-ferred stock to common equity after a designated time period. What this meant in effect was that the state could acquire a major stake in the ownership of private banks. Analysts were quick to point out at the time that within a short period, the government's potential share could reach as high as 60 percent in the cases of Mitsui Trust & Banking and Chūō Trust & Banking. To varying degrees, all the major commercial banks, with the exception of Bank of Tokyo–Mitsubishi, were placed in a similar situation, as can be seen in Table 7.4. In essence, major com-mercial banks gave the state a significant share of stock ownership in exchange for their ability to continue conducting international business. In order to meet Bank of International Settlement (BIS) requirements, banks needed to maintain a capital adequacy ratio of 8 percent, with 4 percent in the category of Tier 1 capital. Selling preferred stocks to the government was a convenient way to address the later requirement since preferred stocks counted as Tier 1 capital.

Table 7.4 Bank recapitalization ratio, March 31, 1999

	BIS ratio (%)	Tier I capital	
		Ratio (%)	Government share (%)
Daiwa Bank	12.7	7.8	48.0
Tōkai Bank	12.6	7.8	37.5
Sakura Bank	12.3	7.2	33.4
Dai-Ichi Kangyō Bank	11.5	5.9	19.3
Industrial Bank of Japan	11.3	6.0	20.0
Fuji Bank	11.2	5.7	21.2
Sanwa Bank	11.1	6.0	28.1
Sumitomo Bank	11.0	5.6	23.0
Bank of Tokyo–Mitsubishi	10.5	5.2	0.0
Asahi Bank	9.4	4.7	41.8

Source: Douglas Ostrom, "Tokyo's Changing Role in Financial Markets," *JEI Report* November 12, 1999.

Perhaps an even more telling example of greater state activism during this period of greater financial liberalization is the increasingly extensive role that the Japanese government played as a direct participant in the financial market. With less regulatory restrictions on entering the Japanese market, foreign investors rushed into the market in an effort to lure away the half trillion dollars in the state-run postal savings deposits that were scheduled to mature starting in April 2000. However, faced with the choice of renewing their 7 percent deposits at 1 percent or investing in mutual funds, roughly 80 percent of the depositors chose to renew their accounts with the postal savings.[47] The state's role on the lending side is equally apparent. Although private financial institutions faced less market restrictions in terms of the financial commodities and services they could offer, private banks retrenched and reduced their volume of lending in order to meet their capital adequacy requirements. It was therefore up to the state to fill in the gap, providing both loans and credit guarantees primarily, though not exclusively,[48] through the Fiscal Investment and Loan Program (FILP). Consequently, as Figure 7.1 below illustrates, both the postal savings share of total deposits and the government's share of total lending rose significantly throughout the 1990s.

The government's role in the bond market is even more conspicuous. As noted earlier, the economic stimulus packages adopted throughout the 1990s, combined with the sharp drop in tax revenues caused by stagnant economic growth during this period, created a huge fiscal deficit. In order to cover the gaping shortfall between tax revenues and public expenditures, the government issued an extensive amount of deficit-financing and other bonds. Hence, whereas the government issued only 7.3 trillion yen worth of bonds in 1990, by 2000 government bond issues reached a record high of 37.5 trillion yen. All told, the total amount of government bonds outstanding stood at 367.6 trillion yen in FY 2000, roughly 71.6 percent of GDP.[49] At the same time, the state was also a major purchaser of these government bonds. Over half the total amount of government bonds outstanding were held by the state itself, with the lion's share in the hands of the Trust

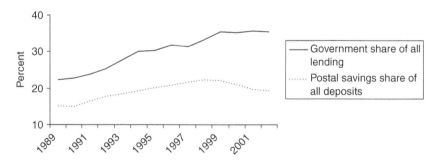

Figure 7.1 Public sector lending and deposit taking in Japan, 1989–2002.

Source: "Guide to Japan's Flow of Funds Accounts," Research and Statistics Department, The Bank of Japan, October 2002. Available online at www.boj.or.jp/en/stat/exp/data/exsj01.pdf. All information last accessed December 16, 2004.

Fund Bureau (a bureau within the Ministry of Finance (MOF)) and the Bank of Japan (BOJ).[50] In short, the state is both a major seller and buyer of central government bonds.

In sum, these measures not only refute the simple notion of a regulatory race to the bottom, but they go well beyond the state renewing its authority in the form of creating and enforcing prudential regulations. Instead, in the case of Japan, the globalization of international finance has been accompanied by active Diet deliberations that culminated in the creation of new public institutions with substantial financial resources and regulatory powers. While the Big Bang was significant, the government also became a more direct and active participant in the financial market by staking out an ownership position in all the major banks, temporarily nationalizing two big banks, and expanding its role as a lender, borrower, credit guarantor, bond issuer, and bond purchaser.

Institutional analysis: the missing key

In this section of the chapter, I advance a historical institutionalist analysis in an effort to address the wide discrepancy between the theoretical assertions about the deleterious effects of global finance on state authority and the empirical evidence in the case of Japan as documented in the introduction. Given the widespread use of the term "institutionalism" in the field of contemporary political science, it is important to make clear at the outset the manner in which the term is used here.[51] Among those working in the forefront of historical institutionalism, the widely accepted definition of "institution" is that of Peter Hall who conceptualizes institutions into three basic categories: "the basic organizational structures we associate with a democratic polity and a capitalistic economy; the basic organization of the state and society; and the standard operating procedures, regulations, and routines of public agencies and organizations."[52]

Many who have examined the political economy of Japan from an institutionalist framework have focused primarily on the third category, namely the standard operating procedures, regulations, and routines of Ministry of International Trade and Industry (MITI) and MOF.[53] To some extent, they have also highlighted *select* aspects of the state structure – such as MOF and MITI's technical expertise, information-gathering capacity, and network linkages – to make the broader claim about how these ministries enjoy a high degree of autonomy from politicians and powerful societal actors in shaping both the agenda-setting process and policy outcomes.[54] In turn, the most vocal critics of this approach have stressed the primacy of parliamentary politics, utilizing a principal–agent model to demonstrate how politicians merely delegate, rather than abdicate, their legislative authority to bureaucrats.[55] In contrast, I stress in this study the centrality of institutions that pertain to the first two categories. This analytic shift provides a useful way to move beyond the contentious debate generated by these two opposing claims toward a broader framework that offers greater comparative utility.

What this means more specifically is the importance of first explicating the ongoing tension that all governments of advanced industrial democracies face in finding an appropriate balance between the role of the state and that of the market in determining how scarce resources are to be allocated. Indeed, what has seemingly been forgotten in the analysis of those who stress the primacy of global market forces are the crucial insights that underscore precisely this point among some of the most classic studies in the field of political economy. The seminal work of Karl Polanyi reveals that the long historical rise of the free-market required a strong and interventionist state in direct and discernable ways.[56] Barrington Moore's comparative study reveals that even in the least obvious case (England), the state was actively involved in the road to the free market.[57] Moreover, this relationship between the state and market is mirrored in the international sphere. Both Charles Kindleberger's oft cited study of the Great Depression and Richard Gardner's work on the sterling–dollar diplomacy reveal that the creation and stability of a liberal international economic system is intimately linked to the underlying political power structure that sustains it.[58]

This is not to suggest that market forces are irrelevant, but rather that the market is inextricably bound in a dynamic and system-like relationship with the state. To be sure, an excessive reliance on the state to make allocative or regulatory decisions based on social and political considerations may indeed create market inefficiencies, or generate a fiscal crisis, as classical economists and globalization theorists insist. However, it is equally plausible that an unfettered market can create its own form of crisis that compels the state to assume a greater role in the market. For instance, financial liberalization may indeed reduce market distortions and provide greater opportunities for banks to make loans, but these can include bad or risky loans that produce a speculative bubble or a crisis of confidence in bank solvency.[59] When financial markets are flourishing, greed mixed with uncertainty about when stock market trends will change could stretch what may be deemed plausible or rational. Whether in the case of Japan in the second half of the 1980s or the United States in the second half of the 1990s, there were no shortages of economic commentators on both sides of the Pacific who argued that the sharp rise in the stock market was sustainable.[60] Under these conditions, investors do not simply purchase stocks based on the price–earnings ratio, but on the expectation of what other investors will do, and how that will influence future stock prices. Accordingly, sharp rises in the stock market can be fueled by a self-fulfilling prophecy that invariably produces an unsustainable asset bubble.

Moreover, once an asset bubble bursts, the state must choose from a variety of different options the manner in which it will deal with the sharp drop in the financial market. These options include the following:

1   simply do nothing and let the market sort out the winners and losers (or let the market sort out winners and losers in conjunction with enforcing prudential regulations such as stricter accounting and disclosure rules, capital adequacy, etc.);

2   insure at a minimum the ability of depositors to safely withdraw their funds with either taxpayers' money or from contributions paid in by the lending

institutions (presumably for the purposes of reducing the systemic risk of a run on the banks);

3   provide public funds to banks to varying degrees for different purposes (i.e. ensure the banks' solvency, meet the capital adequacy ratio set by BIS, provide enough liquidity so that banks will continue to lend to borrowers in order to keep the economy going);

4   nationalize failed private financial institutions (rather than letting them fail as the market sorts out winners and losers);

5   adopt the role of private financial institutions and become a significant player in its own right in financial markets.

Though admittedly crude, these options represent in ascending order the degree to which the state can play a more active role in the financial market, and the Japanese case clearly falls in the higher end of the spectrum.

The same applies to the case of fiscal policy. The globalization of finance and the alleged repudiation of Keynesianism in favor of Monetarism that accompany it may in turn unleash a political backlash at both the domestic and international levels that encourages the resumption of fiscal expansion. At the international level, financial liberalization can intensify, rather than weaken, the political importance of coordinating fiscal policy as monetary policy becomes less effective in stimulating domestic demand and remedying current account imbalances. As the Mundell–Flemming model suggests, an expansionary monetary policy in a world of mobile capital can have the inadvertent effect of encouraging capital outflows that lead to currency devaluation and greater trade surpluses.[61] Moreover, given Japan's large pool of domestic household savings and foreign exchange reserves, there is still room even within the Mundell–Flemming framework for fiscal policy to produce a stimulative effect on the economy.[62] Accordingly, although capital mobility in Japan has risen dramatically since the early 1980s, there has been no corresponding pressure on Japan to adopt austere budgets. To the contrary, international pressures, whether in the form of diplomatic suasion, exchange rate appreciation, or the threat of market closure, continued to encourage Japan to adopt a policy of fiscal expansion, rather than contraction.[63]

At the domestic level, an expansionary monetary policy may provide an attractive alternative to fiscal policy in stimulating the economy, particularly when the government budget deficit is high. However, lowering interest rates will prove ineffective when there is a problem of secular demand and counterproductive when easy credit produces a speculative bubble.[64] Moreover, in a democratic system, the political party in power has no incentive to adopt macroeconomic policies that simply conform to international capital movements if such policies undermine its electoral basis of support. Fiscal austerity during times of economic recession may free up scarce resources but at the cost of a political backlash that no party in power may want to pay.[65] Hence, just as freer trade has led to greater, not less, public spending, freer capital need not force states to adopt uniformly more stringent government budgets.[66]

One key argument of this chapter, therefore, is that this tension between the role of the state and that of the market is never resolved conclusively. That is, the globalization of the international financial market does not lead to a competitive "race to the bottom" either in the case of fiscal policy or financial regulatory policy. Instead, in both these issue-areas, policy decisions that are reached and become entrenched at any one particular point in time – whether they accord greater primacy to either the market or the state to make allocative decisions – simply introduce a different set of challenges that over time generate new negotiations over economic policy. This is not meant to suggest that market forces are irrelevant, or to gainsay those who rightly criticize some of the inefficient, if not outright corrupt, aspects of Japanese financial and fiscal policy that have contributed to the country's economic malaise over the last decade.[67] Rather, it is to make the more basic point that economic policy decisions are *political* decisions, and that among advanced industrial democracies the logic of democratic politics does not simply follow the dictates of market forces in any teleological or uniform manner.[68] Just as left-wing governments cannot privilege employment and income redistribution *at the expense of* economic growth,[69] nor can conservative governments rely exclusively on free market orthodoxy when doing so jeopardizes their ability to secure electoral victory.

What this further suggests is that financial globalization does not produce a uniform response among the advanced industrialized democracies because historical timing and initial conditions matter.[70] That is, while the relationship between politics and markets in Japan reveals the same basic dilemma that all advanced industrial democracies face, understanding the precise manner in which this dilemma unfolds within a particular country also requires a detailed explication of how the second category of institutions – the basic organizations of the state and society – are configured and how this configuration changes over time. More specifically, this entails a clear delineation of the interests of the state and societal actors who compromise Japan's ruling coalition, and the political bargaining and compromises that are struck among them during the policy-making process. Furthermore, because policy decisions that are struck and become entrenched in one period in turn produce unintended consequences over time that help shape and define the political setting in which subsequent decisions are made, identifying economic policy changes requires a careful empirical investigation of these path dependent effects.[71] This institutional approach thus provides the necessary framework to capture both the causes and consequences of economic policy changes. Although it is well beyond the scope of this chapter to present a full historical narrative of this path-dependent process here, a cursory sketch, outlined in the following section, helps illustrate this point.

The case of Japan

In the case of Japan, the institutional pattern that emerged in the early postwar era was a conservative one party dominant system led by the LDP. Relying heavily on the financial support of big business, the voting strength of farmers, and the technical expertise of central economic ministries, the LDP began its long-term dominance by adopting a conservative economic strategy designed to maximize economic growth while minimizing the size of the public sector. Private financial institutions were heavily regulated, compartmentalized, and protected by MOF under a "convoy system" in order to prevent bank failures and to ensure a steady and stable supply of funds from the private household sector to the corporate sector, with depositors receiving below market rates for their savings. The use of fiscal policy as an instrument of economic stimulus was limited; in general, the government budget was balanced and kept small as a percentage of GNP during the first decade and a half of LDP rule (1955–70). Moreover, with exchange rates fixed under the Bretton Woods system, monetary policy was constrained by Japan's balance of payments; as a general pattern, peaks in the business cycle were accompanied by current account deficits, and the government responded by adopting contractionary monetary policies.[72]

With the economy posting roughly a double digit rate of average annual growth in real terms, this economic strategy proved highly successful in keeping the LDP in power during the 1960s. By the following decade, however, the very success of this strategy helped create a setting that would undermine it. Rapid economic growth produced a demographic shift that significantly reduced the relative voting strength of farmers while increasing the electoral clout of white collar middle class voters. This latter group began to throw their weight in key local elections in support of progressive candidates who campaigned and won under a platform that called for an expanded government role in welfare-related programs. Economic success also meant that internationally competitive businesses could finance a larger portion of their investments through retained earnings or the Euromarket, rather than through domestic financial markets that were tightly regulated by MOF. In order to remain in power, therefore, the LDP from the 1970s onward needed to adapt to these changes and adopt an economic strategy that would expand its constituent base and transform the party from one that relied primarily on farmers and big business into one that scholars of comparative politics term a "near catch-all party."[73]

The initial change emerged in the realm of fiscal policy, where the LDP had both the opportunity and the incentive to abandon its policy of fiscal stringency in favor of fiscal expansion throughout the 1970s. With internationally competitive businesses now able to secure funds elsewhere, a greater share of private household savings could be used to finance the public sector debt accrued by the use of fiscal stimulus, and the government bonds issued to cover the budget shortfall would be purchased by an underwriting syndicate led by the main city banks. Predictably, the two budget categories that received the lion's share of the increase in government spending were those that would help bolster and expand the party's constituent base, namely social welfare-related expenditures and public works projects. The former drew the support of white collar middle class voters, while the latter benefited both the construction industry and big business.[74] Moreover, FILP lending to small and medium sized businesses rose dramatically during this period in an effort to draw their support away from the Japanese Communist Party (JCP).[75]

While this strategy was highly effective in keeping the LDP in power throughout the 1970s, it produced by the end of the decade a budget deficit that was spiraling out of control. As can be seen in the right hand column of Table 7.2, Japan's central government financial balance in 1980 stood at −8.6 percent of nominal GDP, a rate considerably higher than those of all other G-5 nations. In the absence of any substantive policy changes related to government taxes or expenditures, government debt was projected to rise at an even higher rate because large volumes of government bonds would mature and propel the share of the budget devoted to debt repayment to a level higher than any other category of government expenditures.[76] Moreover, by the end of the 1970s, the tightly regulated financial market came under strain as banks were no longer willing to continue purchasing rapidly rising levels of government bonds, by then at below market rates, without the ability to sell them back in the secondary market.[77] Furthermore, the financial liberalization adopted in May 1975 by the United States, and then by London in the 1980s, meant that Japanese borrowers could secure better rates than in the heavily regulated Japanese financial market. Overseas financing by Japanese corporations rose from a mere 15 billion yen in 1973 to 421 billion in 1975, and by 1982 the total reached 1.4 trillion.[78]

Accordingly, the strategy adopted by the LDP in the 1980s was one that ostensibly repudiated Keynesian fiscal strategies in favor of an expansionary monetary policy and one that introduced the gradual liberalization of the Japanese financial market.[79] In the realm of fiscal policy, reducing the level of deficit-financing became the main priority, and no new taxes were to be introduced to achieve this goal. In stark contrast to the profligate spending patterns of the 1970s, the government throughout the 1980s adopted "zero ceiling" and "minus ceiling" policies whereby the major domestic spending items in Japan's General Account Budget were first frozen from one year to the next, then cut in subsequent years.[80] To offset this contractionary fiscal policy stance, monetary policy became the chief instrument to promote economic growth. The official discount rate (ODR) set by the Bank of Japan was lowered from 7.25 percent in 1980 to 2.5 percent by 1987.[81]

Here again this strategy proved effective in achieving its economic goals and keeping the LDP in power. Deficit-financing was eliminated in 1990, the concentration of capital shifted from the debt-ridden public sector to a more liberalized private sector, and the economy recorded the second longest period of sustained economic growth in Japanese postwar history during the second half of the 1980s.[82] But this conservative strategy also produced its own unintended consequences in the form of a huge speculative bubble in both the stock and real estate markets. Given the decline in public sector debt and the ability of competitive private corporations to raise money through either retained earnings or the Euromarket, lower interest rates provided large volumes of cheap credit used for speculative investments.[83] Moreover, because financial liberalization was introduced without new safeguards, the collapse of these markets eroded the solvency of Japan's financial institutions.

It is against this backdrop that the Japanese government pursued the particular mix of fiscal and financial policies described in the introductory section.

Although these measures that were adopted clearly ran counter to the expectation of those who argue that financial globalization leads to the erosion of state authority, this path-dependent narrative reveals why such counter-intuitive measures made sense. A macroeconomic strategy, which repudiated Keynesianism in favor of Monetarism, and a financial policy, which promoted liberalization (the policies that globalization theorists predict), failed to revive the economy and keep the political party in power.[84] In fact, there is very clear evidence that no amount of reduction in interest rates could revitalize consumer spending or investor confidence after the bubble collapsed. Moreover, those that sought loans from private commercial banks under a more liberalized system found it difficult to obtain them. In the process of making the transition toward financial liberalization, the banks' efforts to meet the capital adequacy ratio created the unintended consequence of causing them to retrench and reduce their volume of lending.

The problem at the macroeconomic level, therefore, was one of secular demand. Economic growth stagnated not because the cost of borrowing was too high, but because private savings far exceeded private investment demand. Viewed accordingly, the problem with the series of Keynesian stimulus packages that were adopted throughout the 1990s was not their excessiveness but their timidity and inconsistency.[85] Invariably, the actual fiscal impact of each stimulus package was smaller than the announced figures. Moreover, after the two sizeable stimulus packages were adopted in 1994 and 1995, the Hashimoto administration prematurely adopted a contractionary fiscal policy in 1996, effectively killing the economic recovery underway since 1995. It was only two years later, in April 1998, that the LDP implemented another sizeable stimulus package, but by then, the economy had come to another grinding halt, and the budget deficit widened sharply as tax revenues faltered. After adopting three more stimulus packages within the next 30 months, the LDP faced a fiscal crisis even greater than that of the late 1970s.

Conclusion

As Japan's economy continues to stagger, there are many who would squarely put the blame on the inability of Japan's stubborn political and economic institutions to respond to the profound changes in the international economic system. Whereas these domestic institutions may have served Japan well during the early decades of the postwar period, they now simply obstruct the reforms necessary for the Japanese economy to operate efficiently.[86] Over time, however, this 'residual institutional stickiness' will exact a cost too great to sustain, leading to changes in both the state's role in the financial market and the political party system.[87] Some would go further to suggest that these changes are not only inevitable, but beneficial.[88]

In this chapter, I draw very different conclusions about the causes and consequences of Japan's prolonged period of economic stagnation. Japan's long standing political and economic institutions (such as the compartmentalization of the financial industry, the convoy system, and the *keiretsu* system of main banks in terms of the key economic institutions; and the "near catch all," one party dominant political regime) may have exacerbated the economic problem, but it did not cause it. Speculative booms followed by economic collapse are a recurrent theme of free market economies. The liberalization of financial markets allows resources to move more freely according to market principles, offering greater opportunities to make more investments and loans, including riskier and more speculative ones. Viewed accordingly, Japan's bubble economy of the 1980s and its collapse in the early 1990s is merely one example out of many. Although the Great Depression offers the most obvious example, more recent cases can also be found. Switzerland, for example, experienced a similar phenomenon during roughly the same time period; a bubble in real estate prices burst at the beginning of the 1990s, pushing the economy into a prolonged period of stagnation.[89] In the cases of Sweden and Finland during the second half of the 1980s, real asset prices (both stock and land prices) also rose at a rate comparable to that of Japan and dropped precipitously by the end of the decade. Consequently, these Scandinavian governments also injected huge sums of public funds to dispose of nonperforming assets in the banking sector.[90]

A counterfactual example helps illuminate the point. Had prudential forms of regulation been in place during the 1980s, would it have prevented the speculative bubble in the second half of the 1980s? More transparent bank disclosures and stricter accounting standards would not necessarily have revealed fraudulent banking practices during this period given the asset inflation which presumably served to balance the banks' ledger sheet. That is, high yields in the stock and real estate markets during the speculative bubble phase would have minimized the level of banks' nonperforming loans. This is true especially under the prudential regulatory guidelines that prescribe accounting practices based on present book value of stocks, rather than the original purchasing value.

Perhaps it could be argued that had a more prudential regulatory regime been in place, Japan would not have suffered as prolonged a recession as it has since the early 1990s. This may be true, but it misses the broader point; a more prudential regulatory regime by definition requires the state, or other non-market entities, to regulate and enforce market behavior. More importantly, the existence of such entities will not necessarily prevent the rise and bursting of a speculative bubble. Although the United States is often held as the model of a liberalized financial market with prudential regulatory safeguards, such safeguards have clearly failed to prevent serious financial crises. Putting aside the Savings and Loan crisis, Black Monday (October 1987), or the more recent corporate scandals involving Enron, WorldCom and others, the sharp downturn in the stock market since March 2000 illustrates a classic example of a financial bubble that has burst. Moreover, it is only after the bubble bursts that the folly of "irrational exuberance" is met with sober recognition. In a telling remark, the Federal Reserve Chairman, Alan Greenspan, acknowledged that "human psychology, being what it is, bubbles tend to feed on themselves," but that "it was very difficult to definitely identify a bubble until after the fact – that is, when its bursting confirmed its existence."[91]

This chapter also draws very different conclusions about the economic and political consequences of Japan's prolonged period of economic stagnation. If, as

I argue, the rise and collapse of the bubble economy was not caused by Japan's domestic political and economic institutions per se, but rather by the classical free market strategy that the LDP adopted in the 1980s (i.e. rejection of Keynesianism in favor of Monetarism, and a more liberalized financial market), it seems implausible that the Japanese government would simply adopt the very same strategy to work its way out of the economic malaise. Indeed, as the evidence presented in the introduction shows, the role of the state, in the issue-areas of both fiscal and financial policy, expanded rather than eroded throughout the 1990s. This was not simply because greater capital mobility and economic stagnation expanded the number of claimants seeking compensation from the party in power. To be sure, this accounts for part of the story, and the LDP clearly has been more than receptive to these demands. But on a more fundamental level, the market needed the state to assume a greater role in order to remedy the economic instability created by the market itself under a monetarist strategy where cheap credit was more abundant and mobile.

This is not to suggest that the state should necessarily take precedence over the market in determining how scarce resources should be allocated and regulated. Rather, it is to make the more basic point that there is an ongoing tension in the relationship between the market and state, and that any decision that privileges one over the other produces unintended consequences that are apt to spark new decisions in the other direction. What this does suggest, however, is that international economic changes, no matter how compelling, do not produce a teleological end point where all states converge. Structural changes may alter the opportunities and constraints that each state faces, but rarely do they do so in such a way that agency no longer matters. What this further suggests in the case of Japan is that its decade long period of economic stagnation was not based on any intrinsic incompatibility between Japanese institutions and the global economy, but because the LDP simply made bad economic decisions. Instead of adopting a monetarist strategy in the second half of the 1980s, the government could have adopted a Keynesian strategy of stimulating domestic demand through higher levels of government spending. One also wonders whether the economic stagnation of the 1990s would have been as deep and prolonged had the Hashimoto administration not killed the economic recovery underway by adopting a contractionary fiscal policy in 1996.

Notes

1 See Eric Helleiner, *States and the Reemergence of Global Finance: from Bretton Woods to the 1990s* (Ithaca, NY: Cornell University Press, 1994); John Gerald Ruggie, "International Regimes, Transactions, and Change: Embedded Postwar Economic Order," *International Organization*, 36, 1982; Richard N. Gardner, *Sterling-Dollar Diplomacy in Current Perspective: the Origins and the Prospects of our International Economic Order* (New York: Columbia University Press, 1980).
2 Bai Gao, *Japan's Economic Dilemma: the Institutional Origins of Prosperity and Stagnation* (New York: Cambridge University Press, 2001), p. 152; cf. John Eatwell and Lance Taylor, *Global Finance at Risk: The Case for International Regulation* (New York: The New Press, 2000), p. 5.

3 Beth A. Simmons, "The International Politics of Harmonization: the Case of Capital Market Regulation," *International Organization* 53, 3, Summer 2001, p. 589.
4 Helen V. Milner and Robert O.Keohane, *Internationalization and Domestic Politics* (Cambridge: Cambridge University Press, 1996), p. 257. For the definitive text which conceptualizes anarchy as the key ordering principle, see Kenneth Waltz, *Theory of International Politics* (Reading, MA: Addison-Wesley, 1979).
5 In the International Relations literature, see David Andrews, "Capital Mobility and State Autonomy: Toward a Structural Theory of International Monetary Relations," *International Studies Quarterly* 38, 2,1994; Michael C.Webb, "International Economic Structures, Government Interests, and International Coordination of Macroeconomic Adjustment Policies," *International Organization* 45, 3, 1991; Michael C.Webb, *The Political Economy of Policy Coordination: International Adjustment since 1945* (Ithaca, NY: Cornell University Press, 1995); Paulette Kurzer, *Business and Banking: Political Change and Economic Integration in Western Europe* (Ithaca, NY: Cornell University Press, 1993); Susan Strange, *Casino Capitalism* (New York: Basil Blackwell, 1986). The more popular literature includes Thomas Friedman, "DOScapital," *Foreign Policy* 116, autumn 1999. Literature on Japan includes Gao, *Japan's Economic Dilemma*; Henry Laurence, *Money Rules: the New Politics of Finance in Britain and Japan* (Ithaca, NY: Cornell University Press, 2001); Philip G. Cerny, "Financial Globalization and Internalizing Neo-Liberalism in Japan," paper presented at the American Political Science Association (APSA) annual meeting, San Francisco, 2001. See also T.J. Pempel, "Structural Gaiatsu: International Finance and Political Change in Japan," *Comparative Political Studies* 32, 8, December 1999, p. 928, who challenges the notion that "international economics trumps national politics," but concludes that the factor that has prevented it from doing so thus far is "residual institutional stickiness."
6 See for example Michael Bell, "Globalization: Threat or Opportunity?" *International Monetary Fund Issue Brief* April 12, 2000.
7 The outspoken proponent of this position is Jurgen Habermas, who notes: "The trends summed up in the word 'globalization' are not only jeopardizing, internally, the comparative homogenous make-up of national populations – the prepolitical basis for the integration of citizens into the nation-state – by prompting immigration and cultural stratification; even more tellingly, a state that is increasingly entangled in the interdependencies between the global economy and global society is seeing its autonomy, capacity for action, and democratic substance diminish." (Jurgen Habermas, "The European Nation-State and the Pressures for Globalization," *New Left Review* 234, May/June 1999, p. 48). For a similar view, see Ralph Nader and Lori Wallach, "GATT, NAFTA, and the Subversion of the Democratic Process," in Jerry Mander and Edward Goldsmith (eds), *The Case against the Global Economy* (San Francisco, CA: Sierra Club Books, 1996).
8 On this point, see Pierre Bourdieu, *Acts of Resistance: Against the Tyranny of the Market* (New York: New Press, 1999).
9 For some notable examples from this burgeoning literature, see Milner and Keohane, *Internationalization and Domestic Politics*; Philip G.Cerny, "International Finance and the Erosion of State Policy Capacity," in Philip Gummet (ed.), *Globalization and Public Policy* (Cheltenham, UK: Edward Elgar, 1996); Herman Schwartz, "Small States in Big Trouble: State Reorganization in Australia, Denmark, New Zealand, and Sweden in the 1980s," *World Politics* 46, 1994; Andrew Martin, "Labour, the Keynesian Welfare State, and the Changing International Political Economy," in Richard Stubbs and Geoffrey R.D. Underhill (eds), *Political Economy and the Changing Global Order* (New York: St. Martins Press, 1994); Kurzer, *Business and Banking*; Fritz Scharpf, *Crisis and Choice in European Social Democracy* (Ithaca, NY: Cornell University Press, 1991). For the economic model, see Jacob A. Frenkel and Assaf Razin, "Fiscal Policies in the World Economy," *Journal of Political Economy* 94, 3, 1986; Michael Mussa, "Macroeconomic Interdependence and the Exchange Rate

Regime," in Rudiger Dornbusch and Jacob A. Frenkel (eds), *International Economic Policy: Theory and Evidence* (Baltimore, MD: Johns Hopkins University Press, 1979); Robert A. Mundell, *International Economics* (New York: Macmillan, 1968). For an excellent review of this literature, see Benjamin J. Cohen, "Phoenix Risen: the Resurrection of Global Finance," *World Politics* 48, 1996.

10 Robert A. Mundell, "Capital Mobility and Stabilization Policy under Fixed and Flexible Exchange Rates," *Canadian Journal of Economics and Political Science* 29, 4, 1963, p. 478.

11 As Mundell notes: "Monetary policy therefore has a strong effect on the level of income and employment, not because it alters the rate of interest, but because it induces a capital outflow, depreciates the exchange rate, and causes an export surplus" (Ibid., p. 478).

12 Ibid.

13 Ibid., See also Thomas D. Willett, "The Political Economy of External Discipline: Constraint versus Incentive Effects of Capital Mobility and Exchange Rate Pegs," paper presented at American Political Science Association Meeting, San Francisco, CA: August 30–September 2, 2001; Carles Boix, "Partisan Governments, the International Economy, and Macroeconomic Policies in Advanced Nations, 1960–93," *World Politics* 53, 1, 2000, p. 42; Benjamin J. Cohen, "The Triad and the Unholy Trinity: Lessons for the Pacific Region," in Richard Higgott, Richard Leaver and John Ravenhill (eds), *Pacific Economic Relations in the 1990s* (Boulder, CO: Lynne Rienner Publishers, 1993); Louis W. Pauly, *Who Elected the Bankers?: Surveillance and Control in the World Economy* (Ithaca, NY: Cornell University Press, 1997).

14 The term "policy paradigm" is from Peter A. Hall, "The Movement from Keynesianism to Monetarism," in Hall (ed.), *The Political Power of Economic Ideas* (Princeton, NJ: Princeton University Press, 1992). For a related argument, see Albert S. Yee, "The Causal Effects of Ideas on Policies," *International Organization* 50, Winter 1996; Judith Goldstein and Robert Keohane (eds), *Ideas and Foreign Policy: Beliefs, Institutions and Policy Change* (Ithaca, NY: Cornell University Press, 1993); Peter M. Haas, "Introduction: Epistemic Communities and International Policy Coordination," *International Organization* 46, 1, Winter 1992; Kathryn Sikkink, *Ideas and Institutions: Developmentalism in Brazil and Argentina* (Ithaca, NY: Cornell University Press, 1991). On the specific issue of the change from Keynesianism to Monetarism, see Carles Boix, *Political Parties, Growth and Equality: Conservative and Social Democratic Economic Strategies in the World Economy* (New York: Cambridge University Press, 1998); Paul Krugman, "Workers and Economists I: First Do No Harm," *Foreign Affairs* July/August 1996; and Milton Friedman, "The Role of Monetary Policy," *American Economic Review* 58, 1968.

15 For an extended analysis of "the golden age," see Stephen A. Marglin and Juliet B. Schor, *The Golden Age of Capitalism: Reinterpreting the Postwar Experience* (New York: Oxford University Press, 1990).

16 The terms "class compromise" and "embedded liberal compromise" are from Adam Przeworski and Michael Wallerstein, "The Structure of Class Conflict in Democratic Societies," *American Political Science Review* 82, 1982, and John G. Ruggie, "International Regimes, Transactions, and Change: Embedded Liberalism in the Postwar Economic Order," *International Organization* 36, 1982, respectively. For a related argument, see David Cameron, "The Expansion of the Public Economy: a Comparative Analysis," *American Political Science Review* 72, December 1978.

17 On the distinction between "cyclical" and "structural" inflation and its implications for the efficacy of Keynesian policy, see Krugman, "Workers and Economists."

18 Peter Gourevitch, *Politics in Hard Times: Comparative Responses to International Crisis* (Ithaca, NY: Cornell University Press, 1986), p. 185–92; Peter Hall, *Governing the Economy: the Politics of State Intervention in Britain and France* (New York: Oxford University Press, 1986), p. 192–226.

19   Gourevitch, *Politics in Hard Times*, p. 204; Gosta Esping-Anderson, "Single Party Dominance in Sweden: the Saga of Social Democracy," in T.J. Pempel (ed.), *Uncommon Democracies: the One-Party Dominant Regimes* (Ithaca, NY: Cornell University Press, 1990), p. 33–57; Jonas Pontusson, *The Limits of Social Democracy: Investment Politics in Sweden* (Ithaca, NY: Cornell University Press, 1992), pp. 127–61; Jonas Pontusson, "Sweden: After the Golden Age," in Perry Anderson and Patrick Camiller (eds), *Mapping the West European Left* (London: Verso, 1994). The original plan is outlined in Rudolf Meidner, *Employee Investment Funds: an Approach to Collective Capital Formation* (London: Allen & Unwin, 1978).

20   Geoffrey Garrett, *Partisan Politics in the Global Economy* (New York: Cambridge University Press, 1998); Boix, *Political Parties*; Alberto Alesina and Howard Rosenthal, *Partisan Politics, Divided Government, and the Economy* (Cambridge: Cambridge University Press, 1995); Michael R. Alvarez, Geoffrey Garrett, and Peter Lange, "Government Partisanship, Labour Organization and Macroeconomic Performance," *American Political Science Review* 85, 1991; Douglas A. Hibbs, "Political Parties and Macroeconomic Policy," *American Political Science Review* 71, 1977; Douglas A. Hibbs, *The American Political Economy: Macroeconomics and Electoral Politics* (Cambridge, MA: Harvard University Press, 1987). On inflation, see Scharpf, *Crisis and Choice*; Mancur Olson, *The Rise and Decline of Nations: Economic Growth, Stagflation, and Social Rigidities* (New Haven, CT: Yale University Press, 1982); Garrett, *Partisan Politics*; Miriam Golden, "The Dynamics of Trade Unionism and National Economic Performance," *American Political Science Review* 87, 1993; Lars Calmfors and John Driffill, "Bargaining Structure, Corporatism and Macroeconomic Performance," *Economic Policy* 6, 1988; Peter J. Katzenstein, *Corporatism and Change: Austria, Switzerland and the Politics of Industry* (Ithaca, NY: Cornell University Press, 1984); Peter J. Katzenstein, *Small States in World Markets: Industrial Policy in Europe* (Ithaca, NY: Cornell University Press, 1985).

21   Hibbs, "Political Parties and Macroeconomic Policy"; Hibbs, *American Political Economy*.

22   Olson, *Rise and Decline of Nations*; Garrett, *Partisan Politics*; Golden, "Dynamics of Trade Unionism"; Calmfors and Driffill, "Bargaining Structure"; Katzenstein, *Small States in World Markets*. For left-wing governments that do not have an encompassing labor organization, see Scharpf, *Crisis and Choice*. On Keynesian policy and inflation, see Krugman, "Workers and Economists," and Friedman, "The Role of Monetary Policy."

23   For several notable accounts of LDP dominance, see Gerald L. Curtis, *The Japanese Way of Politics* (New York: Columbia University Press, 1988); Ishikawa, Masumi and Hirose, Michisada, *Jimintō: Chōki Shihai no Kōzō* (Tokyo: Iwanami Shoten, 1989); Sato, Seisaburō, and Matsuzaki, Tetsuhisa, *Jimintō Seiken* (Tokyo: Chūō Kōronsha, 1986). For an excellent comparative study, see Pempel, *Uncommon Democracies*.

24   Haruo Shimada, "Wage Determination and Information Sharing: an Alternative Approach to Incomes Policy?" *Journal of Industrial Relations* 25, 2, June 1983. See also Kathleen Thelen and Ikuo Kume, "The Effects of Globalization on Labour Revisited: Lessons from Germany and Japan," *Politics and Society* 27, 4, 1999.

25   Traditionally, Japan's major public union (Sōhyō) has been divided internally along ideological and factional lines, and its major private union (Dōmei) has been unable to effectively control the plethora of individual enterprise unions. It should be noted, however, that in 1990, Sōhyō became a member of "Rengō," an umbrella group that has sought to reunify most unions into one organization. But the crucial question of whether Rengō will be able to consolidate its power and articulate the encompassed interests of all labour workers in a central body remains an open question. On labour fragmentation, see Curtis, *Japanese Way of Politics*, Taishiro Shirai, "Japanese Labour Unions and Politics," in Shirai (ed.), *Contemporary Industrial Relations in Japan*

(Madison, WI: University of Wisconsin Press, 1983). For an account of labour's recent attempt to strengthen its organization, see Lonny E. Carlile, "Party Politics and the Japanese Labour Movement," *Asian Survey* 34, July 1994.

26 On this methodological point, see Gary King, Robert O. Keohane, and Sidney Verba, *Designing Social Research* (Princeton, NJ: Princeton University Press, 1994), pp. 209–12; Alexander George, "Case Studies and Theory Development," in Paul G. Lauren (ed.), *Diplomacy: New Approaches in History, Theory and Policy* (New York: Free Press, 1979); Harry Eckstein, "Case Study and Theory in Political Science," in F.I. Greenstein and Nelson Polsby (eds), *Handbook of Political Science* (Reading, MA: Addison-Wesley, 1975).

27 For a detailed account, see Takaaki Suzuki, *Japan's Budget Politics: Balancing Domestic and International Interests* (Boulder, CO: Lynne Rienner Publishers, 2000).

28 IMF, *World Economic Outlook* (Washington, DC: IMF, 1998), pp.116–17.

29 *Jiji Press Ticker Service* April 24, 1998. See also Adam S. Posen, *Restoring Japan's Economic Growth* (Washington, DC: Institute for International Economics, 1998), pp. 51–54.

30 *Japan Weekly Monitor* November 30, 1998.

31 *Japan Economic Newswire* December 9, 1999.

32 Ministry of Finance, *The Budget In Brief: Japan 2000* (Tokyo: Budget Bureau, Ministry of Finance, 2000), p. 2.

33 For the popular account, see for example, Cerny, "International Finance"; Richard Mckenzie and Dwight R. Lee, *Quicksilver Capital: How the Rapid Movement of Wealth has Changed the World* (New York: Free Press, 1991); Strange, *Casino Capitalism*.

34 See Paul Krugman, "The Myth of Asia's Miracle," *Foreign Affairs* November/December, 1994; Sebastian Mallaby, "In Asia's Mirror: from Commodore Perry to the IMF," *The National Interest* Summer 1998; Laurence, *Money Rules*.

35 George Stigler, "The Theory of Economic Regulation," *Bell Journal of Economics* 2, 1971, pp. 113–21; Sam Peltzman, "Toward a more General Theory of Regulation," *Journal of Law and Economics* August 1976, pp. 211–40.

36 Albert Hirschman, *Exit, Voice and Loyalty* (Cambridge, MA: Harvard University Press, 1971).

37 Philip Cerny, "International Finance and the Erosion of Capitalist Diversity," in Colin Crouch and Wolfgang Streeck (eds), *Political Economy of Modern Capitalism: Mapping Convergence and Diversity* (Thousand Oaks, CA: Sage, 1997) refers to this dynamic as "regulatory arbitrage" which produces a "non-cooperative equilibrium" (pp. 177–78). See also Andrews, "Capital Mobility and State Autonomy," p. 199.

38 Philip G. Cerny, "Paradoxes of the Competitive State: the Dynamics of Political Globalization," *Government and Opposition* 32, 2, Spring 1997, pp. 251–74.

39 Frances M. Rosenbluth, *Financial Politics in Contemporary Japan* (Ithaca, NY: Cornell University Press, 1989); James Horne, *Japan's Financial Markets: Conflict and Consensus in Policymaking* (Sydney: Allen & Unwin, 1985).

40 Laurence, *Money Rules*, pp. 103–44; Rosenbluth, *Financial Politics in Contemporary Japan*, pp. 50–95.

41 Robert Dekle, "The Japanese Big Bang: Financial Reforms and Market Implications," *Journal of Asian Economics* 9, 2, 1998, pp. 237–49; for the official government statement outlining the content of the Big Bang, see www.mof.go.jp/english/big-bang/ebb37.htm, accessed November 30, 2000.

42 Linda Weiss, *The Myth of the Powerless State* (Ithaca, NY: Cornell University Press, 1998); John B. Goodman and Louis W. Pauly, "The Obsolescence of Capital Controls? Economic Management in an Age of Global Markets," *World Politics* 46, October 1993; Jeffry Frieden, "Invested Interests: the Politics of National Economic Policies in a World of Global Finance," *International Organization* 45, Autumn 1991.

43 Steven K. Vogel, *Freer Markets, More Rules: Regulatory Reform in Advanced Industrial Countries* (Ithaca, NY: Cornell University Press, 1996).

44 Rosenbluth, *Financial Politics in Contemporary Japan*; Jennifer Amyx, "Informality and Institutional Inertia: the Case of Japanese Financial Regulation," *Japanese Journal of Political Science* 2, 2001; Laurence, *Money Rules*.

45 In July 2000 the Financial Supervisory Agency was renamed the Financial Services Agency (*Kinyū-chō*), and the Financial Reconstruction Commission, as well as the Deposit Insurance Corporation, were subsumed under it.

46 The two major bills passed were the "Law Concerning Emergency Measures for the Reconstruction of the Functions of the Financial System" and the "Financial Function Early Strengthening Law." Seventeen trillion yen was allocated for the purpose of refunding depositors of failed banks, 18 trillion yen for state-run bridge banks or other forms of public control, and 25 trillion yen for capital injection into solvent banks.

47 James Brooke, "Japan Bursts Merrill's Balloon," *New York Times*, 14 December, 2001.

48 In addition to the public financial corporations that form the core of FILP lending activities, even the BOJ became involved by purchasing commercial papers from corporations unable to raise funds from private financial institutions. Commercial papers are negotiable, short-term, unsecured promissory notes issued in bearer form, usually on a discount basis, by a corporation to raise working capital for any term normally up to 180 days. At the end of September 1998, the BOJ had purchased 5.6 trillion yen worth of commercial paper or 39.4 percent of the total outstanding (Douglas Ostrom, "Central Banks Adjust Monetary Policy to Global Turmoil," *JEI Report*, 23 October, 1998, p. 1).

49 These figures are for central government bonds (i.e. local government bonds not included) and based on settled budget figures (Ministry of Finance, *The Budget in Brief* (Tokyo: MOF Budget Bureau, 2002) p. 172).

50 At the end of fiscal year 1999, the total amount of government bonds outstanding held by financial institutions was 360.6 trillion yen, of which 187.3 trillion were held by the public sector. The Trust Fund Bureau held 79.9 trillion yen, while BOJ held 49.8 trillion. Figures taken from BOJ Research and Statistics Department, "Japan's Financial Structure – In View of the Flow of Funds Accounts," 28 December 2000, chart 15.

51 See Mark Kesselman, "How Should One Study Economic Policy Making: Four Characters in Search of an Object," *World Politics* 44, 4, July 1992.

52 Hall, "Movement from Keynesianism to Monetarism," pp. 96–97.

53 The Japanese name for MOF has now been changed from *Ōkurashō* to *Zaimushō*, but the English name has remained the same; MITI has been renamed METI.

54 The classic study of MITI is Chalmers Johnson, *MITI and the Japanese Miracle: the Growth of Industrial Policy, 1925–1975* (Stanford, CA: Stanford University Press, 1982). For MOF, see William W. Grimes, *Unmaking the Japanese Miracle: Macroeconomic Politics, 1985–2000* (Ithaca, NY: Cornell University Press, 2001); Junko Kato, *The Problem of Bureaucratic Rationality* (Princeton, NJ: Princeton University Press, 1994); John C. Campbell, *Contemporary Japanese Budget Politics* (Berkeley, CA: University of California Press, 1977).

55 Peter F. Cowhey and Matthew D. McCubbins (eds), *Structure and Politics in Japan and the United States* (New York: Cambridge University Press, 1995); Mark Ramseyer and Frances M. Rosenbluth, *Japan's Political Marketplace* (Cambridge: Cambridge University Press, 1993); Samuel Kernell (ed.), *Parallel Politics: Economic Policymaking in the United States and Japan* (Washington, DC: Brookings Institution, 1991).

56 As Polanyi notes: "The road to the free market was opened and kept open by an enormous increase in continuous, centrally organized and controlled intervention... Thus even those who wished most ardently to free the state from all the unnecessary duties, and whose whole philosophy demanded the restriction of state activities, could not but entrust the self-same state with the new powers, organs and instruments required for the establishment of laissez-faire." (Karl Polanyi, *The Great Transformation* (Boston, MA: Beacon Press, 1957), pp. 140–41).

57 For example his portrayal of how "sheep ate men" under the enclosure movement, whereby peasants were driven off the commons "within a framework of law and order" to establish the unrestricted use of private property for personal gain: Moore (1966: 12–29).

58 As Kindleberger notes, "The danger we face is not too much power in the international economy, but too little, not an excess of domination, but a superfluity of would-be free-riders, unwilling to mind the store, and waiting for a storekeeper to appear." Charles P. Kindleberger, "Dominance and Leadership in the International Economy: Exploitation, Public Goods and Free Rides," *International Studies Quarterly* 25, 2, 1981, p. 253; see also Gardner, *Sterling-Dollar Diplomacy*.

59 This point is made most cogently by Kindleberger in *Manias, Panics and Crashes: a History of Financial Crises* (New York: Basic Books, 1978). For an application to contemporary Japan, see Frances Rosenbluth and Ross Schaap, "The Domestic Politics of Banking Regulation," *International Organization* 57, 2, 2003.

60 See for example Karel van Wolferen, *The Enigma of Japanese Power: People and Politics in a Stateless Nation* (New York: Knopf, 1989).

61 This problem becomes particularly acute under conditions of capital mobility. An expansionary monetary policy, such as the lowering of the discount rate, may not lead to domestic demand expansion and smaller current account surpluses. Instead, capital outflow may increase in order to take advantage of higher interest rates abroad. As a result, an expansionary monetary policy can have the unintended consequence of increasing the nation's current account surplus if large volumes of capital outflow leads to currency devaluation. While reducing trade and current account surpluses may not be necessary or desirable from the standpoint of economic efficiency, trade friction and political tensions arise when a nation continues to mount trade surpluses and uses these funds to acquire an increasing amount of foreign property and financial assets.

62 This is because a large pool of foreign exchange reserves and domestic savings can keep Japan's domestic rate of interest at a level lower than that of the world's rate. Moreover, the fact that the state is a major purchaser of government bonds also helps maintain this interest rate spread. Under such conditions, the effects of fiscal expansion on international capital movements and exchange rates are muted. On this point see also M. Feldstein and Charles Horioka, "Domestic Saving and International Capital Flow," *Economic Journal* 90, 1980.

63 The reason for this is straightforward: increasing the level of government spending directly affects the current account balance by increasing domestic demand. In the case where private savings exceed investments, the corresponding pressure toward current account surplus can be offset through expansionary fiscal policy.

64 By "a problem of secular demand" I mean the gap between private savings and private investment demand. Under such conditions, which fit the Japanese case since the mid-1970s, the alternatives are to increase current account surpluses, run government deficits, or stagnant economic growth. I thank Hugh Patrick for pointing this out. For a similar argument, see Paul Krugman, *Return of Depression Economics* (New York: W.W. Norton & Co., 1999), pp. 57–58.

65 This point is made most succinctly by Claus Offe: "The embarrassing secret of the welfare state is that, while its impact upon capitalist accumulation may well become destructive (as the conservative analysis so emphatically demonstrates), its abolition would be plainly disruptive (a fact that is systematically ignored by conservative critics). The contradiction is that while capitalism cannot coexist with, neither can it exist without the welfare state." (Claus Offe, *Contradictions of the Welfare State* (Cambridge, MA: MIT Press, 1984), p.153.

66 For the relationship between free trade and government spending, see Cameron, "The Expansion of the Public Economy."

67 On financial policy, see Peter Hartcher, *The Ministry: How Japan's Most Powerful Institution Endangers World Markets* (Boston, MA: Harvard Business School Press,

1998); Robert J. Brown, *The Ministry of Finance: Bureaucratic Practices and the Transformation of the Japanese Economy* (Westport, CT: Quorum Books, 1999). For public works see Hirose, Michisada, *Hojokin to Seikentō* (Tokyo: Asahi Shinbunsha, 1981); Jacob M. Schlesinger, *Shadow Shoguns* (New York: Simon Schuster, 1997).

68 Indeed, if the rise of global capital truly ushers in a conclusive "race to the bottom," then these changes arguably should have taken place during the height of the gold standard in the late nineteenth century when the world economy reached an unprecedented level of integration on many key measures. See Dani Rodrik, "Sense and Nonsense in the Globalization Debate," *Foreign Policy* 107, Summer 1997; Cohen, "Phoenix Risen."

69 Garrett, *Partisan Politics*, p. 24; Boix, *Political Parties, Growth and Equality*.

70 See Simmons, "International Politics of Harmonization" for a similar argument about historical timing made in a different context; on initial conditions, see Gourevitch, *Politics in Hard Times*.

71 It is this institutional dimension that places this study within the "historical insitutionalist" camp, rather than the rational choice variant. For a useful distinction between these two institutionalist approaches, see Sven Steinmo, Kathleen Thelen, and Frank Longstreth (eds), *Structuring Politics: Historical Institutionalism in Comparative Analysis* (New York: Cambridge University Press, 1992).

72 Gardner Ackley and Hiromitsu Ishii, "Fiscal, Monetary and Related Policies," in Hugh Patrick and Henry Rosovsky (eds), *Asia's New Giant: How the Japanese Economy Works* (Washington, DC: Brookings Institution, 1976), pp. 153–247; Yukio Noguchi, "Public Finance," in Kozo Yamamura and Yasukichi Yasuba (eds), *The Political Economy of Japan*, vol.1, *The Domestic Transformation* (Stanford, CA: Stanford University Press, 1987), pp. 186–222; Koichi Hamada and Hugh Patrick, "Japan and the International Monetary Regime," in Takashi Inoguchi and Daniel Okimoto (eds), *The Political Economy of Japan*, vol. 2, *The Changing International Context* (Stanford, CA: Stanford University Press, 1988), pp. 108–37. Predictably, the incentive to adjust was weaker when running a balance of payments surplus.

73 The term was originally coined by Giovanni Sartori, *Parties and Party Systems: a Framework for Analysis* (Cambridge: Cambridge University Press, 1976), defined as a party system in which one party repeatedly wins a majority of seats in parliament. In the case of Japan, the important exception, of course, was labour, which remained divided and less organized than in other advanced industrial democracies.

74 With the slowdown in the economy in the second half of the 1970s, big business leaders became one of the most vocal proponents of fiscal expansion. For an in depth treatment, see Suzuki, *Japan's Budget Politics*.

75 On this point, see Hirose, *Hojokin to Seikentō*; Kent Calder, *Crisis and Compensation: Public Policy and Political Stability in Japan* (Princeton, NJ: Princeton University Press, 1988).

76 The share of the budget devoted to debt repayment was already quite large by 1980, with only social security expenditures and public works occupying a larger share. By 1985, the share of the budget devoted to debt repayment exceeded that of social security expenditures, making it the single largest expenditure item on the budget.

77 For details, see Rosenbluth, *Financial Politics*, pp. 44–45.

78 Laurence, *Money Rules*, p. 121; Rosenbluth, *Financial Politics*, p. 165.

79 The term "ostensibly" is used here because there were significant discrepancies between rhetoric and reality in the actual policies used to eliminate deficit-financing. A large portion of the spending cuts from the general account budget were merely transferred to other government financial institutions, and sustained economic growth yielded higher than expected tax increases that were used to help balance the budget. For details, see Takaaki Suzuki, "Administrative Reform and the Politics of Budgetary Retrenchment in Japan," *Social Science Japan Journal* 2, 2, 1999.

80 The government also postponed various obligatory payments from the General Account Budget by using funds from other public accounts.

81 Kubota, Isao (ed.), *Zusetsu Nihon no Zaisei: Heisei Ninendoban* (Tokyo: Tōyō Keizai Shinpōsha, 1990), p. 365.

82 According to the EPA, the economic expansion lasted for 51 months, from November 1986 to February 1991. The longest was the "Izanagi" boom, which lasted for 57 months from October 1965 to July 1970 (Okina, Kunio, Shirakawa, Masaaki and Shiratsuka, Shigenori, "The Asset Price Bubble and Monetary Policy: Japan's Experience in the Late 1980s and the Lessons," *Monetary and Economic Studies*, February 2001, pp. 309–402).

83 From September 1985 to December 1989, the Nikkei index rose from the 12,000 to the 39,000 range. By August 1992, the index fell back down to the 14,000, representing a 60 percent drop in stock prices. Similarly, the price index of commercial land in six metropolitan cities tripled between March 1986 and March 1990, but has fallen precipitously since then (Thomas F. Cargill, Michael M. Hutchison, and Takatoshi Ito, *The Political Economy of Japanese Monetary Policy* (Cambridge, MA: MIT Press, 1999), p. 91.

84 Indeed, it was precisely this strategy that helped produce the speculative bubble in the first place.

85 Posen, *Restoring Japan's Economic Growth*.

86 This argument is made most explicitly in Gao, *Japan's Economic Dilemma*.

87 Pempel, "Structural Gaiatsu," p. 928. Note that this point was anticipated much earlier in Pempel, "The Unbundling of 'Japan Inc': The Changing Dynamics of Japanese Policy Formation," in Kenneth Pyle (ed.), *The Trade Crisis: How Will Japan Respond?* (Seattle, WA: Society for Japanese Studies, 1987).

88 Laurence, *Money Rules*.

89 George Rich, "Comment," *Monetary and Economic Studies* February 2001, pp. 104–5.

90 The public funds used for this purpose amounted to 4.7 percent of nominal GDP in the case of Sweden (1991–93) and 7.3 per cent in the case of Finland (1991–92) ("International Banking and Financial Market Developments," *Bank of International Settlements Quarterly Review*, August 1999; (Okina, Kunio *et al.*, "The Asset Price Bubble and Monetary Policy," pp. 404–05).

91 Greenspan's remark reported in David Stout, "Greenspan Says Fed Could Not Prevent Market Bubble," *New York Times* August 30, 2002.

8 Change and crisis in the Japanese banking industry

Mariusz K. Krawczyk

For more than ten years Japan has seemed unable to overcome the repeated sequence of mild recessions followed by periods of stagnation. An average real growth rate of approximately 1 per cent per year between 1991 and 2001 was the lowest among advanced industrial countries. Negative growth rates, falling individual consumption, historically high unemployment and fast growing public debt have stood in such a sharp contrast with relatively stable performance before the 1980s, that Japanese often call the 1990s their 'lost decade'.

The depth and length of Japan's stagnation – the costliest recession suffered by any advanced industrial economy after the Second World War – has led some to predict that Japanese savers, who until now have remained very conservative, may even flee into cash, gold and offshore accounts,[1] corresponding to capital flight from Japan – something unimaginable. Although there are numerous reasons why the Japanese economic performance has continued to disappoint, the weakness of the country's banking industry has been one of the main factors behind the inability to break this prolonged cycle of recessions. For a large part of the last decade or so Japan has experienced a steady deterioration of its banking sector. The decline of the Japanese banking industry began at the end of the 1980s asset bubble and turned into a full-blown crisis in the second of half of 1997 when a number of high profile financial institutions collapsed. There has been no significant improvement since then, despite the enormous amounts of capital allocated for strengthening and revitalising the financial system (approximately 60 trillion yen spent in the last five years, equating to 12 per cent of the country's GDP). This contrasts sharply with the savings and loan association (S&L) crisis of the late 1980s in the US or to the Nordic Banking Crisis of the early 1990s, where the recovery started 2–3 years after the crises had begun. The ailing banking industry has prevented Japan from restoring sound growth rates despite having undertaken structural reforms and substantial fiscal policy efforts. The banking crisis was also one of the reasons why the Bank of Japan (BOJ) policy of quantitative easing failed to stimulate the economy, by impairing the transmission channels of monetary policy.[2]

There exists a big literature analysing the mechanisms that triggered the banking crisis in Japan. Most of the studies, after having identified a reason to blame for the crisis (usually of either a regulatory or macroeconomic nature), and having offered a related solution, conclude, usually optimistically, that the crisis provides a chance for implementing necessary reforms in Japan's economy. Yet despite plenty of advice being offered, the country's continuing banking crisis has not ceased to puzzle for almost a decade.

Contrary to most contemporary studies, it is argued in this chapter that Japan's banking crisis was not caused by a single regulatory or macroeconomic factor but has its origins in a set of deficiencies deeply rooted in the country's post-war institutional and corporate culture. Incomplete liberalisation that was poorly coordinated between sectors, unsustainable macroeconomic policies, ignoring adverse external shocks, combined with poor supervision and regulatory forbearance, as well as bad corporate governance – each of which can be identified as one of the causes of the crisis – are all typical of banking crises in general.[3] However, in the Japanese case, they primarily originate in the specific, bureaucracy-dominated character of economic policies that have prevailed in the Japanese economy since the end of the Second World War. The highly regulated economic system used to perform well until the 1980s, when it became subject to partial deregulation that conflicted with its internal rationality. Since then the country's bureaucratic leadership has been unable to restore the system's internal coherence. Consequently, the banking crisis is viewed here as the result of an incomplete institutional reform effort rather than as a typical financial phenomenon. This observation is important, as successive Japanese administrations have stressed the need for further partial reforms, while at the same time not providing any coherent long-term vision of the country's social and economic system. In this context also, the solution to the current crisis should not be viewed in isolation from the processes taking place in the rest of the economy and must not be reduced to a mere resolution of the non-performing debt problem.

For the purpose of presenting the above reasoning, the rest of the chapter is organised as follows. The section on a brief overview of the Japanese banking crisis sums up the main factors that contributed to the crisis. The section on the conditions of the Japanese banking industry presents the current condition and the main problems that the banking industry has been facing. The section on the solution to the crises defines the conditions necessary for the recovery of the banking industry against the background of economic conditions prevailing in Japan. Finally, the concluding section provides some more general lessons that can be drawn for the future change of the country's institutional framework.

A brief overview of the Japanese banking crisis

The prelude: an asset inflated economy

The emergence of the bubble economy can be attributed to a combination of external pressure, ongoing domestic liberalisation and policy mistakes made by the central authorities. The growing consensus that the US dollar was unrealistically overvalued against other currencies (especially the Japanese yen) resulted in a coordinated policy effort to devalue the US currency, an effort known as the

Plaza Accord (22 September 1985). Consequently, the dollar lost 45 per cent of its value between February 1985 (when it reached a peak of 260 yen/dollar) and May 1987 (141 yen/dollar). The move, primarily aimed at putting a cap on the US trade deficit with Japan, imposed a heavy toll on the Japanese economy, often called the 'High-Yen Recession' (*En-daka Fukyō*). Real economic growth dropped to −0.5 per cent, its first negative rate since the oil shock, and the total unemployment rate reached a historically high level of 3.1 per cent in May 1987. Concerned with the increasing public debt (50.3 per cent of the GNP), the authorities chose monetary expansion with reduction of the official discount rates, hoping for a wealth effect that would increase domestic consumption and investment and, in the end, boost real economic growth.

The scenario worked as expected. In February 1987, the BOJ reduced its discount rate to a historically low 2.5 per cent level and held it constant for two years until mid-1989. The result was a substantial increase in the money supply (defined as M2 plus Cash Deposits), by 10.8 per cent in 1987 and remaining on average 11 per cent until 1990. As shown in Figure 8.1, the policy of easy money supported investment and asset prices increased. Stock prices increased threefold (the Nikkei 225 increased from 13,024 in January 1983 to 38,916 in December 1989) and land prices increased fourfold during the same time. Meanwhile, the BOJ concentrated its anti-inflationary vigilance on consumer price movements, which, thanks to the yen appreciation, were becoming increasingly distorted by the decreasing prices of tradable goods. The Bank's policies largely ignored the surge in asset prices. The unprecedented monetary policy easing coincided with massive privatisation programmes performed by the Nakasone administration (Japan National Railway and Nippon Telephone and Telegraph) and partial liberalisation of financial markets. These two programmes also contributed to the asset bubble getting out of control.

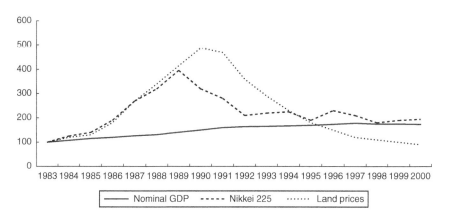

Figure 8.1 Asset prices in Japan (1983 = 100).

Source: Japan Institute for Social and Economic Affairs (*Keizai Kōhō Centre*), *An International Comparison; Japan 2002* (Tokyo: Keizai Kōhō Centre, 2003), p. 14.

The asset bubble was abruptly brought to an end in the second half of 1989 when the BOJ started increasing its discount rate. Share prices collapsed in summer 1990 (the Nikkei 225 dropped from 38,915 in December 1989 to 20,984 in September 1990). Meanwhile, to contain the rise in land prices, the Ministry of Finance (MOF) introduced limits on the total amounts of loans for real estate. The limits resulted in a sudden contraction of real estate lending and were lifted in January 1992, after land prices had started to decline. The overheated economy gradually slowed down.

Banks' response to the asset bubble

The banks actively participated in exacerbating the asset bubble by credit creation. The rapid increase in land prices and the value of shares in real estate related businesses led to a lending boom in this sector. By contrast, lending to large manufacturing corporations was in decline. While the share of lending to big manufacturing companies to total lending decreased from almost 60 per cent in 1985 to less than 50 per cent in 1990 and 40 per cent in 1991, the share of construction and real estate lending increased from 14 to 18 per cent during the same period.[4] The lending to real estate related businesses was based on the misguided expectation that land prices would increase indefinitely, as they had done throughout the post-war years except for 1975. The sharp decline in land prices following the end of the asset bubble caused the quality of loans to the real estate industry to deteriorate rapidly. Banks themselves were to blame for lack of proper risk evaluation. Lending offices were using a simple 'direct capital comparison method', for example, comparing the published land prices of neighbouring properties. Only later did they begin to calculate the value of land collateral based on future income flow. They extended their lending disproportionately to the value of collateral, and these lax policies permitted the use of the same collateral for multiple borrowing.

The large increase in lending to real estate is often viewed as a primary cause of the non-performing loans problem that emerged later in the 1990s. However, it would be a great oversimplification to attribute all the problems of the banking industry merely to irrational lending behaviour during the late 1980s. On the contrary, it is possible to argue that Japanese banks were left with no choice but to undertake risky lending activities in order to survive. Their very unusual lending practices can be linked to two characteristics of the Japanese banking industry at that time. First, partially due to pressure from the US government, the Japanese authorities embarked on the protracted process of liberalisation of the country's financial system. By the mid-1980s the process was only half finished, with the gradual removal of restrictions on access to the corporate bond market and the creation of the commercial paper market on the one hand, but with numerous restrictions on financial institutions' activities still in place on the other. These developments had serious consequences. Incipient liberalisation triggered competition for customers that reduced the already low profit margins of Japanese banks.[5] At the same time large corporations, until then the banks' main borrowers, used their newly acquired freedom of access to corporate bond markets. Enjoying very high credit ratings, the corporations were able to borrow directly from the market at significantly lower cost. Japanese corporations raised approximately 519 billion dollars in the first five years after bond market restrictions were lifted.[6] The long-term credit banks, which enjoyed most protection under the interest rate controls, were among the hardest hit by the new reality. Facing declining profits and losing their traditional corporate customers, the banks had no choice but to look for substitute lending markets. They increased their loan activity not only in the real estate industry, but also in relation to small- and medium-size enterprises, individuals, the finance industry and overseas investment.[7]

Second, the Japanese banking industry suffered from huge overcapacity problems. The industry was designed to provide financing for a Japanese economy that between 1960 and 1973 was growing on average 9.7 per cent. At the same time the average growth in Europe and the USA was 4.8 and 3.9 per cent respectively. Slowing growth (on average 4.4 per cent between 1975 and 1985) and decreasing demand for funds in the second half of the 1970s and in the 1980s were not accompanied by a reduction of banking sector capacity. Fierce competition for lending in a context of heavy overcapacity in the banking industry and the special attention paid by banks to their market shares[8] caused a kind of *cognitive dissonance*. That is, in order to survive, banks had to compete for borrowers even if it meant knowingly loosening credit standards. The myopic character of lending reached almost farcical dimensions, with banks engaging in phoney real estate activities in exchange for kick backs, or, in one case, lending more than 1.8 billion dollars to a small restaurant owner. The fully rational change in lending patterns, which had resulted from changes in the regulatory environment, reached at that stage a state of irrational exuberance.

It was still to be five years, however, before banking sector soundness came into question. During that time the amount of non-performing loans increased steadily, but banks were extremely reluctant to raise their loan-loss provisions. This might have been either due to concerns that an increase in loan-loss provisions could have provided negative signals to markets about future increases in non-performing loans, or because individual banks did not want to draw attention to themselves by breaking ranks with other banks. Banks could not write-off their non-performing loans due to restrictive tax regulations that allowed for write-offs only in cases of bankruptcy or foreclosure proceedings. Given the average speed of legal proceedings in Japan this substantially slowed down the writing-off of non-performing loans. The close relationship between banks and their borrowers, integral to the main bank system, might have been yet another important reason why banks were slow to clean their balance sheets of non-performing loans. The main bank may have been reluctant to identify a troubled borrower because this in turn could raise questions about its own monitoring abilities, and because the main bank would usually be required to absorb the bulk of the losses incurred by creditors. Moreover, when the main bank itself comes under stress it may result in the bank's becoming a captive of its own borrowers. Finally, the poor corporate governance of Japanese banks may have been one of the main factors behind the growing amount of non-performing loans. The weak corporate governance of Japanese banks originated from the fact that banks' major shareholders have had little incentive to confront management. The main groups of shareholders have either been dependent on management (banks' employees and banks' corporate borrowers) or had a close relationship with management (other banks and insurance companies through cross shareholding). Members of boards of directors are usually promoted from the ranks of employees at the end of their careers and resign after their terms expire in order to be replaced by more junior employees. This, combined with weak internal and external audits, creates incentives during their terms for managers to conceal problems rather than take decisive steps. During the five years following the collapse of the bubble economy, Japanese banks chose not to make determined efforts to solve the problem of mounting non-performing loans. Instead, they preferred to wait for stock and land prices to recover to their previous highs.

The banking crisis

The beginning of instability (early 1995–Autumn 1997)

The instability in the Japanese banking industry came into public view in early 1995. Two insolvent credit cooperatives, Tōkyō Kyōwa and Anzen, collapsed at the end of 1994, and two more, Cosmo and Kizu, had followed by August 1995. In August 1995 Hyōgo Bank, one of the regional banks, was ordered to suspend its operations. These closures of insolvent financial institutions marked the end of the policy of not allowing depository institutions to fail. Adding insult to injury, a scandal over concealment of losses forced Daiwa Bank to close its operations in the USA later in the year. These events coincided with controversy surrounding the *jusen* (housing loan) companies.

The *jusen* companies, established in the 1970s by banks and other financial institutions for lending in the home mortgage market, engaged in real estate lending in the late 1980s and at the beginning of the 1990s. With funds from agricultural cooperatives, the *jusen* companies increased their lending to real estate businesses, filling the gap left by commercial banks that had to follow restrictions on lending to real estate imposed by the MOF.[9] Already by early 1992 the quality of the lending of the *jusen* companies had raised serious concerns, but it was only in 1995 that the authorities decided to intervene. By that time, three quarters of *jusen* loans were already non-performing loans.

Soon the *jusen* problem became a major political issue. It was the first time that the government attempted to use public funds to solve problems with weak financial institutions. In that sense, the discussion surrounding the *jusen* companies set an important precedent. Facing a clear public dislike of the idea of using taxpayers' money for rescuing banks, the authorities reached a consensus that the problems of the financial institutions should be solved as far as possible without the direct involvement of the government. In the case of the *jusen* companies, 55 per cent (or 3.5 trillion yen) of their losses had to be covered by their founding banks, 27 per cent (1.7 trillion yen) by the lending banks, 8 per cent (530 billion yen) by the agricultural financial institutions and the remaining 10 per cent (680 billion yen) by public funds.[10]

The collapse of insolvent financial institutions together with the *jusen* confusion heavily damaged the image of the Japanese banking industry. It was then that the 'Japan Premium' (premium on lending to Japanese institutions) appeared for the first time on international financial markets and international rating agencies, which had already been downgrading Japanese banks since 1989, radically reduced the credit ratings for 1996. As shown in Table 8.1, while there was no major Japanese bank with a B rating in 1995, a year later four were classified as BBB and only one reached an AA rating. Despite this, inaction and the regulatory forbearance of the financial authorities continued until 1997, substantially undermining public confidence in the country's banking industry.

Crisis (Fall 1997–mid 1999)

The increase of the consumption tax rate in April 1997 marked the beginning of another recession. Economic conditions deteriorated, and by November 1997 the Japanese financial industry faced several spectacular bankruptcies. On 3 November 1997, Sanyō Securities, a second tier security company, defaulted on the inter-bank

Table 8.1 Credit ratings of major Japanese banks

Bank	3/90	3/95	3/96	3/97	3/98	3/99	3/00	3/01	3/02
Industrial Bank of Japan	AAA	A+	A	A	A−	BBB	BBB+	BBB+	A
Long-Term Credit Bank[a]	AA	A−	BBB+	BBB+	BBB−	BB−	BBB−	BBB−	BBB−
Nippon Credit Bank[b]	AA+	A	BBB−	BB+	BB+	BB−	BB−	BB	BBB−
Dai-Ichi Kangyō	AA	A+	A	A	BBB+	A	A	A	BBB
Sakura	AA+	AA−	A−	A−	A−	BBB	BBB	A−	A−
Fuji	AA	A+	A−	A−	BBB+	A	A+	A+	BBB
Mitsubishi[c]	AA+	AA−	A+	A+	A	A−	A−	A−	BBB+
Asahi	AA+	A	A	A	A	BBB	BBB	BB+	BB+
Sanwa	AA	AA−	A	A	A	BBB+	BBB+	BBB+	BBB
Sumitomo	AA+	A+	A	A	A−	BBB	BBB	BBB+	BBB
Daiwa	AA+	A−	BBB+	BBB+	BBB−	BB+	BB+	BB+	BB+
Tōkai	AAA	A	A	A	A	BBB−	BBB−	BBB	A
Hokkaidō Takushoku	AA	A	BBB−	BBB−	BBB−				
Tōkyō[c]	AA+	AA+	AA+	AA+					

Source: Hideaki Miyajima and Yishay Yafeh, 'Japan's Banking Crisis: Who Has the Most to Lose?', *Waseda University Financial Paper* 03/02, 2003, p. 26.

Notes
a Since 1999 Shinsei Bank.
b Since 1999 Aozora Bank.
c In 1996 merged into Bank of Tokyo Mitsubishi. For mergers after 1999 see Table 8.2.

loan market. This was followed by the collapse of Yamaichi Securities, one of the country's big four securities companies, and of Hokkaidō Takushoku Bank, one of the city banks, then numbering 12. The events resulted in serious disruptions on the inter-bank market and a sell-off of banking shares on the Tokyo Stock Exchange. Unable to continue its non-interference policy, the government used the newly enacted Financial Stabilisation Law (*Kinyū Anteika Kinkyū Sochi Hō*), to establish a 30 trillion yen fund for capital injection into troubled banks. The Law was an important novelty in the authorities' response to banking problems. Loosely modelled after the US Prompt Corrective Action regulations, the law provided for the introduction for banks of well-defined self-assessment procedures and their external audit and, no less important, clearly defined the capital threshold ratios for intervention by the authorities in an individual bank's management affairs (e.g. restricting dividend payments and management bonuses, closing branches and suspending operations). This reduced the scope for regulatory inaction so often exercised before 1997.

In March 1998, four months after the crisis had begun, the newly created Financial Crisis Management Committee (*Kinyū Kiki Kanri Shinsa Iinkai*) presided over a capital injection of 1.8 trillion yen for 21 major banks in the form of subordinate debt. The injection of public funds was intended to help the banks to meet their capital requirements. In order to avoid drawing attention to weaker banks, all banks applied for the same amount (100 billion yen) of capital. However, this calm did not last long. The collapse of the Long-Term Credit Bank, the largest bank failure in post-war Japan, brought new waves of instability. In October 1998, the Financial Function Early Strengthening Law (*Kinyū Kinō Sōki Kenzenka Kinkyū Sochi Hō*) replaced the earlier Financial Stabilisation Law. The new law was designed to help banks with insufficient capital. The Diet authorised the use of 25 trillion yen for this purpose, and 15 major banks received 7.4 trillion yen at the beginning of 1999. In contrast to the 1998 public fund injection, this time around banks were required to submit rehabilitation plans. Moreover, the amount of public capital varied between banks. The capital injection took the form of preferred stock that could be converted into common stock and used to exert pressure on a bank's management if the implementation of a rehabilitation plan was not satisfactory. Of the major banks, only the Bank of Tokyo Mitsubishi, the biggest and soundest of Japanese banks at the time, turned down the offer of public funds.

A second law introduced in October 1998, the Financial Reconstruction Law (*Kinyū Kinō Saisei Kinkyū Sochi Hō*), was designed to deal with failed banks. Under this law, 17 trillion yen was set aside on special account to become a deposit guarantee for failed banks, and another 18 trillion was held for purchasing shares (nationalisation) of failed banks and for supporting the Resolution and Collection Corporation (RCC) (*Seiri Kaishū Kikō*) to purchase non-performing loans. Finally, as a recognition that bank supervision had not been sufficient, the Financial Supervisory Agency (FSA) (*Kinyū Kantoku Chō*) was established and took over supervision of banks from the MOF in June 1998.[11]

In late 1998, under the new legal framework, the Financial Reconstruction Committee (*Kinyū Saisei Iinkai*) decided to place the Long-Term Credit Bank and

Table 8.2 Consolidation of the banking industry

Date of merger	Merging parties	New financial group
September 2000	Dai-Ichi Kangyō Bank, Fuji Bank, Industrial Bank of Japan	Mizuho Holdings
April 2001	Sakura Bank, Sumitomo Bank	Sumitomo Mitsui Banking Corp. (SMBC)
April 2001	Bank of Tokyo Mitsubishi, Mitsubishi Trust and Banking, Nippon Trust Bank, Tokyo Trust Bank	Mitsubishi Tokyo Financial Group, Inc.
April 2001	Sanwa Bank, Tōkai Bank, Tōyō Trust and Banking	United Financial of Japan (UFJ) Group
March 2003	Asahi Bank, Daiwa Bank	Resona Group

the Nippon Credit Bank under public administration (i.e. effective nationalisation). Both of these banks had been indispensable participants in Japan's rapid economic growth in the early post-war period.

The merger wave (1999–2003)

Capital injection under the Financial Function Early Strengthening Law required receiving banks to clean up their balance sheets of non-performing loans and strengthen their capital positions. Restructuring and cost cutting was an obvious way to become profitable and be able to return public funds as soon as possible. This triggered a series of mergers. The 23 large banks that existed in 1985 have been reorganised into four groups, as shown in Table 8.2.[12] The number of regional banks also slowly decreased, from 133 to 118, mainly in the second half of the 1990s.

The long awaited liberalisation of financial services (the Japanese 'Big Bang') finally started being implemented. Under the new rules, the restrictions that once separated banking, securities and insurance businesses were lifted. In order to survive in a new environment, banks had to look for new partners.

What caused the crisis?

The given story of the unfolding banking crisis in Japan shows, there was no single cause that triggered the meltdown of the industry. Instead it is possible to identify a set of factors that contributed to the worsening of the crisis. Undoubtedly, monetary policy mistakes by the BOJ in the second half of the 1980s generated asset inflation and provided excessive liquidity to a financial system that was unprepared for its absorbtion.[13] It is also possible to argue, as do Jinushi and others,[14] that an excessively tight monetary policy at the beginning of the 1990s further aggravated the crisis that was already well under way.

A second factor was that the Japanese financial system was an instrument of industrial policy aimed at supporting re-industrialisation, supporting investment and export-led growth, protecting domestic businesses from international competition and providing liquidity at as low a cost as possible. This set of objectives produced a highly bank-dependent, rigid system full of administrative controls and guidance. The system fully met its objectives and served well during the period of high growth of the Japanese economy in the 1960s. The authorities were very slow however to modify the system once it accomplished its mission.[15] Japan, Germany and France are usually given as examples of bank-oriented financial systems, but, as shown in Figure 8.2, while the rate of bank deposits to total financial assets in Germany was 39.3 per cent in 1999 (down from 67.9 per cent in 1971), Japan's ratio remained almost unchanged over the same period, standing at 62.9 per cent in 1998. As a result, when the asset inflated bubble economy arrived, Japan was still reliant on its highly bank-dependent financial system, lacking in transparency and only partially liberalised. This led to a third factor, extremely poor supervision and regulatory forbearance on the part of the Japanese financial authorities. Various reasons may be suggested for this: ineffectiveness on the part of the authorities, including lack of political leadership, the 'cosy' relationships between the regulators and the regulated that originated from *amakudari*[16] and just the poor quality of staff working on banking issues, on which more will be said later. One other possible factor in the crisis may have been opposition from the taxpaying public to the use of public funds to rescue ailing financial institutions, opposition that became even stronger when a series of scandals at the MOF and the BOJ was revealed.

It is likely that each of these factors contributed to the depth and the length of the crisis. Together they can fully explain the unfolding of the banking crisis in Japan, and there seems little need for 'revisionist' theories claiming that Japanese bureaucrats intentionally planned and implemented the crisis as Lee[17] suggests.

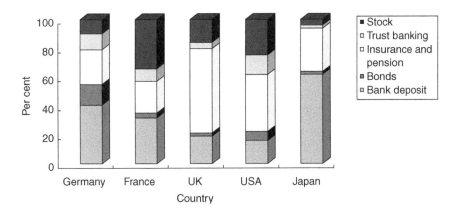

Figure 8.2 Breakdown of financial assets in the household sector.

Source: Bank of Japan, *Comparative Economic and Financial Statistics*, 1999.

The condition of the Japanese banking industry

Increasing non-performing loans

Japanese banks accumulated losses of approximately 88.2 trillion yen in disposing of non-performing loans. Despite such enormous losses, they still had more than 38 trillion yen of disclosed non-performing loans at the end of fiscal year 2002 , in March 2003, as shown in Table 8.3. This amounted to more than 5 per cent of their portfolio, yet there are some analysts who argue that the disclosed amount of non-performing loans is somewhat underestimated. Fukao, for instance, points out that the rules of the *FSA Bank Examination Manual* contain a very narrow definition of non-performing loans. Others, like Horie, argue that there is a bias towards big companies in estimation of their financial position and thus also overestimation of the performance of funds loaned to these companies.[18]

The prolonged recession has been partially to blame for the increasing amount of non-performing loans since more and more firms have faced financial distress. Their loans increase the amount of non-performing loans. On the other hand, banks have tended to be willing to underestimate their non-performing loan positions. Apart from the peculiarities of Japanese corporate governance mentioned in the preceding section, the banks were under heavy external and internal pressure. Within the *keiretsu* (industrial group) framework, which big Japanese firms still prefer, classifying a certain loan as risky puts not only a particular borrower in a difficult position, but also the group as a whole.[19] The bank, in many cases itself a member of such a group, can hardly afford to alienate its other members. Furthermore, disposing of a bad loan and placing a borrower under bankruptcy means a reduction of tax income for local authorities. This, combined with the presence of 'politically well-connected firms', results in an external pressure on banks not to classify loans as non-performing. Similar internal pressure originates from the banks' top management, which tends to avoid public fund injections associated with restructuring conditions, not least because it may reduce their own retirement bonuses.

Japanese banks have not maintained sufficient loan loss reserves. This happens due to the lenient reserve policy of the FSA regarding reserve ratios, restrictive tax deduction guidelines on specific loan-loss provisions and also unrealistically low limits on general loan-loss provisions.[20] Compared to US banks, which maintain a ratio of loan-loss reserves to bad loans of more than 160 per cent, the ratio maintained by the Japanese banks has been in the range of 40–60 per cent since 1994.

Weak capital position

Under the lenient supervision that has prevailed despite reorganisation, Bank of International Settlement (BIS) capital rules have often been manipulated. First, lower reserves for non-performing loans increase the banks' capital base. Second, banks are allowed to retain large amounts of deferred taxes as a part of their

Table 8.3 Loss on disposal of bad loans in all banks (billion yen)

	FY'92	FY'93	FY'94	FY'95	FY'96	FY'97	FY'98	FY'99	FY'00	FY'01	FY'02
Loss on disposal of bad loans	1,640	3,872	5,232	13,369	7,763	13,258	13,631	6,944	6,108	9,722	6,658
Net transfer to loan-loss reserves	945	1,146	1,402	7,087	3,447	8,402	8,118	2,531	2,732	5,196	3,101
Direct write-offs	424	2,090	2,809	5,980	4,316	3,993	4,709	3,865	3,072	3,975	3,520
Incl. loss on bulk sales etc.	219	1,855	2,103	4,259	3,343	3,142	2,332	1,984	552	770	1,357
Other	271	636	1,022	302	0	863	804	548	304	552	37
Summing up from FY 1992	1,640	5,512	10,744	24,113	31,877	45,135	58,766	65,710	71,818	81,540	88,198
Summing up direct write-offs	424	2,514	5,322	11,302	15,618	19,611	24,320	28,185	31,256	35,231	38,751
Risk management loans	12,775	13,576	12,548	28,504	21,789	29,758	29,627	30,366	32,515	35,231	38,751
Loan-loss reserves outstanding	3,698	4,547	5,536	13,293	12,334	17,815	14,797	12,230	11,555	13,353	12,585

Source: Compiled by the author from the data disclosed yearly by the Financial Services Agency (Kinyū Chō), Furyō Saiken Shori Son no Sui-i.

capital. However, in order to recoup the deferred taxes, banks need to be profitable. Since Japanese banks have been losing money during the post-bubble period, the deferred taxes should not appear in their capital base. It was a stricter application of this rule that is said to have contributed to the failure of the Resona Group in May 2003.[21] Finally, cross holding of shares between banks and insurance companies is shown as capital although the shares' are nothing more than mutually held debt. Fukao's estimation of Japanese banks' capital base assuming strict application of the BIS rules suggested that, in 2001, 4 out of 15 major banks had negative capital bases, while the capital base at the remaining 11 banks was less than 2 per cent.[22]

Historically, Japanese banks have faced no limits on the number of corporate shares they could hold, but large share holdings are, of course, very sensitive to stock price fluctuations. The situation became very serious when the Nikkei 225 fell below 10,000 yen in 2002 and fluctuated in the range of 8,000 yen until the summer of 2003. Banks having difficulties with maintaining the BIS capital rules have tended to reduce their lending, creating a credit crunch that results in financial distress for non-financial corporations, further reducing the value of shares held by banks and causing even more difficulties for the banks themselves.

Low profitability

Results released in March 2003 showed that most Japanese banks were losing money.[23] In fact, most of the Japanese banks have been unprofitable for the last ten years, surviving mainly by realising capital gains from shares and real estate sales. There are several reasons for the banks' current weak profitability. First, Japanese banks did not undertake serious restructuring until the late 1990s. Not only did the number of banks not decrease significantly despite heavy overcapacity in the banking industry (contrary to the USA where the number of banks decreased by 15 per cent, Norway by 10 per cent, and Sweden by 80 per cent during the first two years after the banking crises began), but banking employment actually increased by 3 per cent. This compared to −5 per cent in the USA, −25 per cent in Norway and −8 per cent in Sweden. Personnel costs in Japanese banks also increased by more than 15 per cent in the first half of the 1990s, compared to the decrease of 15 per cent in the USA and Norway, and of 12 per cent in Sweden.[24] Intensive cost cutting at the end of the 1990s reduced operating costs, but the pace of improvement is likely to be difficult to sustain because of long overdue investment in infrastructure, without which banks will further lose their market share to convenience stores and foreign financial institutions.[25]

Second, the deposit interest rate controls that existed until the early 1990s allowed banks to maintain relatively high lending margins. However, after the controls had been lifted, deteriorating market conditions prevented banks from significantly increasing their lending rates. While real interest rates (lending rates adjusted for inflation) have remained high for borrowers due to the deflationary environment of the Japanese economy, they have hardly been covering banks' operating costs. Another reason for banks' poor profitability is the fact that they have had to compete with the government sponsored financial institutions, which account for almost 40 per cent of the market. It is hard to compete with housing loan programmes that offer longer maturity and accept prepayment without penalties. In the deposit market, the postal savings system has more than 24,000 offices around the country, against 600 for the largest banking group, Mizuho. It does not charge account maintenance fees and offers deposit interest rates similar to those of private financial institutions. Needless to say, the government sponsored financial institutions benefit from a comprehensive governmental guarantee.

Finally, technological change has resulted in the emergence of new types of banks. These include, for instance, the IY Bank, which specialises in payment and settlement services for individual customers. Established in May 2001 by the largest Japanese supermarket chain Itō Yōkado, the bank operates by using ATMs installed in the chain's convenience stores. Others, like Sony Bank, eBank or Japan Net Bank, established by interests such as trading companies, manufacturers of electronic products or information services companies offer bank services via the Internet or mobile phone networks. This makes the competitive position of traditional banks even more tenuous. The environment of the Japanese financial market thus prevents banks from restoring profitability.

Macroeconomic effects of the banking crisis

The banking crisis is responsible for the serious macroeconomic difficulties that the Japanese economy has been facing. Struggling to improve their capital base and profitability, banks have reduced their lending and contributed to further deterioration of economic conditions through a credit crunch. Instead of lending to private businesses, banks have chosen to purchase government bonds and effectively prevent the diffusion of the effects of the BOJ's expansionary monetary policies, as it is the government, not private businesses, that end up holding the increased money supply. Despite growing deposits, bank lending declined 3.4 per cent on average between June 2001 and June 2003. This makes the use of expansionary monetary policies or inflation targeting in Japan at least impractical.[26] Such policies cannot succeed without a healthy banking industry, unless the BOJ directly lends to private businesses – an uncommon practice for a central bank.

Apart from impairing the effectiveness of the BOJ monetary policies, the banking crisis has also had other effects. First, the currency to bank deposit ratio has been growing steadily,[27] indicating a lack of confidence in the banking system. At the same time, the share of postal deposits to total deposits has almost doubled.[28] Given this relative inefficiency of the investment of postal deposits, this may contribute substantially to the severity of the current recession. Second, the attitude of the banks impairs other policies aimed at revitalising businesses: for instance, the efforts of the Industrial Reconstruction Agency, launched in May 2003, to buy-back some of non-performing loans of small and medium enterprises in local economies.

On the other hand, Miyajima and Yafeh see some positive aspects of the banking crisis in Japan. They argue that the credit crunch resulting from the crisis affects mainly small low profit companies in low-tech sectors with limited access to bond markets. In contrast, companies with high R&D investment in high-tech sectors can easily find their way to direct financing. In this way the banking crisis contributes to the 'natural selection' of firms and banks and, therefore, helps to transform Japan's heavily bank oriented financial markets into a more direct financing system.[29]

Solution to the crisis

A solution to the crisis should include two groups of measures. One set of measures should strictly target the banks and include tackling the problem of the non-performing loans and improving bank supervision. The other should comprise of macroeconomic policy measures aiming at revitalising the economy. Unfortunately, despite the highly publicised policy steps very little has changed in terms of the relations between banks and their regulators. Even now, under the FSA supervision banks are allowed to under-disclose non-performing loans and poor profitability. Only in July 2003, the FSA issued profitability warnings to several banks for the first time ever. The implicit policy, adopted by the FSA, of not interfering with the internal management of the banks receiving public funds results in the management of the banks not being held responsible for their actions. Announcements of non-interference in the rehabilitation of the de facto nationalised Resona Group seem to confirm this policy trend. However, this attitude has been further undermining public confidence in the financial sector and may result in an even stronger opposition to using public funds in future. The government must stringently assess the real quantum of non-performing loans, make banks provide for sufficient loan-loss reserves, make public funds injections without bank management consent and rehabilitate them under conditions of effective nationalisation.[30] This is how Komiya Ryūtaro once described the role of the *main bank* in the economy. Now the banks themselves need the same service.

However, cleaning the banks' books of non-performing loans alone is not sufficient. Decisive actions must be undertaken in order to restore a sound economic growth without which the banks cannot improve their profitability. The Japanese government tried to revitalise the economy through such policies as promoting information technology-led growth (an 'IT revolution'), liberalisation and opening of the Japanese economy (including the highly publicised 'Japanese Big Bang'), stimulating stock market prices in order to support the value of banks' shareholdings and massive public spending. All of these ultimately failed to live up to expectations because it seems that none of these attempts were actually sufficiently oriented to consumers. Most of the regulatory changes as well as the fiscal stimuli have been strictly business-oriented measures aimed at providing relief not even to the economy as a whole but to particular industries. Most of them have not improved the welfare of the individual consumer. The same can be argued about the changes to the pension system, health insurance, social security, environment protection regulations and so on. In reality, policy measures have had somewhat adverse effects on consumer spending, while not providing enough relief to businesses.

Increased spending on public works projects failed to stimulate individual consumption because the Japanese public is aware of the negative fiscal effects of such projects and their rather limited rationality. Numerous scandals relating to bid rigging, corruption among bureaucrats and politicians involved in public work projects, the poor quality of construction work and the involvement of organised crime have further undermined the confidence of the Japanese public, which seems to view such spending as a waste of public funds rather than genuine steps leading to an economic recovery. This, not less than deflation itself, has discouraged consumer spending. Anecdotal evidence says that for similar reasons the companies participating in public works projects have used leased machinery and equipment and hired a poor quality, part-time labour force, instead of making capital investments and hiring full time employees, which ought to be the primary objective of such public spending.

In order to restore public confidence, it is necessary to make substantial changes restoring rationality to the national pension system, health insurance, education and other areas of public spending. At the same time, in order to make a one-time boost to consumer spending, certain goods, such as housing, vehicles, electric and electronic appliances, could be exempted from consumption tax for a limited period of time, for instance one year. Because the CPI deflation rate is still lower than the rate of consumption tax, this could result in a substantial increase in consumer spending. By contrast, increasing the rate of consumption tax, as advocated by some business leaders, could result in a 1997-like recession, with similar results for the economy in general and the banking system in particular. Given rapidly dissipating public confidence and, much worse, the government's fiscal position, the recovery from such a recession could be even more difficult than the last time. By reducing its transfers to thousands of government and semi-government agencies of questionable usefulness, which have been in receipt of hefty subsidies or at least do not pay taxes, the Japanese government would still have enough scope for a substantial fiscal improvement. Therefore, the adverse fiscal effects of such a consumption tax reduction need not be catastrophic.

No less important is a resolution of the problems arising from the presence of government sponsored financial institutions. This applies especially to the postal saving service, which currently accounts for more than 20 per cent of total funds raised, and is effectively crowding the banks out from their primary deposit market. However, privatisation of postal services, promoted as a trademark for structural reforms, is not likely to provide a sound solution to the problem. If it was simply privatised, as proposed by the current administration, postal savings activity would become a near monopoly in the country's deposit market, several times bigger than the biggest of the banking groups. Additionally, transforming postal savings into ordinary banking business would require finding a solution to its insufficient capital base (currently its own capital is less than 1 per cent of its total assets, so the remaining part would have to be provided by an injection of public funds) and building up its lending facilities from nothing. Experience suggests that this is no simple task. Needless to say, it would require a substantial fiscal effort while at the same time creating a lot of confusion in the financial markets. Unless this issue is addressed, a fragile recovery in the banking industry may be seriously damaged.

Conclusion

The experience of Japan's banking crisis provides some more general lessons that may be of some importance in considering the future shape of the country's social and economic system. Although the banking crisis in Japan has often been viewed as *a crisis that triggered a change*, the crisis was, in fact, *the product of a change*. Poor coordination and sequencing of liberalisation allowed for '*regulatory arbitrage*', the unequal treatment of different institutions engaging in similar activities, while failure to address the problem of overcapacity in the banking industry led to '*survival myopia*', that is, engaging in increasingly risky activities in order to survive in the market. Similarly, a specific Japanese corporate governance system including such factors as the presence of a main bank, weak corporate management and low profitability, that worked almost flawlessly in the highly regulated environment of the post-war growth era, was bound to fail when confronted with the new conditions of a (partially) liberalised economy. The origins of this failure can be traced to the simplistic view of a market mechanism as a straightforward demand-supply game. In contrast, viewing the market as an internally coherent set of institutions that have to be created could result in much better prepared reforms.

It is very difficult to develop economic policies in isolation. Although perhaps not directly responsible for the banking crisis in Japan, the Plaza Accord led to a series of events that ultimately triggered the crisis and aggravated its severity. The ability to foresee the outcome of a particular policy is a very important but often neglected element of policy making. Making short-term, *ad hoc* international policy commitments without undertaking proper adjustments continued in Japan well after this, as proved by the liberalisation of imports within the WTO framework often blamed for the ongoing consumer price deflation. In the era of growing globalisation of the world economy a future Japanese system cannot ignore the influence of the outside world as often happened in the past.

Many policy mistakes made by the authorities may be attributed to the specific character of policy making in Japan. The policy-making process has been under the control of bureaucrats, and therefore the quality of bureaucratic cadres is essential to its effectiveness. The central bureaucracy has been largely comprised of graduates from schools of law (it should be noted that in the Japanese education system this means approximately two years of general education and two years of rather general studies of law). Bureaucracy has been generally closed to economists (Takenaka Heizō's appointment as Minister for Finance and Economy is a very rare exception), and for that reason economics, finance and economic policy are self-taught subjects at the highest level of the Japanese decision-making process.[31] Profound changes to the bureaucratic selection process as well as to the

Japanese education system in general may be a necessary part of any future attempt to improve the system's performance.

Once hailed for its ability to forgo short-term profits in favour of a long-term view of growth, and for its ability to achieve consensus among principals and agents, Japan is now increasingly viewed as a symbol of bureaucratic indolence. This chapter has attempted to shed some light, within its limited scope of analysing the banking crisis in Japan, on the ongoing changes in the country's social and economic system. The main lesson is that each attempt at reform needs to be internally coherent, based on cooperation with the outside world and reform of the country's bureaucratic structure.

Acknowledgement

While preparing my paper for the 10th EAJS conference in Warsaw I benefited greatly from conversations with professors Hirashima Shinichi and Suzuki Masao from Senshū University, Iwata Kenji from Kyūshū University, Yuno Tsutomu from Ryūgoku University and Seo Junichirō from the Bank of Japan. Private conversations with officials of regional banks and stock exchanges as well as with members of the Japan Society for Monetary Economics also provided me with a rich factual knowledge about the Japanese financial industry. However, the paper reflects my own view on the banking crisis in Japan, and my interlocutors may not necessarily agree with all of my judgements.

Notes

1 Adam Posen, 'The Looming Japanese Crisis', *International Economics Policy Brief* 02–05, Institute for International Economics, 2002.

2 For instance, Tamim Bayoumi, 'The Morning After: Explaining the Slowdown in Japanese Growth in the 1990s', *IMF Working Paper*, 1998; Toshitaka Sekine, 'Firm Investment and Balance Sheet Problems in Japan', *IMF Working Paper*, 1999; David Woo, 'In Search of Credit Crunch: Supply Factors Behind the Slowdown in Japan', *IMF Working Paper*, 1999 and others.

3 David Mayes, Liisa Halme and Aarno Liuksila, *Improving Banking Supervision* (Basingstoke: Palgrave, 2001).

4 Fujiwara, Kenya, 'Ginkō Shisutemu no Kijakusei – Saiken e no Mondaiten', in Ishigaki, Ken'ichi and Hino, Hiroyuki (eds), *Nihon no Kinyū Shisutemu no Saikōchiku* (Kōbe: Kōbe University Research Institute for Economics and Business Administration, 1998), p. 26.

5 Yoshinori Shimizu, 'Convoy Regulation, Bank Management, and the Financial Crisis in Japan', in Ryoichi Mikitani and Adam S. Posen, *Japan's Financial Crisis and its Parallels to US Experience* (Washington, DC: Institute for International Economics, 2000), p. 163.

6 Tomohiko Taniguchi, 'Japan's Banks and the "Bubble Economy" of the Late 1980s', in William M. Tsutsui (ed.), *Banking in Japan* (London: Routledge, 1999), p. 194.

7 Yoshinori Shimizu, 'Problems in the Japanese Financial System in the Early 1990s', in Tsutsui, *Banking in Japan*, pp. 164–67; Shimizu, 'Convoy Regulation', pp. 63, 67–69.

8 Japanese banks' obsession with their market share has been in a sense a remnant of the overly regulated financial system. Under the interest rate controls, banks' lending spreads were more or less fixed, and the size of their net income was determined by

the sheer size of their outstanding loans (Akihiro Kanaya and David Woo, 'The Japanese Banking Crisis of the 1990s: Sources and Lessons', *IMF Working Paper*, 2000).

9 The agricultural cooperatives were under the supervision of the Ministry of Agriculture, and the limits on real estate did not apply to them.

10 The largest creditor group of the *jusen* companies, the agricultural cooperatives, were charged with only a minor part of the bail out costs due to political pressure from the Ministry of Agriculture (Kanaya and Woo, 'Japanese Banking Crisis of the 1990s').

11 The FSA took over the supervision of banks, insurance and security companies and non-bank financial institutions from the MOF; *shinkin* credit associations from regional financial bureaux and credit cooperatives from local governments. As one of its first changes, the FSA started making its own investigations into non-performing loans; until then banks had calculated them themselves. In July 2000, the Financial Supervision Agency was renamed the Financial Services Agency (*Kinyū Chō*), and from January 2001 it took over the duties of the Financial Reconstruction Commission.

12 A fifth one, the Resona Group, was launched in March 2003, only to file for protection two months later.

13 Much of the criticism direction at BOJ policies during the Bubble economy is based on our current knowledge of the events that took place later and our much-improved modern analytical tools. It is, however, very hard to estimate how aware of the problem officials were at the time. This argument has been raised by, for instance, Shiratsuka (Shigenori Shiratsuka, 'Asset Prices, Financial Stability, and Monetary Policy: Based on Japan's Experience of the Asset Price Bubble', *IMES Discussion Paper*, 2000). Kosai, Yutaka, Itō, Osamu and Arioka, Ritsuko, 'Baburu-ki no Kinyū Seisaku to sono Han'ō', *IMES (Institute for Monetary and Economic Studies, Bank of Japan) Discussion Paper*, 2000, argue that the BOJ, while concentrating on consumer price stability and liquidity issues, ignored the asset price inflation in the 1980s, wrongly interpreting it as a result of market liberalisation. On the contrary, Ben Bernanke and Mark Gertler ('Should Central Banks Respond to Movement in Asset Prices?', *American Economic Review* 91, 2, 2001, pp. 253–57), and Kunio Okina and Shigenori Shiratsuka ('Shisan Kakaku Baburu, Kakaku no Antei to Kinyū Seisaku: Nihon no Keiken', *IMES Discussion Paper*, 2001) argue against including asset price stability in the central bank's policy objectives. The discussion on responsibility for creating the asset bubble economy in Japan seems to be far from closed.

14 Toshiki Jinushi, Yoshihiro Kuroki and Ryuzo Miyao, 'Monetary Policy in Japan Since the Late 1980s: Delayed Policy Actions and Some Explanations', in Mikitani and Posen, *Japan's Financial Crisis*, p. 132.

15 Thomas F. Cargill, 'What Caused Japan's Banking Crisis?', in Takeo Hoshi and Hugh Patrick (eds), *Crisis and Change in the Japanese Financial System* (Boston, MA. Kluwer Academic Publishers, 2000), p. 44; Shimizu, 'Convoy Regulation', p. 61.

16 The practice whereby top bureaucrats assume management posts in private businesses after retirement contributes greatly to the supervision failures (it happens that government controllers have to control their own mentors) and policy mistakes. Although the practice of *amakudari* seems to have subsided in recent years, between 5.7 per cent of top management posts in regional banks and 9.6 per cent in second tier regional banks are still occupied by former bureaucrats (*Asahi Shinbun* 13 September 2003).

17 Jongsoo Lee, 'The "Crisis" of Non-Performing Loans', in Tsutsui, *Banking in Japan*, pp. 240–41.

18 Mitsuhiro Fukao, 'Barriers to Financial Restructuring: Japanese Banking and Life Insurance Industries', paper presented at conference on 'East Asian Monetary and Financial Cooperation: Concepts, Policy Prospects and the Role of the Yen', Hamburg Institute for International Economics, 29 May 2002; Horie, Yasuteru, 'Shinyō Kakutsuke to Furyō Saiken no Kibo', paper presented at the annual conference of the JSME (Japan Society for Monetary Economics), 31 May 2003.

19 For more on *keiretsu*, see Moerke's chapter (Chapter 6) in this volume.

20 Fukao, 'Barriers to Financial Restructuring'; Kanaya and Woo, 'Japanese Banking Crisis of the 1990s', p. 11.
21 In March 2003 (end of fiscal year 2002), deferred taxes accounted for 60.8 per cent of Mizuho Group's own capital (in September the share had decreased to 43.6 per cent). In Mitsui-Sumitomo it was 58.7 per cent (51.5 per cent in September), in Mitsubishi Tokyo 41.6 per cent (26.8 per cent in September), in UFJ 59.4 per cent (51.5 per cent in September) and in Resons 99.3 per cent (12.6 per cent in September). The low September figures for Resona are due to an injection of public funds (*Asahi Shinbun* 26 November 2003).
22 Fukao, 'Barriers to Financial Restructuring'.
23 Although the half-yearly results released in November 2003 showed substantial improvement (except for the Resona Group), there remained certain doubts about the sustainability of the recovery in the banking industry (*Asahi Shinbun* 26 November 2003).
24 Iwatsubo, Kamon and Hino, Hiroyuki, 'Ginkō Shisutemu no Kiki to Makuro-Keizai', in Ishigaki and Hino, *Nihon no Kinyū Shisutemu no Saikōchiku*, p. 9.
25 Because their outdated fund transfer system has been unable to accept the Chinese characters necessary for the transliteration of personal names, banks cannot compete with the 24-hour bar code reading terminals at convenience store chains.
26 Ben Bernanke, 'Some Thoughts on Monetary Policy in Japan', speech delivered before the 60th Anniversary meeting of the Japan Society for Monetary Economics, Tokyo, 31 May 2003.
27 It grew from 7.1 per cent in the first quarter of 1993 to 9.1 per cent in the first quarter of 2002 (Iwatsubo and Hino, 'Ginkō Shisutemu no Kiki to Makuro-Keizai', p. 10; Posen, 'The Looming Japanese Crisis', p. 6).
28 Iwatsubo and Hino ('Ginkō Shisutemu no Kiki', p. 13) estimate that postal deposits are at least 20 times less effective in generating growth.
29 Miyajima and Yafeh, 'Japan's Banking Crisis', p. 19.
30 This is more or less exactly what happened in Korea after the 1997 crisis. See Nakai, Hiroyuki, 'Nihon no Furyō Saiken Shori ni kansuru Hikaku Seidoronteki Kōsa', paper presented at the annual conference of the Japan Society for Monetary Economics, Tokyo, 31 May 2003, for comparison of the Japanese and Korean approaches to banking crises.
31 Cargill, 'What Caused Japan's Banking Crisis?', p. 53.

9 International mergers and acquisitions with Japanese participation

Two cases from the automotive industry

Sigrun Caspary

Introduction

For many years, Japanese companies were not considered targets for international mergers and acquisitions (M&A). During the 1970s and 1980s, there were hardly any examples of Japanese companies being taken over by foreign ones. Domestic partners would usually bail out a Japanese company if it was in trouble. However, times have changed. The 1990s, called the 'lost decade' as growth rates bobbed up and down around the negligible growth mark, were characterised by a persistent downturn of the economy, sick companies and banks revealing a massive accumulation of bad loans and an increasing number of bankruptcies as well as unemployment. As a consequence, a greater number of potential take-over candidates appeared. The number of M&A cases in Japan has increased over the last few years and so have the number of international M&A with Japanese participation. In this chapter, we focus on those cases in which foreign companies have merged with or acquired a Japanese company (so-called OUT-IN), thereby gaining control over the Japanese counterpart.

In general, cross-border M&A can be expected to face double the difficulty in the integration process because of the necessity of merging different 'company cultures' as well as different 'national cultures'. However, research on European cross-border M&A has revealed that national cultures have not been considered so much of a problem. Instead, organisational similarity was found to be a crucial factor for the success of any merger.[1] Based on these findings, we investigate why the number of OUT-IN cases in Japan was, and still is, extremely low by international standards.[2]

Three alternative hypotheses can be considered. As described elsewhere, psychological barriers have been mentioned as an important obstacle to engaging in business in Japan.[3] If this were to be true in the case of foreign M&As also, the number of OUT-IN mergers would still remain small even after the abolition of formal hurdles (*Hypothesis I*). Our period of analysis relates to a time of rapid change in formal institutions, and we may well obtain mixed results. However, it is possible that the change of legal institutions may enable a greater number of M&A cases regardless of the buyers' nationality (*Hypothesis II*). Furthermore, it may be the case that differences in national cultures play a crucial role, and hence the number of OUT-IN cases will remain relatively low (*Hypothesis III*).

Based on this finding that organisational similarity matters, the automobile industry is an appropriate sector in which to examine these hypotheses. Since 1985, changes in consumer behaviour have led to global consolidation in the industry, which could imply that differences in national cultures matter less than differences in company cultures. With the mergers of Renault–Nissan and DaimlerChrysler–Mitsubishi Motor Company, two of the most prominent cases of M&A with foreign participation have taken place in the Japanese automobile industry in the 1990s.

The first task is to check how far Japan may, or may not, be different. Japanese companies are well known for their special form of organisation,[4] and we can examine if the unique form of Japanese corporate organisation helps us to understand the pace of M&A activity. We will present Aoki's concept of the J-firm,[5] since it refers to the supplier *keiretsu* type of organisation, and both Nissan and Mitsubishi Motors displayed this kind of corporate organisation.[6] In addition to the differences in the organisation at a company level, there are also differences in the organisation of company groups in Japan. This is important because *keiretsu* were accused of being a hurdle to foreign M&A because of their group behaviour regarding strategic manoeuvres, share-holdings and networking.

As Japanese companies have been engaged in a process of restructuring for the past decade, we can examine the changes in their formal structure in terms of whether they have become similar to their foreign counterparts. Second, we will also analyse whether changes in informal institutions are supporting or impeding the transformation of the J-firm. If in a merger both companies are J-firms, a change of J-firm-type of company organisation may not necessarily occur. However, in the case of a foreign company buying into a Japanese counterpart, a J-firm will have to change its organisation to avoid difficulties in the merger process. Therefore, in case of a merger with a foreign company causing changes in ownership and control, a J-firm may be expected to change its organisational structures in the direction of the foreign company's organisation. By doing so, post merger integration (PMI) will be supported. As mentioned, national differences can be overcome more easily in cases where companies with a higher level of organisational similarity merge, as compared to cases with a higher degree of differences in company cultures.[7] Following this, we put forward the hypothesis that if a Japanese firm reorients its company structure to make it more similar to the foreign buyer's structure, differences in national cultures can be regarded a minor problem (*Hypothesis IV*), as the research on European firms suggests.[8]

Furthermore, we also need to examine any differences between firms organised in vertical and horizontal *keiretsu* types. An example of the former would be the formation of a group of suppliers surrounding a final assembler along the line of value-adding in production. Such a form of company organisation is called a 'supplier *keiretsu*'. In contrast, horizontal *keiretsu* include independent companies (which by themselves may be supplier *keiretsu*) from various industries grouping around a bank and a trading company.[9] We can also suggest the hypothesis that due to the complicated structure intertwining other group members, companies that are a member of a horizontal *keiretsu* might be more difficult to integrate into a foreign company (*Hypothesis V*) than are vertical *keiretsu* or independent Japanese firms.

To prove our hypothesis we will proceed as follows. In the section on OUT-IN cases, we will look at the development of M&A cases in Japan. We list possible reasons for the low number of foreign M&A and check whether they have an impact on formal and/or informal institutions. In the section on different types of organisations we present Aoki's concept of the J-firm as the traditional mode of company organisation. Then we look at the recent changes in company organisation. The section on the global and the Japanese car industry gives a brief overview of the development of the international automobile industry. Increased global competition and changes in consumer behaviour pushed car makers to consolidating into five major groups. This trend was accompanied by a transformation of organisational structures which can be considered as making international M&A more likely to occur. We add a brief history of the Japanese automobile industry to show the organisational changes on a national level. Then, in the section on two case-studies, we introduce two case studies of international M&A in the Japanese automobile industry, the cases of Renault and Nissan, and of DaimlerChrysler and Mitsubishi Motor Company. We show that the stock market evaluation is positive for both cases. However, analysis of organisational changes in PMI (section on organisational changes) shows certain differences. We sum up our findings in the concluding section.

OUT-IN cases

As mentioned in the introduction, the number of cases in which a foreign company merges with or acquires a Japanese firm (OUT-IN) is low by international standards, as shown in Figure 9.1. In other countries, OUT-IN numbers are almost as high as IN-OUT and also considerably larger than those for Japan.[10] This calls into question the international openness of Japan towards M&A.

In every merger there are differences between companies which have to be overcome. As mentioned earlier culture as such is widely believed to be an important barrier, and cultural differences are blamed more frequently if a merger does not work out. Regarding the term 'culture' we have to distinguish between differences in corporate cultures as well as national cultures. As mentioned, findings from M&A among companies from European countries revealed that national culture as such is regarded as a factor of limited importance in impeding mergers.

However, in the case of Japan, analysts have come to the following conclusion, namely that the big problem is that 'There is no "market for corporate control" in Japan. Companies are only sold just before they would go bankrupt, no other time'.[11] This judgement points to structural differences which have historical reasons but which may also be rooted in psychological reasons. It seems from this judgement that Japan is a special case in which differences in national culture compound differences in company culture.

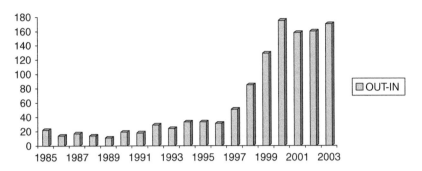

Figure 9.1 OUT-IN cases in Japan, 1985–2003.

Source: Marr September 2002, Recof, quoted by www5.cao.go.jp/keizai1/2002/112tainichi/1121item1-e.pdf and http://www.recof.co.jp/web/fm/graph.

Note
Figures for 2002 and 2003 are writer's estimations from the internet graph's view of the second source. According to e-mail conversation of August 2003 with Recof, the number of OUT-IN deals into the Japanese auto parts industry as of August 2003 was 7 cases in 2001, 5 cases in 2002 and 2 cases in 2003.

Hence, in order to answer the question of why the number of OUT-IN mergers is low for Japan, a number of factors have to be checked. First, we have to distinguish between the willingness of foreign companies to engage in M&A in Japan and the willingness of Japanese companies to accept foreign M&A. There may be economic as well as psychological reasons for foreign firms not engaging in M&A activity in Japan or for Japanese firms not welcoming foreign investment. Further, we need to analyse how far formal and informal rules on the Japanese side may pose a hurdle for foreign companies. Table 9.1 lists a number of possible macro- and micro-economic, legal, cultural and psychological reasons.[12]

Admittedly, it is difficult to assess to what extent any one particular factor has contributed to hindering overall M&A activity. Inhibiting factors have emerged over a period of more than a century, along with the historical development of formal and informal institutions. The net effect was that until 1990, OUT-IN cases in Japan were extremely rare.[13] For Japanese companies facing managerial and/or financial difficulties there was, on the one hand, a safety net of *keiretsu* business partners who would help with personnel, technology and/or orders. On the other hand, public or semi-public financial institutions would provide assistance, mostly in the form of favourable loans. Large companies especially would benefit from such policy measures. The assumption was that their bankruptcy should be avoided because of fears of rising unemployment and adverse reputational effects.[14] In addition, the *keiretsu* system was a guarantee that a certain amount of stocks would be kept in the hands of companies belonging to the same group. Cross-shareholding agreements made it difficult for a foreign investor to buy into a company and/or try a hostile take-over.[15] This manner of achieving control over a company, in most cases a competitor, was instead a means of M&A used in the United States and Europe.

Table 9.1 Barriers to foreign M&A in Japan

	The Japanese side	The foreign side
Economic reasons	• Company groups (*keiretsu*) with long-term relationship • Special distribution system • Special Japanese management system (life-long employment, seniority based wage system, intra-firm unions) • Special Japanese education system which is dedicated to the Japanese employment system • Ambiguity of adapting to international standards and maintaining the Japanese way	• No international market for M&A • High investment cost over a long period until investment pays off • High cost of non-tariff barriers, for example importance of having access to inner circles of the business community • Difficult labour market with only recently increasing job hopping of middle managers • Necessity to adapt to Japanese way to organise work • Unwillingness of own headquarter to provide necessary understanding and/or resources • High living costs in Japan • Limits to exports and technology transfer[a]
Political and legal reasons	• Government protection of some industries against foreign entrants[a] • M&A regulations limiting foreign ownership • Capital market law, for example exchange rate regulations limiting investment • Stock market regulations restrict exchange of shares in case of M&A • Special board member regulations make integration difficult	
Social and psychological reasons	• Japanese society was (and still is) kind of a 'closed-shop' towards foreigners[b] • Language barrier due to poor education in foreign languages • Foreign employers are regarded as minor to Japanese ones • Japanese working for a foreign firm regarded as below standard	• Unwillingness of foreigners to work in Japan • Japan is believed to be a closed and difficult market • Cultural barriers of 'Japanese-ness' • Feeling of uncertainty, unpredictability, non-transparency of Japanese behaviour • Language barrier, unwillingness to learn Japanese • Fear of being misunderstood and laughed at as a foreigner

Notes

a Does not directly apply for car industry, except sometimes indirectly, for example protection of the oil market leads to high gasoline prices and thus impacts on consumer behaviour towards car driving.

b Referring to the overall low number of foreigners as well as immigrants living in Japan.

The changes which the Japanese economy and society have witnessed over the last decade or so are remarkable. As mentioned earlier, the Japanese economy did not show convincing signs of recovery for years. The so-called 'hollowing out', as well as the dissolution, of the *keiretsu* structures increased the pressure for restructuring and the need to look for new partnerships. The credit market has remained tight, which pushes firms into searching for new sources of finance abroad. Due to the sluggish economy, domestic demand has remained low, increasing the need to develop new markets at home and abroad. Another problem is the increasing international integration of business and hence the increasing vulnerability of a single nation, with the consequence (among others) that the exchange rate impacts on export profits. Further, the process of globalisation goes hand in hand with the development of new technologies, and hence Japan, too, faces the need to adapt to international standards. One crucial problem that needs to be solved is the crisis in the banking sector, as well as the deflation, both of which impede restructuring processes at the company level.[16] It is in this context that the Japanese government is required to proceed with institutional reforms. The Japanese government has also started to promote M&A actively as a solution for troubled companies.[17] Formal, legal institutions have been changed to achieve this goal (Table 9.2).

Looking at the timing of these legal changes and comparing it with the rise in the numbers of OUT-IN cases shown in Figure 9.1, a clear correlation is apparent. It seems highly likely that the steep increase in M&A numbers, both IN-IN and OUT-IN, can be explained purely by changes in the legal framework. For instance, governmental publications state that 'changes to Japan's Commercial Code in 1999 have made it possible to acquire companies through an exchange of shares, giving a big boost to overall M&A activity in Japan'.[18] This casts doubt on our *Hypothesis I* that states that if psychological barriers remain high, the number of OUT-IN mergers is likely to remain small even after the abolition of formal barriers. These findings instead support our *Hypothesis II*, that the change of legal institutions will enable a greater number of M&A cases regardless of the buyers' nationality. We can conclude that it was formal barriers that in the first place kept the barrier to M&A high. It should be added that if the effects of changes in formal institutions are this apparent, then the changes in informal institutions must already have been well under way.

Regarding the fact that the increase still leaves the number of OUT-IN cases below international standards, this might be taken as evidence in support of our *Hypothesis III*, namely that differences in national cultures play a crucial role, and hence the number of OUT-IN cases is likely to remain relatively low. However, it is important to distinguish between public opinion and the opinion of employees whose position depends on the survival of the company. For the latter a merger is related to the maintenance of their workplace, and thus they will estimate a solution with a foreign buyer as something better than a bankruptcy and cast aside their negative attitude towards foreigners.[19]

Acceptance of the foreign buyer also has implications for the results of a merger. For example, if a foreign CEO is popular, he may be accepted despite

Table 9.2 Recent legal changes promoting international M&A in Japan

Year	Commercial law	Other laws	Accounting	Tax system
1997	• Simplification of merger process	• Lifting ban on forming holding companies by general companies		
1998				
1999	• Equity-swap system • Equity-transfer system	• Special measures law on industrial revitalisation	• Adoption of tax effect accounting	
2000	• Corporate divestiture systems (spin-offs)	• Civil Rehabilitation Law	• New consolidated accounting standards • Valuation of financial products at market prices (except for corporate cross shareholding)	
2001	• Treasury stock system		• Valuation of corporate cross shareholdings at market prices • Retirement benefit accounting	• Corporate reorganisation tax system
2002	• Class share system • New stock option system			• Corporate reorganisation tax system
2003	• Purchases of treasury stock authorised in the articles of incorporation	• Full modification of corporate reorganisation law • Modification of industrial revitalization law	• Standards for accounting for the impairment of assets	

Source: http://www.recof.co.jp/english/ma.html

pushing through unpopular measures; or if it is more valuable for all stakeholders to keep the brand name alive, then even a high rate of job losses may be acceptable. The response to our *Hypothesis III* thus depends on the specifics of each case. Here, we can only state that successful mergers between Japanese and foreign companies may increase the overall acceptance of foreign leadership. Assuming that changes in the Japanese economy as well as in Japanese society are leading to a more open-hearted attitude towards foreign investment and management, opportunities for foreign M&A are likely to rise further as well.

Different types of organisations

The changes in formal institutions comprised by the above-mentioned legal changes may be expected to cause changes in other formal (and informal) institutions as well. This is already evident in the form of changes taking place within the corporate structures. In order to highlight these changes, we will make use of Aoki's concept of company organisation and the comparison of information processing in firms within select countries.

Aoki developed a model for a number of company types which show special features due to their historical development in different business environments.[20] The model indicated the existence of different intensities in hierarchical organisation which cause differences in information processing and exchange between company units or among firms.[21] For example, in the Japanese 'suppliers *keiretsu*', Aoki identified the following features: 'In this architecture T_1 [i.e. period one] and each unit at the T_2-level [i.e. period two] share information regarding the systemic segment of the environment to a certain degree within a general framework of a functional hierarchy.' He explicitly cites the automobile industry as providing 'a rough analogue of this architecture'.[22]

This contrasts to the pattern of information flow in more hierarchically organised firms such as German firms,[23] which allows participation in decision making. If we look at Figure 9.2, we see that this kind of firm is located to the left of the J-firm (but not right at the left side). On the right side of the J-firm are located organisations with a more horizontally organised pattern of information flow among small units, as in the case, for example of the small firm communities in Italian industrial districts.[24]

Two points need to be made regarding Aoki's concept. The first is that studying different types of organisations provides a framework for analysing the question of how similar companies are during mergers. In the two cases presented in the latter part of this chapter, we can identify the Japanese companies Nissan and Mitsubishi Motors as supplier *keiretsu* of the J-firm type. By contrast, the foreign firms Renault (France) and DaimlerChrysler (Germany) are located more to the left in terms of Figure 9.2, that is, both companies are assumed to be more hierarchically organised in terms of information processing, with DaimlerChrysler belonging to the 'participatory hierarchy type' and Renault slightly more to the left of DaimlerChrysler. In the latter case, the idea of looking for a Japanese partner bore the strong stamp of Jürgen Schrempp, DaimlerChrysler's CEO. Hence, it seems that the German influence was, and remains, greater than that of the original American type company organisation of Chrysler.[25] In this chapter we thus take DaimlerChrysler as a company with a German type of organisation of Aoki's concept of participating hierarchies.

Aoki's observations relate to organisations within a more or less stable environment. However, as already mentioned, a decade of changes in Japan has led to changes in the business environment which have caused changes in the way companies are organised as well. The trend towards the dissolution of company groups (*keiretsu*) is one example of the changes that are occurring. Consequently, companies increasingly have to operate independently of their groups and are forced to find new methods of undertaking things like financing and partnership building. Hence information processing, too, may be expected to be subject to change.

Systemic information / Local information	Hierarchical	Strongly assimilative	Weakly assimilative
Encapsulated	Functional		Silicon Valley
Assimilated (network-induced)	Network integrated f-hierarchy		
	h-controlled teams	Participatory hierarchy (*)	Japanese *keiretsu*
(Contextual)			

Figure 9.2 Types of organisational and quasi-organisational architecture.

Source: Aoki, *Toward a Comparative Institutional Analysis*, p. 117.

Note
(*) refers to the G-Firm, Japanese *keiretsu* to the J-firm.

In the event of a J-firm agreeing to form a partnership or alliance, a number of changes are likely to take place. A change in ownership structure may also necessitate changes in inter-company information-processing. Where the merger is between two J-firms, changes may be relatively minor, but a merger with a non-J-firm is likely to result in the development of a new system of information processing different from that of the original J-firm. We can assume that a change in organisation will definitely occur when the nationality of top management changes.

As mentioned earlier, if a foreign company buys into a Japanese one, a typical firm will undergo organisational change to reduce possible difficulties in the PMI process. Achieving higher organisational similarity will support PMI. Hence, where a merger with a foreign company causes changes in ownership and control, a J-firm will change in terms of its organisational structure (albeit unwillingly) to move closer to the foreign company's organisation. Depending on whether the new company is more hierarchically or more horizontally organised, the new system of information processing that will emerge will cause the new company organisation to be located more to the left or more to the right of its original location according to Figure 9.2. Hence, we can assume that foreign M&A causes the merging Japanese company's organisation to change in the direction of that of the foreign company acquiring it.

In the cases observed here, we have a German firm and a French firm buying into Japanese companies. Both foreign companies can be considered as having a more hierarchical form of organisation than the J-firm. Information processing in these firms will thus turn out to be organised in a more hierarchical form as well. However, because of the fact that both Japanese firms are still embedded in the environment of the Japanese economy (and not in a German or French environment), we may expect the new patterns to be located closer to that of the J-firm than, for instance, to the participatory hierarchy of the G-firm found in the case of the DaimlerChrysler–Mitsubishi merger.[26]

In order to find out whether or not a change in information processing took place in the wake of the mergers we have looked at the manner in which knowledge creation in cross-functional teams (CFT) occurred. The use of CFT as such is not a purely Japanese idea, but Japanese companies made substantial use of CFT for knowledge creation with considerable success.[27] Hence, this practice has been labelled a special Japanese method of information exchange. From the late 1980s other companies copied this way of organising production too, in order to reduce lead times, waste of resources and costs. The Japanese automotive industry had taken the lead in developing a production process CFT especially in combining R&D, production and sales (i.e. 'lean production' or Toyotism), and car makers in North America and Europe were keen to copy the concept.[28] This leads us to the assumption that the global car industry looks very similar in terms, of production processes, and that differences can be pinpointed by looking at the use of CFT.

The global and the Japanese car industry

Regarding the changes in the Japanese economic landscape, there are obviously differences in the need for restructuring depending on the industry. In the finance, banking and insurance sector, for example, companies have faced enormous losses due to bad loans, and hence have found themselves in a weak position, and as almost every domestic player has faced enormous financial constraints foreign investors have been the only alternative sources of 'good' money. The chemical industry has also recently witnessed an increasing amount of M&A activity. Among the most significant and spectacular cases of mergers or acquisitions, however, were those in the automobile industry, which were closely watched by the public. The two alliances we present here are Renault–Nissan and DaimlerChrysler–Mitsubishi Motors, both of which entail capital. There are, in fact, four different forms of M&A. These are purchase (e.g. AXA/France–Nihon Dantai Life Insurance in 2000), transfer (e.g. Dupont/US–Teijin in 1999), capital participation (e.g. Renault/France–Nissan in 1999 or DaimlerChrysler/Germany–Mitsubishi Motors in 2000) and investment expansion (e.g. Boehringer Ingelheim/Germany–SSP in 2000).[29] However, because of space constraints we can only focus on type 3, that is, capital participation.

The spread of M&A cases varies throughout the industries, but there are several reasons why our two examples are of particular interest. First of all, they are important for the whole automotive industry due to the continuing trend towards consolidation initiated by the DaimlerChrysler merger. Second, they are of major concern to nations that host major automobile manufacturers because of the importance the car industry has for economic development in industrialised and industrialising countries across the world. Third, as the automotive industry can be called an internationally leading industry, it is likely that other industries will closely observe what is happening to it, and if alliances turn out to be successful they may be copied. Finally, the car industry is of intrinsic interest because of the large number of consumers in each country. As cars are branded products and the consumer relationship is highly important for the development of further models, car makers themselves, as well as their respective governments, cannot ignore consumers' opinions and reactions. Thus, the mass media will also watch closely what happens in the automobile industry.

Almost every car manufacturer is active on the domestic as well as the international market. Following a global trend towards consolidation, the car industry shows a high degree of international integration. Since 1985, increasing competition has forced the global players to increasingly form alliances or co-operate with each other. The latest wave was initiated in 1996 by the acquisition of British Rover by German BMW.[30] Groups are now arranged around the 'Big Five' which consist of General Motors (GM) and Ford of the United States, DaimlerChrysler and Volkswagen (VW) of Germany, and Toyota of Japan (Figure 9.3 and 9.4).

On the one hand the car market has become more and more integrated, but on the other hand consumer demand has become more and more individualised.[31] Companies have faced the challenge of building a large number of cars on a smaller platform, that is, by increasing the total number of cars by increasing the number of models, and variants within the models, so that the number of each model or variant actually decreases. Hence, they have to develop structures that lead to synergies among companies, while at the same time remaining flexible in

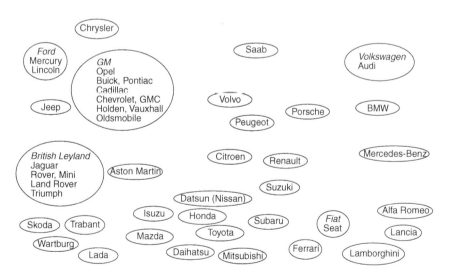

Figure 9.3 Groupings in the world car industry in 1985.

Source: Jakob, 'Die Entwicklung des Weltautomobilmarktes seit 1985', p. 14.

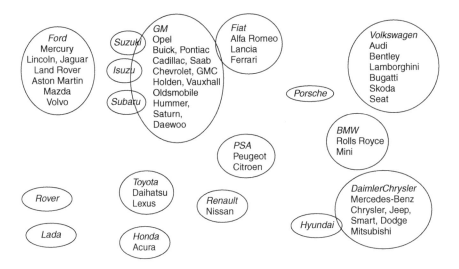

Figure 9.4 Groupings in the world car industry in 2002.

Source: Jakob, 'Die Entwicklung des Weltautomobilmarktes seit 1985', p. 15.

response to customer demand. As a consequence, the car industry has already established itself in a leading position regarding production methods and knowledge creation. In this sense, automobile companies increasingly look alike, and we can assume the existence of a degree of open-mindedness towards new ideas in management and organisation. Building on the interrelationship between company organisation and the business environment, the car industry has become one of the leading international industries in relation to production technology and information processing. This leads us to the assumption that on a national level institutional changes are likely to react to what is already common practice in car industry.

The Japanese car market

Japan is a leading player in the international car market along with North America and Europe, and the Japanese automobile industry has become a symbol for Japan's economic success since the Second World War. At present, 1 in 10 people employed in the manufacturing sector is employed in the automotive industry. Japanese car makers produce about 10 million passenger cars annually, which is about one-sixth of world output.[32]

The history of the Japanese car industry began with the investment of American car manufacturers in Japan in the 1920s. However, foreign firms retreated from production in Japan in early 1940 and did not re-enter the market until after the Second World War. Leaving aside some limited instances of co-operation with foreign car makers, the development of the car industry in Japan since the 1950s is very much a Japanese story of indigenous development. Looking at the market share of Japanese companies over time,[33] Toyota and Nissan have been the market leaders, with Mitsubishi Motors, Honda and Mazda always striving to catch-up with the first two and a third group consisting of manufacturers with a strong share in the mini-car market (Daihatsu, Isuzu and Fuji/Subaru). Foreign cars only had a small percentage of the Japanese market, but it has been increasing recently.[34]

Over time, the automobile industry has increasingly become global. The Japanese makers, too, followed this trend at a time when not too many Japanese companies went overseas for production. Here, 'going abroad' meant the establishment of a dealer network for exports, followed by an investment in production facilities, initially in Asian countries and later in North America and Europe, to cater to regional markets.[35] Almost every Japanese maker has engaged in one or more instances of collaboration with foreign companies. Examples include the famous 'New United Motor Manufacturing, Inc.' (NUMMI). 'NUMMI is the pioneering joint venture of General Motors Corporation and Toyota Motor Corporation. Established in Fermont, California, in 1984, NUMMI helped change the automobile industry by introducing the Toyota Production System and a teamwork-based working environment to the United States.'[36]

Thus, although domestic development was almost purely Japanese, the history of international co-operation is not new for Japanese car makers. However, a look at the regional distribution of such collaboration reveals that Japanese companies go abroad and invest in production in Asia, North America and Europe (IN-OUT), whereas until relatively recently foreign companies have not tended to invest in production facilities in Japan nor has any collaborative agreement led to an investment by a foreign company in Japan. The only exception to this was Ford holding 20 per cent of Mazda shares.

Following decades of expansion, the Japanese domestic market in the 1990s was characterised by sluggish domestic demand. Many automobile manufacturers also faced setbacks during this period. Depending on the company, the effect of management mistakes became apparent, including incorrect market forecasting and delaying reductions in excess asset and employee capacity. Nissan, for example, faced huge losses and was replaced by Honda as the number two producer in 1999. By contrast, Toyota was able to enlarge its market share, enjoying historically high profits in 2001 (Table 9.3).

The trend in global development in the automobile industry changed in 1998 when Daimler and Chrysler signed their 'mega-merger'.[37] The restructuring process spread through the entire industry, including final assemblers and suppliers. This time a new wave of consolidation in the global automotive industry reached Japan for the first time.[38]

In this context, in 1998 DaimlerChrysler started discussions with Nissan Motor and Nissan Diesel Motor. As an immediate reaction to this, Toyota strengthened its share holding position in Daihatsu (to 37 per cent) and Hino (to 50 per cent) to avoid possible takeover manoeuvres from foreign companies (Table 9.4). Ford, too, intensified its existing ties with Mazda. In early 1999, after DaimlerChrysler

Table 9.3 Market shares of Japanese companies

Company	1993 (%)	2002 (%)	Ranking	Change in %
Toyota	33	35	1	+2
Nissan	16	14	2	−2
Mitsubishi	12	8	5	−4
Honda	11	13	3	+2
Mazda	9	8	5	−1
Suzuki	7	10	4	+3
Daihatsu	5	6	7	+1
Subaru	4	4	8	—
Isuzu	3	2	9	−1

Source: Figures taken from www.jama.org; percentage related to number of vehicles produced.

Table 9.4 Percentage of shares in Japanese companies held by foreign companies

Japanese car maker	North America	Europe
	Company/country – share (%)	Company/country – share (%)
Fuji Heavy Industries (Subaru)	GM/USA – 20	
Isuzu	GM/USA – 49	
Mitsubishi Motors		DaimlerChrysler/ Germany – 37.3
Nissan Motors		Renault/France – 44.4
Nissan Diesel		Renault/France – 22.5
Suzuki	GM/USA – 20	

Source: Own research (homepages of respective companies as of August 2003) and data of JAMA 2002: 17–19.

withdrew from consultations with Nissan, the latter agreed on an alliance with Renault buying 34 per cent of Nissan's shares. DaimlerChrysler started talks with Mitsubishi and finally invested in 44 per cent of Mitsubishi Motor Company's shares. We will go into more detail on these developments in the following section.

Two case-studies

As indicated in the previous section, two alliances have been selected for presentation in this chapter, that between Renault and Nissan and that between DaimlerChrysler (DC) and Mitsubishi Motor Company (MMC). Some of the reasons for selecting these two cases were mentioned earlier, but need to be elaborated on here. First, the automotive industry is a strong industry with an important home market in all four countries concerned, France, Germany, Japan and the USA, with these countries leading the car market internationally. Moreover, these two cases would seem to be important for a further consolidation of the international automotive market. In addition, public opinion is keen to get information on the speed and success of the merger process in both cases and so are internal as well as external stakeholders in the process. The respective governments will also watch closely these cases, because of the effects the restructuring process will have on the international reputation of the respective country and its industry, for example in relation to things such as the employment effects of cutting the workforce and the management qualities of the company taking over. In this sense, too, both cases give important signals to the rest of the industry and/or the economy as a whole. The impact of the activities of such renowned companies as these means that it is relatively easy to get reliable information on both cases.

Reasons for M&A

Although both the above examples belong to the same industry, and we can identify fairly similar reasons for foreign companies' investing in Japan, the reasons why these two Japanese companies became targets for take-over are actually quite different. All companies face the decision of what to produce themselves and what to buy in, and over time, as the market develops, there may be a need to change overall corporate strategy. Strategy may change in response to horizontal diversification or perhaps vertical diversification. This might in turn compel the board of the company to make a decision regarding whether to build up a new division or to co-operate with a company within the same market segment or regional market. Forms of co-operation can differ, from a limited time partnership for a specific project to a tight, formal tie between the two companies. The latter can take the form of either a merger or an acquisition.

In most cases, reasons for M&A are supposed to be strategic. What differs, of course, is the interpretation of the term 'strategic', but cases in which there is no financial necessity or pressure from the market to consolidate ('no reason' cases), such as the merger between the two Japanese steel-makers Ishikawajima and Harima in the 1960s, are an exception. In many cases at least one of the following reasons is given: (1) access to a market without making own investment, (2) cost reduction through synergy effects, (3) technology is cheaper to buy than to develop, (4) reduction of excess capacity, (5) maintenance of market dominance and (6) 'merge before being merged'. This list is not compiled in order of importance, nor is it completely comprehensive. What is of interest here is that each of the above-mentioned strategic reasons for M&A can be expected to be followed by a change in organisation. Aoki's concept, therefore, is only likely to be applicable to companies without a history of mergers.

In many cases, the companies involved talk about an 'equal partnership' when announcing a merger. However, in practice there is always a power imbalance, and equal partnership is difficult to maintain. In most cases the company with the greater financial power is going to take the lead. In the two cases presented here it was the foreign companies that were definitely the more powerful ones. The bargaining power of the Japanese companies was weak, as without an injection of fresh capital, Nissan as well as MMC would have had to exit the market.

Non-realisation of the respective 'alliances' would have led to bankruptcy.[39] However, both companies, Nissan as well as Mitsubishi Motors, had enough strategic value (and therewith bargaining power) for the foreign companies, Renault as well as DaimlerChrysler, to decide to invest good money in them.

Whether the market thought that the alliances were a good strategy or not can be judged by analysing the share prices, and this will be explored in the section on stock market evaluation. However, both alliances are still relatively recent. For a decision on how successful both alliances will be in the long run we need to wait for more time to pass. Nevertheless, what we can definitely state even after a short period of time is that both alliances have given out certain signals to the automobile industry as a whole and to other foreign companies considering the question of whether or not to acquire or merge with a Japanese partner.

The Renault–Nissan case

Nissan Motor Company's roots date back to the year 1933, and the company was re-established in 1949.[40] After the Second World War, the company was initially allowed to engage in truck production but soon turned back to car maintenance services with the support of MITI. It then came to compete with Toyota, and since the 1960s it has consistently ranked number two among Japanese car producers in terms of market share, production volume and employment. Nevertheless, from the mid-1990s Nissan was losing market share due to organisational problems within the company, including problems with its management structure. These structural problems had contributed to the building up of excess capacity and financial troubles. The Nissan management was bureaucratic and not courageous enough to push through unpleasant decisions. In 1998, Nissan faced huge losses[41] and was desperately looking for a partner. The company had to find additional financial and managerial support in order to achieve its ambitious goal of getting back into the black by 2000. With no Japanese company willing to step in to bail Nissan out, finding a foreign partner was imperative. A secondary objective which could be achieved by finding an appropriate partner would be the enlargement of Nissan's business base outside Asia and the USA. Nissan secretly started consultations with both DaimlerChrysler and Renault. Although financially with its back against the wall, Nissan insisted on forming an alliance to maintain its independence as a Japanese company, and its name as an internationally renowned brand.

As already mentioned, the negotiations with DaimlerChrysler did not work out successfully. Instead, it was Renault that in spring 1999 agreed to sign an alliance partnership with Nissan. The world had witnessed a number of international mergers just prior to this, and Renault was facing increased pressure to engage in M&A as well. The French company had enjoyed high profits, peaking at 1,337 million euros in 1998, and thus had the necessary financial reserves to invest abroad. One strategic goal was to strengthen its presence in Asia, which at that time accounted for a mere 3.4 per cent of the company's production volume (number of cars). The best way to achieve this goal was believed to be through investment in an existing company. Renault enjoyed governmental backing for such a step, which was necessary because the French state still held more than 40 per cent of the company's shares.

After ten months of consultations, the CEOs of both companies, Luis Schweitzer of Renault and Yoshikazu Hanawa of Nissan, signed the alliance agreement on 27 March 1999. The agreement provided for Renault to purchase 36.8 per cent of Nissan for 4.610 billion euros (590.7 billion yen), 22.5 per cent of Nissan Diesel and to take over 100 per cent control of the 5 Nissan financial subsidiaries in Europe.[42] The deal also resulted in a reduction of the French government's ownership in Renault from 43.8 per cent down to 37.6 per cent. In addition, the agreement included an option for Renault to increase its share in Nissan to 39.9 per cent within four years and further to 44.4 per cent in the fifth year (up to 28 May 2004). With this agreement, the third largest alliance after DaimlerChrysler and Ford–Volvo was created, and Renault–Nissan became the fourth largest car manufacturer in the world.[43]

In October 1999 the 'Nissan Revival Plan', containing the 'Core Alliance Principles', was made public. Goals included a return to the black by 2000, a profit margin of 4.5 per cent by 2002, and for the same year a reduction of the company's debt to below 700 billion yen. Although these goals seemed more than ambitious at first sight, financial success would in fact be reached as early as 2000, when Nissan's operating income reached 290 billion yen, achieving a profit margin of 4.75 per cent and reduction of the debt to 953 billion yen.

Following the agreement the company structure was changed along the following lines. First, a 'Global Alliance Committee' was created, consisting of 1 co-president and 5 executives on each side, plus 11 cross company teams and 9 functional task teams. Both companies remained more or less independent brands under a newly created headquarters called 'Renault Nissan BV Holding', with a 50 : 50 share located in the Netherlands. Renault's CEO Carlos Ghosn was appointed president, Nissan's CEO Shemaya Levy vice-president.

DaimlerChrysler–Mitsubishi Motors

MMC belongs to the Mitsubishi Group. Its car production dates back to as early as 1917. After the Second World War the Mitsubishi conglomerate (*zaibatsu*) was dismantled, and during the Allied Occupation period the car and truck producing facilities were spread over a number of group companies. This situation was maintained throughout the following years, with each plant specialising in a certain model. In the 1960s the Mitsubishi Colt proved to be so successful that there was overwhelming pressure to concentrate on automotive production, but it was not until 1970 that the group decided to form a separate Mitsubishi firm called MMC. MMC soon enjoyed an international reputation because of the Colt's success, its racing activities, and, last but not least, because of the fact that it was a member of the strong Mitsubishi group and was hence allowed to use the three-diamond Mitsubishi trade mark. The affiliation with a horizontal *keiretsu* provided the company with a number of advantages, including access to resources which enabled MMC to access the group's network for things like information, purchasing and sales. Cross-shareholding impeded hostile take-overs and preferential sales within the group provided a stable customer base. However, affiliation with a horizontal *keiretsu*, particularly the intertwining of MMC with the Mitsubishi group, could be a problem when it came to financial issues, especially as decisions could not be made independently. As a member of the Mitsubishi *keiretsu* MMC had to rely upon 'group-leaders' in making decisions on issues such as investment in a new plant.[44]

Over time competition in the domestic as well as in the foreign car market became stronger. Although belonging to a strong group meant that MMC could count on a stable inter-group business base as well as financial or managerial assistance, the company faced a number of problems from the mid-1990s. Sales and profits were declining because of problems with management, a number of coincidental circumstances led to changes in the presidency, and a sexual harassment case in an MMC plant in the USA in 1998 seriously damaged the company's reputation. When, in August 2000, it became public that MMC had not for decades reported claims from customers to the Ministry of Transport, the supervisory body in charge,[45] MMC sales and reputation dropped to a historic low. By the end of that month, the company had had to recall 200–250,000 cars. The company's problems continued, and sales and hence profits dropped further. Under the circumstances, MMC became a problem for the entire Mitsubishi group and especially for the Mitsubishi trade mark.[46]

Fortunately, DC was looking for a Japanese partner to strengthen its position in Asia and approached a number of potential partners. When Honda refused participation by DC (or any other foreign company), and the extent of Nissan's problems was revealed to be so enormous that DC's CEO Jürgen Schrempp decided to withdraw from consultations, investment in MMC was the next best opportunity for DC.

The parties were not totally unknown to each other. Chrysler, for example, had been the first company to agree on a North American–Japanese joint venture with Mitsubishi in 1971.[47] However, in the early 1990s a financially shaken Chrysler had sold all stakes in MMC and their joint venture. There had also been co-operation with the German Daimler company, in engine projects and in the aerospace division.[48] In 1999, consultations between MMC president Kawasoe Katsuhiko and DC CEO Jürgen Schrempp started in secrecy. After ten weeks, on 27 March 2000, both announced that DC would take over 34 per cent of MMC shares.[49]

DC therewith became a major shareholder with the right to nominate 3 of the 10 board members. Its presence in Asia increased from *c*.4 to 21 per cent in terms of sales volume. This was due to MMC's strategic position, including its strong dealer network within Japan, a market share of 26 per cent in ASEAN countries and of 10 per cent in the Pacific region. Supplementary or synergy effects were identified in the small car and sedan segment as well as in the mini-car segment, with MMC providing engine know-how for a future four-seater Smart Car.

Stock market evaluation

In order to be able to judge the success of both alliances, we briefly make use of stock market evaluations. Rohde convincingly concludes that in the case of

Renault–Nissan, the figures for the return on capital (ROC) which developed after the alliance had been announced were positive, at least from the second year onwards.[50] Increasing Renault ownership of the alliance partner's shares was regarded positively by the stock market, whereas a reduction of shares was seen in negative terms.

The reason for this positive stock market development was that soon after the alliance was signed a Nissan Revival Plan was announced, and it soon became clear that the goals, although ambitious, could be reached far ahead of schedule. As a consequence, Renault had already increased its stock holding ratio to 44.4 per cent on 28 February 2002, and, via capital injection, provided Nissan with as much as 15 per cent of its own shares. This latter step reduced the share of the French government in the company, which was welcomed by Renault's shareholders as well.

The second case, of DC–MMC, showed a similar positive development. The alliance of DaimlerChrysler and Mitsubishi Motors Company was made public in 2000, a year later than the Renault–Nissan alliance. Thus, in this case it may be premature to try and make any objective judgement of the return to capital. However, on a short-term perspective, MMC's shares were rising even before the alliance with DC was announced. This could mean that the shareholders anticipated and hence welcomed a potential investment. By contrast, DC did not 'lose' as much share value as might normally be expected in the case of an acquiring company. This shows that the market was not inclined to 'punish' DC for its investment in MMC.[51] However, we should keep in mind the fact that in both cases the period of PMI is still short. We need to wait for a couple of years before giving a final answer to the question of whether or not the decisions of the foreign companies to acquire their Japanese counterparts were good ones.[52]

Organisational changes

Notwithstanding the conclusion that the market evaluated both alliances positively, we still have to look at the organisational changes which the foreign firms introduced to their Japanese partners.

Renault–Nissan

In the case of the Renault–Nissan alliance, as indicated earlier, a holding company was set up in the Netherlands under the name 'Renault–Nissan B.V', in which Renault and Nissan hold equal shares.[53] Both companies exchanged 'non-executives' with the other partner in order to participate directly in daily business operations. 'At the end of 2001, 47 Renault employees had joined Nissan and 56 Nissan employees had joined Renault. In addition, a total of 250 Renault and Nissan employees were directly involved in Alliance cooperative ventures.'[54] Further, bi-national teams were formed for special tasks. Under this new umbrella both companies were able to maintain their brand names independently. Further, there are two fully owned subsidiaries called Renault–Nissan Purchasing Organization and Renault–Nissan Information Services. These were created to achieve synergy effects in both areas.

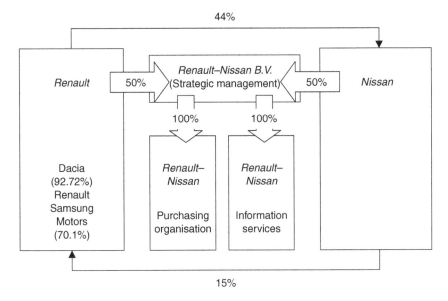

Figure 9.5 Structure of the alliance of Renault–Nissan (as of 31 December 2002).

Source: www.renault.com, Renault 2003 Atlas.

Note
The figures stand for percentage of ownership.

Thinking back again to Aoki's concept of different types of company organisation, we assume that Nissan can be labelled a 'J-firm', as Aoki himself gave the Japanese car industry as an example of this architecture.[55] Being a partly public owned company, Renault instead was a much more hierarchically organised company. Hence, with an alliance of both companies we can assume the appearance of a new type of organisation in Aoki's terms.[56] While further research is needed to confirm any conclusions, it may be suggested that the following facts point in this direction. First, when the new CEO, Carlos Ghosn, took the helm, he immediately introduced his 'turn-around plan'. This plan left Nissan as an independent brand name but with some organisational changes proceeding immediately such as streamlining of procedures, co-operation in R&D and increasing the number of parts in common. In other words, organisational changes had to take place to achieve the strategic goals and realisation of synergies in areas like product development and purchasing. Because Renault was the partner with the greater financial strength, Nissan's organisation had to adapt. The new structure of the alliance is shown in Figure 9.5.

DaimlerChrysler–Mitsubishi Motors

In the case of DaimlerChrysler and MMC, the changes in organisation were different because of the different organisational structures of both companies and the different circumstances to the Renault–Nissan case. DaimlerChrysler had just merged and were still to complete their own PMI phase. On the DC side, a holding company had already been established for the merger of Daimler and Chrysler, and MMC was simply embraced within this structure. On the other side, MMC belonged to a horizontal *keiretsu*, thus dissolution of any structures integrated with other Mitsubishi companies was more complicated. As in the Renault–Nissan case, MMC needed to remain an independent brand, too, but collaboration with DC in R&D also needed to be strengthened. Furthermore, it was also necessary to co-ordinate long run sales and purchasing. This meant that integration of operations to achieve synergies led to a number of organisational changes at MMC. As far as car operations were concerned, changes were introduced in two stages.[57] As the first step, organisation was transformed from a functional organisation with weak project teams to a cross-functional organisation that encouraged project teams. This goal was achieved by June 2001. The second step was realised one year later. Horizontally arranged 'competence centres' were set up, with project teams working in the respective centres under the leadership of a project manager. The organisational structure after the second step is shown in Figure 9.6.

In the case of the car R&D department, this concept of horizontal competence centres led to a division of R&D work by car segments. This means that one centre became responsible for small and mini-car development (so-called A and B segment), and a separate one for sedans (so-called C and D segments). Within these two centres R&D work is jointly organised and conducted with DC staff. The Recreational Vehicle (RV) Centre, by contrast, is independently run by

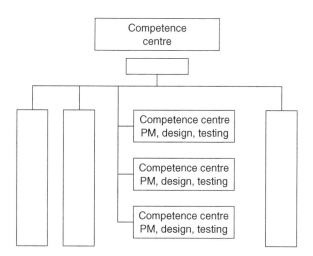

Figure 9.6 Mitsubishi Motors R&D organisation change by June 2002.

Source: http://www.mitsubishi-motors.co.jp/docs4/ir/e/other/info/product_strategy. pdf

Note
PM is project manager.

MMC. The vertical bars shown in Figure 9.6 represent an Advanced Engineering Block, a Vehicle Common Technology Block, a Powertrain Common Technology Block and a Development Support Block. The establishment of a 'research block' is also planned.

In addition to these changes in the organisation of the R&D division, changes were also implemented in the procurement division. In order to achieve cost saving by global procurement, MMC organisation was again changed to cross-functional project teams and a target system introduced. In co-operation with DC Europe and DC America, a global procurement network was established to realise consolidation of volumes. Sourcing could be done jointly to achieve cost reduction on the one hand and an increase in the ratio of common parts used on the other.

The introduction of CFT by DC was considered essential in achieving the changes that DC thought were necessary to achieve a turn-round at MMC. This raises the question, of course, of whether MMC had already used CFT before the alliance was signed. In quality terms, MMC is believed to have been at least as good as DaimlerChrysler.[58] In order to achieve good quality in production, co-operation across functions is essential, and must have been practised at MMC for some time.[59]

Another question is how far MMC fitted into Aoki's type of J-firm mentioned earlier. The company's integration with other companies as a group member of a horizontal *keiretsu* might lead to organisational differences as compared to supplier *keiretsu*. What is significant here is that being a group member makes the organisation of information processing more complicated because of the larger number of contact points to which the information has to be delivered when such information is critical for the decision-making process. Still, in comparison with other company types identified by Aoki, these differences are likely to be of minor significance in terms of information processing. Further, as a single unit MMC was also a supplier *keiretsu* and therefore we can categorise MMC as a J-firm. So, the formation of an alliance with a foreign company must have created a new organisational form in this case too.

Organisational changes

Although the circumstances surrounding both our examples are not identical, with the foreign companies coming from different national environments and the Japanese companies belonging to different *keiretsu* forms, in both cases the new organisations that have evolved since the mergers look similar. The holding structure ensures the maintenance of all brand names, and synergies are achieved by integrating R&D as well as purchasing, with the goal of increasing the share of common parts and platforms.

We saw earlier that the number of foreign companies buying into Japanese firms, and hence gaining control over organisational issues as well, has been increasing. If the number of cases reaches a significant level,[60] we may soon see a new organisational type developing. In terms of information processing, this new type is likely to be highly dependent on organisation in teams which have to be cross-cultural (both national culture and company culture) and cross-functional. The former is necessary for smooth information flow between the merging firms and the latter is necessary for smooth information flow between the divisions within the respective companies.

We need now to return to our hypothesis that if a Japanese firm adapts its company structure in the direction of the foreign buyer's structure, then differences in national cultures can be regarded a minor problem (*Hypothesis IV*). In the two cases presented here all companies are final assemblers surrounded by groups of suppliers. We find that in both cases the achievement of synergies by integration of purchasing is a major issue. An increase in parts commonality will lead to a reduction of the number of suppliers. Increasing competition with other car makers increases the competition among suppliers as well, and hence from this viewpoint supplier relations are changing too. The former *keiretsu* way of privileging long-term relations over profitability cannot be sustained under such circumstances. With ongoing *keiretsu* dissolution, supplier relations will also change, becoming closer to those adopted by the foreign companies. In this area, assimilation is already under way. In R&D, cultural differences might not be so much of an issue.[61] However, following the list of cultural differences in Table 9.1 we can identify a number of differences in dealing with people that could impede PMI. We have tended to work on the assumption that differences in national culture are likely to lead to a problem when one partner in the alliance comes from the West, and the other one from the East. However, what counts more is the objective of the merger. If survival is the first problem, everybody will strive to overcome these hurdles of company and national culture to maintain his or her own future employment.

In the two cases reviewed here, both Japanese companies had their backs against the wall. It may be suggested that the above hypothesis, on the significance of cultural differences, will hold true as long as there is no alternative solution to the merger. The real question is what happens when the Japanese companies recover. Will they still accept foreign ownership and, in a Japanese tradition of *giri* and *ninjō*,[62] never forget that they have received a helping hand in times of trouble? Or will nationalistic tendencies become stronger when financial stability returns? This will depend on management's foresight in integrating or assimilating differences or in maintaining independence where employees feel that is most appropriate.

Again, the issue for a successful merger is organisational similarity and strategic fit. A number of factors in Japanese company organisation have been identified,[63] but it is the *keiretsu* structure with its practice of cross-shareholding that has been identified as impeding (foreign) M&A. It was mentioned earlier how the lost decade caused a number of changes in the Japanese firm as well as in the structure of Japanese *keiretsu*. With increasing international competition, integration with other Japanese companies in a *keiretsu*-like structure is under review, as revealed by the dissolution of the *keiretsu*. In the case of supplier *keiretsu*, final assemblers are quite independent and are already working on streamlining their supplier base. In the case of horizontally organised *keiretsu*, integration is much broader. Grouped around a bank, these *keiretsu* face greater changes because of the changes that have been taking place in the financial sector. Further practices such as the exchange of board members, presidential meetings or preferred contracting among group members are more difficult to terminate, especially at short notice. It is these practices that make it more difficult for a Japanese company which is a member of a horizontal *keiretsu* to integrate into a foreign company (*Hypothesis V*) than for a vertical *keiretsu* or an independent Japanese firm. We predict that over time these structural differences are likely to become visible in the outcome of both the cases presented here. It may be expected that it will take DC–MMC more time to achieve success than Renault–Nissan because of the greater independence Nissan enjoys when compared with Mitsubishi Motors.

We will, however, have to wait before we can come to any convincing conclusion on the impact of national cultures on success, keeping always in mind the eagerness of many to acclaim cultural differences in case of failure. In that context, the most effective way forward must be to pursue a case-by-case analysis of differences in company cultures, rather than sweeping generalisations.

Conclusion: a model to copy

In this chapter, we have analysed how M&A have occurred in recent years involving Japanese companies. The number of OUT–IN M&A cases has been low for the reasons listed in the section on OUT-IN cases. The correlation of changes in the law with an increasing number of M&A cases, however, strongly suggests that legal constraints have been an important factor. This dismisses our first hypothesis, namely that psychological barriers in Japanese culture impeded M&A. Instead, we conclude that the steep increase in the number of cases proves that it was formal barriers in the form of legislation that were a fundamental barrier to M&A. Hence, if changes in formal institutions had such an evident result, then changes in informal institutions must already have been well under way. This proves our second hypothesis, which predicted that a change of legal institutions will increase the number of M&A cases regardless of the buyer's nationality. However, as the number of cases in Japan did not rise as high as in other industrialised countries, this suggests support for the third hypothesis, that differences in national cultures still matter. These findings lead us to agree with the findings of Jansen and Körner, and Schewe *et al.*, that organisational similarity matters,[64] and we can state that this holds true for international M&A with Japanese participation as well. However, in the case of Japan, differences in national culture seem to matter more than the findings suggest for European countries.

In addition, we find differences in company organisation among Japanese firms which have to be taken into account. Although the automobile industry can be regarded as internationally similar in terms of company organisation, there are differences between Japanese companies which may impede the success of foreign M&A. For a long time the *keiretsu* structure was identified as an important hurdle, and we considered Aoki's labelling of supplier *keiretsu* as J-firms.

However, a rising number of OUT-IN cases must necessarily have caused a change in the organisational structures of so called J-firms. When ownership shifts to a foreign company, changes in organisation are bound to follow. Hence a different type of organisation will appear that in terms of Figure 9.2 will be located in between the J-firm and more hierarchically organised firms as the G-firm, situated to their left. It must be acknowledged that a critical number has still to be reached that will allow us to define clearly the features of information flows in this new type of organisation.

In both cases presented here, a holding company forms an umbrella for the merging companies, which allows them to remain independent to a certain extent. Brand names are maintained and thus marketing will continue independently. Still, in both cases purchasing organisations have been set up jointly to reduce costs. This will result in joint product development (increasing commonality of parts) and vice versa. Thus, in terms of parts production cars will become more alike. With joint production agreements under way the same can be said for organisations. The challenge for car makers therefore will be how to continue to be able to maintain an independent identity. This can only be achieved with more distinctive differentiation, which will appear in the organisation through a separation of the whole development and production process by car segment, as shown by the introduction of competence centres in the case of DC–MMC.

The most important reason why both models are likely to be emulated is the fact that in both cases the respective companies were organised under the umbrella of a holding company, a legal form of organisation that has only recently been again permitted in Japan. In this context one issue which will take more time to change will be Japanese board practices, in terms of both targets and institutional investors. Nevertheless, with a rising number of foreign companies buying into Japanese counterparts we can be sure that a new kind of organisation will be born. For this to happen, however, we must look to a further increase in the number of OUT-IN cases in the future, which will enable the creation of a stable environment in which this new organisational type of company can firmly establish itself. Allowing for the fact that the cases presented here are still from the recent past, our findings tend to support our fifth hypothesis, namely that because of the intensity of existing first relationships, buying into a company that is part of a horizontal *keiretsu* brings with it more complications than buying into the more independent supplier *keiretsu* or completely independent companies. However, as described in the two sections on case-studies and organisational changes, both alliances have been quite successful in terms of market acceptance by internal and external stakeholders and in terms of realising the objectives of turning around the companies (most of them on schedule, some even ahead of schedule). As a consequence, public opinion has been favourable concerning both alliances. This is particularly important in the light of the view that psychological barriers are likely to result in most M&As in Japan being failures. Reducing this negative psychological barrier could be a positive signal for other companies to become more active in acquiring businesses in Japan.

Notes

1 Stephan A. Jansen and Klaus Körner, *Fusionsmanagement in Deutschland – Eine empirische Analyse von 103 Zusammenschlüssen mit deutscher Beteiligung zwischen 1994 und 1998 unter spezifischer Auswertung der Erfolgswirkungen des Typus der Fusion, der (Inter-)Nationalität, der Branche und der Unternehmensgröße* (University of Witten/Herdecke Discussion Paper, April 2000), pp. 2–3. On the importance of culture in M&A, see also the 7-K Model of Stephan A. Jansen *Internationales Fusionsmanagement: Erfolgsfaktoren grenzüberschreitender Unternehmenszusammenschlüsse* (Stuttgart: Schäffer Poeschel Verlag, 2000), p. 4. For culture as one of the factors influencing costs of integration, see also Pascal Clerc, 'Managing the Cultural Issue of Merger and Acquisition: the Renault–Nissan case' (1999 Master thesis available at http://www.handels.gu.se/epc/archive/ 00001319/01/ Clerc_1999_32_inlaga.pdf, accessed February 2004), p. 31. Both are also quoted in Marco Böhmer and Jörg Hübner, 'Nationales Image und Philosophie in Japan', in Sigrun Caspary, Kazuma Matoba and Dirk Schierek, *Mergers and Acquisitions in der japanischen Automobilindustrie* 2 (*Wittener diskussionspapiere* no. 124, May 2003), pp. 41–43. See also Gerhard Schewe and Johannes Gerds, 'Studie zum MPI-Management: Erste empirische Ergebnisse', *Arbeitspapiere des Lehrstuhls für Betriebswirtschaftsehre, insb. Organisation, Personal und Innovation der Westfälischen Wilhelms-Universität Münster* 11, 2000, p. 15.
2 See http://www.recof.co.jp/web/fm/graph and http://www.jetro.go.jp/en/invest/ whyjapan/advantage/10a_6.html
3 'According to the Japanese Ministry of Finance (MOF) and the Legal Affairs Bureau (the Ministry of Justice department responsible for keeping the companies register), it seems that it would be against the spirit of the law to permit a Japanese corporation to engage in such businesses as selling its own assets or other corporations' (Clerc, 'Managing the Cultural Issue of Merger and Acquisition', p. 1. Clerc refers to the work of Kanji Ishizumi, *Acquiring Japanese Companies* (Oxford: Basil Blackwell, 1990). See also Yoshio Sugimoto, *An Introduction to Japanese Society* (2nd edn, Cambridge: Cambridge University Press, 2003), pp. 3–5.
4 Among the classic readings on Japanese companies (lifelong employment, seniority based wages, company-wise organised trade unions) are Ronald Dore, *British Factory, Japanese Factory* (Los Angeles, CA: University of California Press, 1973); Rodney Clark, *The Japanese Company* (New Haven, CT and London: Yale University Press, 1979); James C. Abegglen and George Stalk Jr, *Kaisha: The Japanese Corporation* (Tokyo: Charles E. Tuttle, 1985); Noboru Yoshimura and Philip Anderson, *Inside the Kaisha: Demystifying Japanese Business Behavior* (Boston, MA: Harvard Business School Press, 1997), p. 2; Clerc, 'Managing the Cultural Issue', p. 1; and Ikujiro Nonaka and Hirotaka Takeuchi, *The Knowledge Creating Company: How Japanese Companies Create the Dynamics of Innovation* (Oxford: Oxford University Press, 1995), p. 125ff.
5 Masahiko Aoki, *Toward a Comparative Institutional Analysis* (Cambridge, MA: MIT Press, 2001).
6 MMC itself is a supplier *keiretsu*, but the company also belongs to the Mitsubishi group, a horizontal *keiretsu*.
7 Jansen and Körner, *Fusionsmanagement in Deutschland*.
8 For the importance of information and communication within the merging companies as well as with external stakeholders, refer to Gerhard Schewe, Claudia Michalik and Christian Hendtker, 'Kommuniaktionsgestaltung bei Post Merger Integration', *Arbeitspapiere des Lehrstuhls für Betriebswirtschaftslehre, insb.Organisation, Personal und Unnovation der Westfälischen Wilhelms-Universität Münster* 8, 2003, p. 17.
9 For a description of *keiretsu* characteristics, see for example Michael Gerlach, *Alliance Capitalism: The Social Organisation of Japanese Business* (Berkeley, CA: University

of California Press, 1992), p. 103ff; or Yishay Yafeh, 'Japan's Corporate Groups: Some International and Historical Perspectives', Dept of Economics, The Hebrew University, February 2002 (http://www.nber.org/~confer/2002/struct02/yafeh.pdf), p. 2ff. See also Moerke's chapter in this volume.

10 For details see H. Richard Nakamura, 'Preliminary Report on the Current State of Mergers and Acquisitions in Japan'. *European Institute of Japanese Studies Working Paper* no. 140, Stockholm, January 2002, p. 2ff; (http://www5.cao.go.jp/access/english/jic/19960426b-jic-e.html, accessed February 2004).

11 Quoted from www5.cao.go.jp/keizai1/2002/112tainichi/1121item1-e.pdf, accessed February 2004.

12 A discussion on 'Japaneseness' (*Nihonjinron*) is beyond our scope here. Sugimoto, *Introduction to Japanese Society*, pp. 28–30, gives a good summary on the 'double codes' of *tatemae-honne, ura-omote* and *uchi-soto*. For the impact of ideology on *Nihonjinron*, see Nagao Nishikawa, 'Two Interpretations of Japanese Culture', in Donald Denoon, Mark Hudson, Gavan McCormack and Tessa Morris Suzuki (eds), *Multicultural Japan: Palaeolithic to Postmodern* (Cambridge: Cambridge University Press, 2001), pp. 246–48.

13 In Japan, there was only one case which at the time attracted a lot of attention because of its rarity: the American T. Boone Pickens in the late 1980s surprised Japanese and international investors by becoming a major shareholder in Koito Manufacturing through purchasing stocks in the market (Robert A.G. Monks of Japan Investor Relations Association, Tokyo, 2 November 1994 (http://www.lens-library.com/info/viner.html)).

14 Yoshimura and Anderson, *Inside the Kaisha*, p. 76.

15 Gerlach, *Alliance Capitalism*, pp. 180–81.

16 See the chapters by Suzuki and Krawczyk in this volume.

17 'M&A is the only mechanism by which Japan can hope to achieve significant and stable increases in FDI' (www5.cao.go.jp/keizai1/2002/112tainichi/1121item1-e.pdf, accessed February 2004). See also www.investment-japan.net/statements/files/19960426-2.htm

18 http://www3.jetro.go.jp/iv/cybermall/whyjapan/faq1.html, accessed February 2004. The same source comes to the conclusion that '(t)he steady increase in foreign direct investment inflows into Japan is primarily the result of three interrelated trends: globalization, the rapid pace of technological change and deregulation and regulatory reforms in Japan'.

19 In the case of the German firm BMW buying into British Rover in 1996, in the UK the public feared another 'Third Reich invasion', whereas Rover employees welcomed the merger as a workplace guarantee (Schewe *et al.*, 'Kommuniaktionsgestaltung bei Post Merger Integration', pp. 5, 16).

20 Aoki, *Toward a Comparative Institutional Analysis*.

21 'Any organizational architecture fundamentally exhibits a hierarchical structure in the way in which interrelated activities are modularized into disparate task units.'(p. 98).

22 Ibid., p. 113.

23 Ibid., p. 112.

24 Ibid., pp. 114–15.

25 This assumption is supported by Sven Eppert, 'Compare the Two Mergers: Daimler–Chrysler and Renault–Nissan: Any Implications for the IMGT Framework?' 2003, (available on http://www/sven-eppert.de/downloads/daimler-chrysler_nissan-renault.pdf, accessed February 2004), p. 4, who claims that cultural differences meant that the merger did not turn out equal. With Daimler dominating the management, the structure and spirit of DaimlerChrysler's decision-making process can be labelled 'German'.

26 A definitive conclusion on this requires further research, but this requires the collection of further information from inside the respective companies and is ongoing.

27 Nonaka and Takeuchi list a number of cases; among them Nissan's Primera Project (*The Knowledge Creating Company*, pp. 206–07).

28 MIT conducted a survey on the success of Japanese companies in the automotive and electronic industry pointing out the important role of CFT, which resulted in the publication of the best-seller, James P. Womack, Daniel T. Jones and Daniel Roos, *The Machine that Changed the World*. I have used the German translation, *Die zweite Revolution in der Automobilindustrie: Konsequenzen aus der weltweiten Studie des Massachusetts Institute of Technology* (Frankfurt: Campus Verlag, 1991). See especially pp. 119–20 on team work, p.124 on transfer of practices from Nissan Japan to Europe and the USA.

29 Http://www.jetro.go.jp/en/invest/whyjapan/advantage/10a_6.html, accessed February 2004.

30 See Schewe *et al.*, 'Kommuniaktionsgestaltung bei Post Merger Integration', p. 1. Christoph Jakob ('Die Entwicklung des Weltautomobilmarktes seit 1985', in Caspary, Matoba and Schierek (eds), *Mergers and Acquisitions in der japanischen Automobilindustrie*, pp. 9–11) believes that the DaimlerChrysler merger marks the peak of the last wave of M&A activity in the global car industry.

31 For further reading on changes in the production philosophy from 'Fordism' to 'Toyotism' or 'mass production' to 'lean production', see for example Womack *et al.*, *Die zweite Revolution*; for an explanation of the latter see Ōno, Taiichi, *Toyota Seisan Hōshiki – Datsu Kibō no Keiei o mezashite* (Tokyo: Daiyamondo, 1978, repr. 1998) or Imai, Masaaki, *Kaizen: der Schlüssel zum Erfolg der Japaner im Wettbewerb* (Berlin: Ullstein, 1998).

32 Sigrun Caspary, 'Wirtschaft und Automobilindustrie in Japan', in Caspary *et al.*, *Mergers and Acquisitions in der japanischen Automobilindustrie*, p. 19.

33 Because of space constraints, trucks are not included here.

34 For details, see for example Sigrun Caspary, 'Zur Management-Struktur japanischer Grossunternehmen', and Caspary, 'Wirtschaft und Automobilindustrie in Japan', both in Caspary *et al.*, *Mergers and Acquisitions in der japanischen Automobilindustrie*; Akira Kawahara, *The Origin of Competitive Strength: Fifty Years of the Auto Industry in Japan and the US* (self-published, 1997); or Hiromichi Mutoh, 'The Automotive Industry', in Ryutaro Komiya, Masahiro Okuno and Kotaro Suzumura (eds), *Industrial Policy of Japan* (Tokyo: Academic Press, 1988).

35 With the exception of VW in China, it was almost only Japanese companies that heavily invested in production facilities in Asian countries. See Matthias Fechner, 'Der Marktauftritt der japanischen Automobilhersteller in Südostasien, 2000 (http://webdoc.sub.gwdg.de/diss/2000/fechner/fechner.pdf), p. 27f. The investment in production facilities in Europe was believed necessary with the European decision to form a unified market within the European Union in 1992 and hence to increase requirements for local content (see, for example Japanologisches Seminar, Universität Bonn (ed.), 'The EC Common Market and the Japanese Trade and Industries: 8 Case Studies of Japanese Enterprises in Germany', *Occasional Paper* 1, May 1991.

36 Quoted from http://www.nummi.com/co_info.html; on the success of NUMMI see also JAMA, *The Motor Industry of Japan*, 2002, (www.jama.org/library/brochures2002MIJReport.pdf, accessed February 2004), pp. 17–19, and Toshihiro Nishiguchi, 'Beyond the Honeymoon Effect', in *INSEAT Information*, Summer 1991, pp. 8–9. Here, team-work of course includes CFT.

37 As mentioned earlier, other analysts view the BMW-Rover case of 1994 as a turning point when a number of companies realised that they could be take-over targets.

38 For details and development since 1985 see Jakob, 'Die Entwicklung des Weltautomobilmarktes seit 1985', p. 11ff.

39 It is unclear whether the Japanese government would have been pushed to intervene if one of these companies had had to announce its bankruptcy, because Nissan as well as

Mitsubishi are renowned companies and thus too important for the economy and the nation as a whole to let them disappear.

40 Unlike Mitsubishi, Nissan was one of the 'new *zaibatsu*'. For details on the company's history see http://www.nissan-global.com/EN/DOCUMENT/PDF/FF/2003/ff2003_ 21.pdf, accessed February 2004; www.nissanmotors.com, http://www.nissan. co.jp/ALLIANCE/alliance-e.html, accessed February 2004; or Ivonne Rohde, 'Der Hahn im Reisfeld: die Allianz zwischen Renault und Nissan, in Caspary *et al., Mergers and Acquisitions in der japanischen Automobilindustrie*, p. 43ff.

41 Figures vary from 20 to 32 billion yen. See Rohde. 'Der Hahn im Reisfeld', p. 48. The true amount will be hard to bring to light, partly because of the different accounting standard in Japan.

42 Located in Germany, Italy, the UK, Spain and the Netherlands, the Nissan financial subsidiaries were 'established . . . (i) to improve the financial efficiency of the Nissan Group by centrally controlling the raising and deployment of funds for the Parent's subsidiaries and affiliates in Europe; and (ii) to supplement the financial operations of Nissan's head office by directly approaching the European financial markets' (http://www.nissan-global.com/EN/DOCUMENT/PDF/EMNT/2004/emnt_ program_05.pdf, accessed February 2004).

43 Rohde, 'Der Hahn im Reisfeld', p. 53ff.

44 'Group-leaders' here means the so called 'go-san-ke', the three presidents of Mitsubishi Heavy Industries, Mitsubishi Bank (now Bank of Tokyo Mitsubishi) and Mitsubishi Trading Company. For details, see for example Sankei Shinbun, *Burando wa naze Ochita ka: Yukijirushi, Sōgō, Mitsubishi Jidōsha Jiken no Saizō* (Tokyo: Kadokawa Shoten, 2001), p. 216.

45 'Mitsubishi said it hid complaints from car owners and information on possible defects that it was supposed to report to the Japanese government. The company also said it had secretly recalled and fixed several models without telling the ministry as required' (http://www.financialexpress.com/fe/daily/20000824/fco24065.html, accessed February 2004).

46 Sankei Shinbun, 'Burando wa naze Ochita ka', p. 211ff.

47 Chrysler bought 15 per cent of MMC, and Mitsubishi produced Dodge Colt and Plymouth for Chrysler; in 1978 a contract to buy a million MMC small engines for Chrysler's K-series was signed. When Chrysler's financial crisis deepened during the mid-1980s, MMC provided the company with credit to maintain production.

48 This collaboration was in the context of MMC being part of the Mitsubishi Group. Since the late 1980s the aerospace division of the then Daimler Benz AG had been engaged in consultations on a partnership with the aerospace division of Mitsubishi Heavy Industries. For various reasons, however, this did not turn out to be permanent co-operation. See also Clerc, *Managing the Cultural Issue of Merger and Acquisition*, p. 17ff.

49 The price of 450 yen per share was 50 per cent higher than the previous day's stock market price of 243.2 yen. At the same time, a capital increase of 51.1 per cent was agreed on, and DC bought 500 million new shares. Hence, the total price for the whole package was around 2.1 billion euro (David Klett, 'Zuwachs für die Hochzeit im Himmel: DaimlerChrysler AG und Mitsubishi Motor Company', in Caspary *et al., Mergers and Acquisitions in der japanischen Automobilindustrie*, p. 81ff).

50 Rohde, 'Der Hahn im Reisfeld', p. 55ff.

51 Klett, 'Zuwachs für die Hochzeit im Himmel', p. 81ff.

52 In the case of BMW-Rover it took the German luxury car maker six years from the acquisition (1994) to come to the conclusion that the deal could never be success-ful. When BMW finally sold the 'English patient' in 2000, its share price rose by 30 per cent. For more details, see http://www.automobear.com/PDFs/(AutomoBear) %20The%20BMW-Rover%20story.pdf, accessed February 2004.

53 BV is *besloten vennootschap met beperkte aansprakelijkheid* (private company with limited liability). The Renault group includes Renault, Dacia (92.72 per cent held by Renault) and Samsung Motors (70.1 per cent).

54 *Renault 2002 Atlas* (http://www.renault.com/docs/atlas_gb/2002/atlas_2002_gb.pdf, accessed February 2004).

55 Aoki, *Toward a Comparative Institutional Analysis*, p. 116. Details on the organisation of product development at Nissan are given by Nonaka and Takeuchi (*The Knowledge Creating Company*, p. 200ff). They show that CFT were common practice in product development from the mid-1980s.

56 Research on this specific issue is ongoing.

57 The following information is mainly extracted from a joint presentation made on 6 December 2002, by Ulrich Walker, Executive Vice President, Car Product Operations, Kai-Uwe Seidenfuss, Car Product Planning and Product Management Office, and Akira Kijima, Car Research and Development Office (http://www.mitsubishi-motors.co.jp/docs4/ir/e/other/info/product_strategy.pdf, accessed February 2004).

58 Insiders believe the production quality of MMC superior to that of DC, see for example Tokudaiji, Atsutane, *Jidōsha Sangyō Shinkaron: Nissan Kakumei ga Kaeta Mēkātachi no Sekai Senryaku* (Tokyo: Kōbunsha, 2001), pp. 192–93.

59 In an interview with a manager from the aerospace division of MHI in Ōe plant in March 1996, the author was told that the lean production method was copied from the *keiretsu*'s car production. Lean production including cross-functional research and development was practised at MMC.

60 We agree that it is not easy to figure out the number of cases necessary to produce a new type of organisation. Assuming that the number of *keiretsu* companies is high enough for the creation of a type (Aoki), a critical number may be reached when about 5–10 per cent of *keiretsu* have agreed on foreign participation. With increasing M&A among *keiretsu* groups, the absolute number of new-type companies will become lower.

61 There are national differences in the way of doing research as well. For example, Boeing engineers working on the development of the 777 admitted that they were shaking their heads at watching their Japanese counterparts in Seattle being able to continue the work of their colleagues located in Japan overnight using time difference in both locations to speed up operations. 'We never could do that. They must be able to look into the others' heads.' (interview with the author in June 1995). Another example would be the acknowledgement of differences between German and Indian engineers in the logic of software development, as a Siemens manager revealed to the author in May 2000.

62 *Giri* means 'obligation/bound in honour' and *ninjō* means 'human feelings' with both being central to the concept of the samurai's 'culture of honour' which shaped Japanese society. See for example Eiko Ikegami, *The Taming of the Samurai: Honorific Individualism and the Making of Modern Japan* (Cambridge: Cambridge University Press, 1995), p. 22.

63 Other characteristics of Japanese companies are lifelong employment, seniority based wages and company-based trade unions. These institutions are changing as well.

64 Jansen and Körner, *Fusionsmanagement in Deutschland*; Schewe *et al.*, 'Kommuniaktionsgestaltung bei Post Merger Integration'.

10 Environmental protection and the impact of institutional changes in Japan[1]

Ilona Koester

Introduction

There are many books and papers dealing with environmental problems and economic policy in Japan. Depending on the viewpoint of the author, the Japanese policy is either a near-miracle of support for industrial growth or a nightmare of environmental neglect. But – to my limited knowledge – no one has put the crucial question concerning environmental policy in Japan, that is, why does it work at all? Environmental theory is a fairly well-developed branch of economic theory as a whole and has established a set of trusted instruments for the alteration of industrial outcomes in order to protect the environment. A close look at the Japanese situation shows that Japanese regulation often does not follow the established counsel of economic theory. On many occasions it even contradicts the orthodox economic modelling. This allows only one conclusion, namely that there have to be important factors that go beyond the usual reasoning. In this chapter I argue that informal institutions have up to now played an important role in enabling the Japanese bureaucracy to achieve a sufficient extent of environmental protection. This dependence on mechanisms unexplained by neoclassical economic theory has meant that there has been little need for the political instruments considered necessary in many foreign countries such as Germany. As a result, those 'classical' instruments remain underdeveloped in Japan. I further propose that the incipient change of these informal institutions endangers the quality of environmental protection in Japan because of the lack of culturally embedded alternatives. Deregulation has become a widespread topic of political initiatives in Japan. This deregulation often means that the overwhelming power of Japanese bureaucrats has to be reduced and the reliability of regulation has to be created by strengthening written law and reducing the scope and importance of administrative guidance. This is because so-called arbitrary decisions by central and local officials are considered a cost factor for the economy according to the neo-liberal credo. In the field of environmental protection this institutional change may well turn out to be fatal.

In order to prove my propositions, I will start by giving an overview of the ideas governing the neoclassical approach to environmental problems. For readers unfamiliar with environmental economics, I will put special emphasis on the instruments discussed in this branch of economic theory and also sum up the points in favour of and against each of these instruments. This discussion will constitute the basis for the later analysis. As a next step I will introduce some of the results from my field studies undertaken in Japan during 1999 and 2000. Because this material is mostly based on interviews with environmental experts, it has not been previously available in written form in English. Water pollution control in Japan will be taken as a case study in this paper, because it offers a good example to illustrate the points that need to be made. This case study will first be analysed in the light of orthodox environmental theory which will show that social institutions play a crucial role in explaining the efficiency of environmental policy in Japan. It is the use of these informal institutions that enables Japanese officials to alter cost–benefit expectations concerning environmental protection activities for Japanese industry. It will be concluded that the outcome of administrative guidance cannot be explained on any other basis than the existence and usage of social institutions. It is this that leads to the above-mentioned assumptions concerning the direction of institutional change in the field of environmental protection in Japan. On this basis it becomes possible to assess the impact of institutional change on the future prospects of environmental policy in Japan, which I will do in the last part of this chapter.

Environmental protection – the neoclassical approach

Nature as a public good

Standard economic theory addresses the environmental issue as a cost problem.[2] Resources for production are usually costly so is the disposal of waste in any form – solid, liquid and gaseous. Under circumstances of perfect competition, production costs determine the price of a certain good, and the price determines the demand. If producers can avert some of the production costs, for example, by disposing of their waste into nature or by using natural resources for free, the price of the market good is lower than it should be and consumption is higher. Economists refer to this underlying phenomenon as a negative externality. Producers and consumers do not carry all the costs connected to a product in this case. Society as a whole, or some third person, has to pay for the disadvantages that derive from the environmentally harmful activity. This payment can take the form of actual monetary transfers (if, for example, the government pays for the restoration of historic buildings damaged by acid rain) or missed opportunities (if a river cannot be used for recreational activities any longer). The term external costs is often used because of these payments.[3]

Basically nature and its many services can be used by everybody without any charge and without loss in opportunities for further usage by other persons. Goods characterized by this non-rivalry in consumption are classified as public goods. The other criterion for public goods is the fact that nobody can be excluded from their usage. Air is a good example of such a public good. Under normal circumstances everybody breathes, uses oxygen for combustion, or disposes of exhausts into the atmosphere. The breathing of one person does no harm to the breathing possibilities of any other person, and nobody can be excluded from breathing (again, under normal circumstances). However, if many factories and cars emit more and more exhaust gases, the atmosphere's carrying capacity for pollutants becomes more and more stressed and eventually might even break down. The costs of this pollution will come down on everybody who needs fresh air, and the society as a whole pays for side effects such as dying forests, deteriorating public and historic buildings and rising health care costs. Individuals pay in the form of increasing respiratory diseases and so on.

The problem of public goods lies in the fact that it is economically rational on an individual basis to use as much of them as possible whenever they are a substitute for other costly resources. This excessive usage ultimately results in the damaging or destruction of the public good.[4] As a consequence, usage of the public good has to be limited or restricted to some extent. It is normally only in very small and closed communities that an agreement is reached upon by spontaneous and independent cooperation. As soon as the relevant group exceeds the limits of repeated face-to-face contact the situation becomes problematic, as indicated by the so-called prisoner's dilemma in game theory. A prisoner's dilemma can be described as a situation in which individual and total (or social) benefit are highly dependent on cooperation (Table 10.1). If everybody cooperates the social benefit is maximized. If, on the other hand, one of the parties chooses defection over cooperation that player maximizes his or her individual benefit, while the others end up in the worst possible outcome. As every player wants to be in the superior position nobody cooperates and the social benefit is minimized.

Situation   Each country (A and B) in Table 10.1 is free to decide whether to act solely to its own advantage (defection) or to contribute to a globally beneficial outcome (cooperation). Noted are the pay-offs for each possible outcome.

The same kind of pay-off chart as in Table 10.1 is often used to describe the situation in environmental protection. The trade-off between environmental goals and economic welfare is the reason behind the difficulties in global environmental protection.[5] However, even in a national or even local framework situations similar to the prisoner's dilemma quite often arise and usually require some kind of regulation by a governing institution if they are to be solved.[6] In order to achieve

Table 10.1 The typical prisoner's dilemma

	Defection		Cooperation	
	Country A	Country B	Country A	Country B
Defection	2	2	10	1
Cooperation	1	10	8	8

a reduction in emissions a number of instruments are discussed by economic scientists and politicians.

Instruments for emission reduction

Because of the basic principle of nature being a public good described in the previous section, most political instruments aim at the internalisation of external costs. This means they put additional costs on environmentally harmful production or consumption.[7] This can be done through regulation, special ecological taxes or tradable emission permits (Table 10.2). Regulation can be shaped in the form of obligations to use certain technologies, for example to treat wastes or exhaust gases, or as limits concerning the amount and/or the composition of emissions. Economists consider especially the first alternative to be highly inefficient in economic terms. In this case the companies do not have much freedom to adapt to environmental standards according to their own technological and economic needs, which creates unnecessary high costs. Furthermore government officials have to keep track of technological developments to decide upon the 'current state of the art' of emission reduction technology, because this becomes the standard of judgement whether or not a production unit is obliged to use it by law. If, on the contrary, emission limits are set, companies can decide upon the way in which they are going to comply with those limits on their own. This creates at least some dynamic incentives for technological development, because suppliers of environmental technology can compete on purchasing or running costs. In both cases the reduction of emissions ceases the moment the governmental regulations are fulfilled. For this reason politicians often prefer ecological taxes in order to ensure continuous relief for the environment. As a result, the German social democratic government has introduced ecological taxes on the use of fossil energy. Reactions to this step show one problem that all kinds of taxation and regulation have in common. They put a burden on national competitiveness, and multinational enterprises in particular are tempted to blackmail governments to lower taxes – or alleviate the burden in some way, threatening otherwise to shift jobs abroad. At least taxation gives the company the freedom not only to pick an appropriate environmental technology but also to choose an economically rational mix of emission reduction and tax payment.[8] The dynamic incentives for technological development can be strengthened further by the use of tradable emission permits, and it can be ensured that investments in order to reduce emissions are carried out by those companies best suited for the task (best allocation).[9] On a national or even international scale the overall costs of environmental protection are thus minimal.

The instruments of environmental policy all follow the neoclassical theory and mostly put a burden on producers or consumers. Because of the political problems relating to measures that can damage economic growth, instruments aimed at lowering the costs of environmental protection have also been discussed, with subsidies being the most prominent. In theory the effect of taxation and subsidies should be the same, but experience shows that this is not the case. Companies

Table 10.2 Instruments for environmental policy – pros and cons

Name and description	Advantages	Disadvantages
Regulation: orders and prohibitions • Limits to emissions • Prohibitions of production and so on	• Fixed amount of emission reduction • Clear-cut standards for official controls of emissions	• Difficulties in determining optimal emissions • High costs of bureaucracy • Few dynamic incentives for development • Bad allocation
Regulation: prescribed technology • Certain technologies have to be used	• Technologies can be specifically targeted	• High costs of bureaucracy • No dynamic incentives • No choice of action for the companies • Bad allocation
Ecologic taxation • Taxes harmful activities • Optimal taxation according to Pigou	• Broad liberty of action for the companies • Good allocation • Normative foundation: responsibility principle	• Difficult assessment of optimal taxation • High costs of bureaucracy • Resistance of producers and consumers
Tradable emission permits	• Best allocation • Dynamic incentives for technology development and further emission reduction	• High costs of official controls • High financial burdens for certain industries • Risk of local emission concentration
Subsidies • Subsidies up to the amount of external costs	• No burden on enterprises	• Very unclear amount of emission reduction • High budgetary burden • Normative problems
Support for R&D • Subsidies for R&D concerning environmental technology	• No burden for enterprises • Supports for developing new industries and technologies	• Very unclear amount of emission reduction • Only vague connection between R&D and the actual implementation of new technologies
Liability • Lawsuits for appropriate compensation, adjustment of insurance premiums according to risks	• Economically rational because of the careful fixing of insurance premiums • Limited bureaucracy • Broad freedom of action for the companies	• Large numbers of lawsuits • Problems of evidence • Uncertainty among companies • Difficulties in attributing damages to emitting plants (especially in the case of global problems)

Source: Compiled from Xepapadeas, *Advanced Principle in Environmental Policy*, supplemented by the author.

often just take the subsidy for investment projects that they would be carrying out anyway. There is no inevitable connection between subsidies and a measurable reduction of emissions.[10] Moreover, it is quite difficult to explain to taxpayers why they should compensate companies for reducing their pollution. There are even problems with agreements on international tariffs that can derive from subsidies (e.g. according to GATT or inside the EU). Normally this can be avoided if the subsidies are connected to technology promotion, but the connection of R&D and emission reduction is even weaker than in the case of subsidies for investments. If firms do not buy and use environmental technology there is no use of developing it.

The last instrument discussed here is liability.[11] There are some points in favour of liability in order to enforce environmental protection. Not much bureaucracy is required for it. There are no officials adjusting or controlling emission limits, only courts where victims can sue offenders. In order to protect their companies against enormous compensation claims managers would be most likely to obtain insurance. If those premiums are adjusted carefully by environmental experts they are likely to reflect risks quite accurately, so that enterprises would be interested in reducing pollution in order to decrease insurance payments. This system, however, also has its difficulties. It works properly only if the victims are able to establish the responsibility of certain polluting companies, and such proof is difficult to come by, especially in the case of global pollution, when many emission sources contribute to a single problem. Moreover, there is the matter of uncertainty on the side of the producers about the amount of compensation to be paid.[12] For example, a German or Japanese enterprise is simply unable to pay levels of compensation quite common in the USA because it is not prepared for such a situation. For these reasons liability is a good instrument to fill the gaps left by other regulatory approaches but should not be used as a main pillar of environmental protection.

In concluding this overview of the instruments for environmental policy, however, it should be noted that in the end it is up to political traditions and the personal preferences of policymakers which instruments are most heavily used, as will be shown in the remainder of this chapter.

Preferences for political instruments in Germany and Japan

Germany's philosophy of sustainability explicitly states the aim of combining economic welfare in a social market economy and responsibility for creation.[13] The principles of precaution and responsibility for damage caused govern the decision making. Therefore a mix of all the instruments mentioned above is used, with a preference for those instruments that at least in theory provide dynamic incentives for further emission reduction and technological development. Whenever feasible, ecological taxation is used, and the German government is almost on the verge of introducing tradable emission permits now. Many emission limits and standards considered essential for human health and the preservation of nature are enforced by controls and fines, up to temporary shut-downs of production. Wherever possible prescribing technological components is avoided because of its bad effects on allocation and technological development. Subsidies for the use of environmentally friendly products are often directed towards private households, and R&D in the field of the environment is subsidized in various forms (such as tax exclusions, transfers, funding of research facilities). Liability is used only as an option of last resort in order to close the gaps left by the other instruments. All these activities put together show that the German government has a vital interest in environmental issues and is acting according to the prescriptions of environmental economy as a branch of neoclassic modelling.

The situation in Japan is completely different. In fact at first sight it is difficult to determine much environmental policy at all. The year 1992 marks one turning point in environmental protection in Japan, as in this year the basic principles of environmental policy were laid down in the Environmental Basic Law (*Kankyō Kihon Hō*). In spite of many discussions in advance, concerning, for example, whether citizens should be given an enforceable right to enjoy nature, no such ideas were included in the final version.[14] In the Environmental Basic Law as much as in everyday policy there is only one principle recognizable. That is: *What has to be done in order to protect human life and health has to be done. Otherwise economic interests have precedence.*[15]

If we take a closer look at the various instruments for environmental policy in Japan, not one of them is used in a particularly distinct fashion. There are a growing number of laws dealing with environmental issues, but typically there are only a few emission standards or other orders stated in these laws or the decrees connected with them. Laws are commonly only understood as declarations of intent to show that the government is interested in finding solutions for the relevant problems.[16] Interestingly enough, the Japanese bureaucracy quite often uses prescribed technologies in order to protect the environment, although this instrument is most heavily discredited in economic theory. Ecological taxation or even tradable emission permits have been discussed, especially in the former Environmental Agency (*Kankyō Chō*), but realizing their implementation was never considered in earnest at least up to the present.[17] Surprisingly, subsidies never played a major role in environmental policy either, as the budget of the central government for economic policy shows. Payments are concentrated on R&D projects of major companies, and even in this case, the total amount of funding cannot be considered as the outcome of political influence on environmental protection activities.[18] Certainly, liability cannot be considered to be a very effective tool for environmental protection in Japan if we look at the aftermath of the Minamata case.[19] Policy-makers seemed to be at least as much concerned for the survival of the pollution-generating enterprise as for the compensation of the victims. As a result the company still exists but under a different name. Today it operates in the field of environmental technology[20] among other businesses.

In concluding this section, it can be deduced that Japanese policymakers have virtually no preferences for specific environmental policy instruments or the ideologies for evaluating them. In fact it is difficult for a traditional Western economist to understand how and why the Japanese environmental policy works at all. In order to explain the effectiveness of Japanese policy, we will have a closer look at two case studies in the next sections.

Case study on environmental protection in Japan and its interpretation

Policy for water pollution protection

The main guidelines for the protection of surface (and underground) water quality are laid down in the Law for the Prevention of the Deterioration of Water Quality (*Suishitsu o daku Bōshi Hō*) which fixes the circumstances under which waste water can be emitted in so-called public water usage areas (which consist of virtually every water body except the public sewers). Its main purpose is to prevent the contamination of water resources with pollutants that are hazardous for human health or which are carcinogenic. Especially substances that accumulate in the human body are targeted here because of the disastrous experiences in Japan in the past. For this reason the law relies upon quality standards for water bodies. These standards can be divided roughly into two groups. First of all there are standards with respect to human health (*kenkō kōmoku*). These were decided upon in 1970–71, with small modifications in 1975 and 1993. The list contains 23 substances such as lead, PCB or arsenic which are considered highly dangerous for human life[21] and is (since 1993) consistent with the recommendations made by the UN.[22] The second group of standards is concerned with the preservation of natural living space (*seikatsu kankyō kōmoku*) and includes important biological indicators such as pH, biological oxygen demand (BOD) or oxygen concentration. In recent years, because of the algae problem in coastal regions of Japan, phosphorus and nitrogen compounds tend to be included as well. These standards depend on the existing usages of the respective water bodies. If, for example, a river is used for the production of drinking water or fish-hatching, it will be assigned a higher standard than another one which is only used for industrial purposes.[23]

The interesting part of Japanese policy for the protection of water quality is the way the standards are enforced among the industry. This, again, is quite a confusing subject. First of all, any plant or facility has to adhere to the 23 standards concerning human health.[24] The emission standards are roughly 3–100 times higher than the quality standards for the environment. If those waste waters flow into public sewers there can be exemptions from this general rule according to special agreements between an enterprise and the local government operating the sewers and the subsequent waste water treatment plants. These agreements often result in the payment of higher treatment fees in exchange for highly contaminated waste water.[25] The second group of standards (those with respect to nature) is only relevant for 'designated' facilities. This refers to plants in branches of the industry, which are known for large and dangerous waste water amounts. Moreover, it only concerns plants with a waste water emission of more than 50 cubic metres per day. The difference between designated and non-designated facilities lies mainly in the instruments for which bureaucrats have to enforce emission standards. Designated plants can be fined for exceeding standards or can be subject to temporary (partial) production shut-downs. For non-designated plants there exists only administrative guidance as a tool to alter management behaviour.[26]

With the term 'administrative guidance' we have touched on the main subject of this chapter, the way environmental protection has been enforced in Japan. In interviews carried out with members of the municipalities of Osaka, Shizuoka and Kyoto, the officials were friendly enough to describe the way they usually succeeded in changing the environmental behaviour of enterprises in their regions.[27] This process consists of various steps. The first, and probably the most important, factor is to determine the occurrence of unusual pollution and to identify its source. For this purpose the (waste) water departments conduct regular surveys of water contents especially in the public sewers. The city of Osaka has established an automatic monitoring system at strategic points of the public sewer network in order to detect sudden changes of pH in the waste water as an indicator for changing waste water contents. This is to trace the sources of illegal infusions into the sewers, which can damage waste water treatment plants operated by the city.[28] Once the offender is identified, the enterprise is informed of this fact and is requested to change its facilities in such a way that the emissions conform with current local or national environmental standards. All interviewed officials stated that most enterprises usually change their behaviour after this notification or commence negotiations about time limits and other circumstances associated with the necessary changes. If this first official measure brings no satisfactory result, the offending company finds itself subjected to continued 'attention' from the municipal officials in the form of repeated controls and on-site visits. At this stage the bureaucrats offer help, too, if the respective enterprises are not able to carry out changes in their production facilities, due to lack of technical knowledge, for example. The last step in the administrative pressure is the threat to make the name of the offending company public. Only official sanctions such as fines or temporary (partial) shut-downs constitute a greater sanction than the publication of the names of unrelenting companies, but these are almost never carried out. All interviewed officials stressed that the informal instruments are usually sufficiently influential to achieve their goals. The question that arises now is why and how these instruments seem to work.

Interpretation from a neoclassical point of view

The first point that needs to be discussed here is the effort put into the detection of illegal emissions and the identification of their sources. In this case neoclassical theory is in line with common sense. The critical factor is the probability of an illicit emission being detected and traced back to the emitting enterprise.[29] A rational management[30] takes this probability into account when determining its optimal reaction on environmental standards and official sanctions. Even high fines and strict shut-down orders have only a small effect on decision making if the probability of being discovered is small, although this combination might have a negative effect on business performance because of the high uncertainty of the possibly fateful event of detection. This situation would only be tolerable if the enterprises were able to insure themselves against official sanctions. On the other hand, rather small fines or other sanctions would be fully considered in decision making if the probability of detection was very high. Companies would invest in environmental technology in order to adopt standards up to the point where these costs would equal the financial burdens deriving from sanctions. In this respect, Japanese officials behave closely according to neoclassical predictions when they try to improve automatic and manual controls of waste water qualities, and there is no need to introduce special assumptions or social institutions to explain the effectiveness of this measure.[31]

The next point is the reaction of companies to notifications of their illegal behaviour. To explain this within the neoclassical methodology, we can draw on the possibility of official sanctions again. If the offending emission of a company has already been detected, the possibility of further and more intense controls rises dramatically, because this is the first step in the chain of measures described in the previous section. With intensifying controls the risk of further detections and possibly expensive sanctions increases too. Rationally it would pay for a company in this situation to invest in avoiding these consequences as long as the necessary investments are not more expensive than the sanctions themselves. It all comes down to one critical factor, namely the monetary value of the sanctions that can be inflicted upon offenders by public officials. Therefore these sanctions need to be analysed in more detail.

Unfortunately, and in spite of many inquiries, it has not been possible to get confirmed facts about the amount of fines levied for illicit waste water emissions, either from written sources or from the interviews conducted with various officials of major Japanese municipalities.[32] The only information given was the obvious dependency of fines (and other measures such as production shut-downs) on the gravity of the pollution. The impression given was that fines were meant more as a symbolic act than as an actual economic incentive according to the neoclassical logic explained earlier. Again, the interviewed officials stressed most explicitly the fact that it was almost never necessary to fall back on official sanctions. As a final instrument, if all forms of persuasion failed, the bureaucrats seemed to prefer shut-downs compared to drastic fines because this measure would guarantee the end of dangerous emissions for the time being, although they admitted that this was an extremely rare event.

A neoclassical interpretation of the facts presented in the previous paragraph is quite difficult. As only monetary incentives are considered in neoclassical analysis, we really need to know the exact value of fines or production losses because of shut-downs, which are not available. Following the equilibrium model these possible financial losses would only exert actual incentives for changes of behaviour if they were bigger than the savings accruing from avoiding investments in environmental technology. According to all information from the interviewed municipalities, the fines imposed on offending companies are in no way sufficient to satisfy this criterion. That leaves only the possibility of shut-down orders as a reason for companies to conform to emission standards in Japan.[33] Of course no production means no revenues, so the financial loss from shut-downs may be a sufficient incentive for additional investments in pollution regulation technology, or at least it would be if this was a consequent that was closely related to the occurrence of illegal emissions. However, even if we exclude the fact that most enterprises are not subject to such sanctions, we do need to take account of the fact that such official reactions are extremely rare.[34] Neoclassical economists would argue that it did not matter whether such sanctions were actually carried out or not, but that the mere possibility would be taken into account by the companies. They would assume that the shut-down was threatening their facility if they did not comply with regulations, and they would avoid doing this so that the actual sanction would in most cases be unnecessary. We need to ask, however, if this is true.

In order to analyse the effectiveness of production shut-downs we must take a closer look at the circumstances in which these sanctions might be imposed. As a matter of fact, it is necessary to examine whether this consequence occurs automatically whenever a company fails to give way to official pressure or whether we have to consider merely the probability of this happening, in the same way as we did for fines above. The statement of the interviewed municipalities, that they almost never resort to this action, is not sufficient evidence in this respect because it can be interpreted in different ways, as explained earlier.[35] A new perspective can be found if the 'social' context of the regulating officials is considered. First, the competition of municipalities for tax revenues and jobs has to be taken into account.[36] This means that there is pressure to avert any unnecessary burden on enterprises in order to make the region an attractive location for both future and existing industrial facilities. Also, the official stance of the central government, which is quite influential even in the municipalities, is biased in favour of growth rather than environmental protection. As a result, officials who act too strictly against environmental offenders tend to face problems, including deteriorating career prospects. Second, the 'socialization' of bureaucrats plays an important role. Administrative guidance, that is exerting influence through informal, personal channels, has been a major element in governmental work for several decades.[37] The use of official sanctions can well be seen as indicating incompetence when it comes to influencing managers in the traditionally approved way. Again, incompetent persons will have poor career opportunities and a bad reputation among colleagues. Additionally the officials themselves have learned their trade by training on the job, which concentrates on the importance of personal interaction between (local) government and companies.[38] After this learning process, the officials themselves expect to be able to handle problems on an unofficial basis. Failure to do this means disappointment and loss of self-esteem for them. As long as the socialization of bureaucrats and the stance of local and central government fail to change in favour of stricter environmental protection and a new model of governmental work it can be concluded that municipal employees who use shut-downs (or fines) on a regular basis will suffer various disadvantages. This not only considerably reduces the probability of these sanctions being implemented but also the (neoclassical) effectiveness of this instrument. Managers know that officials use this last tool only if it is absolutely unavoidable to stop dangerous emissions in order to prevent human damage. Other problems are solved consensually, for example, by raising waste water fees or by imposing more or less generous time limits for investments in environmental technology.

After discussing this last tool of municipalities to make enterprises adhere to environmental standards, we can come to the conclusion that, in line with neo-classical arguments, no single one of the instruments is likely to be sufficient in altering company behaviour. However, as the situation of the environment in Japan shows, industry has made progress in protecting the environment from threatening emissions, and this cannot be explained by neoclassical arguments. We have to set aside this model, or at least some of its assumptions, and turn to social factors in order to explain the effectiveness of environmental policy in Japan.

Social institutions as an explanatory factor

In the task of ensuring environmental protection, the interviewed officials were overwhelmingly confident that any offenders would relent when faced with the 'soft' instruments of intervention: official notifications, intensified attention and finally the threat to publish the company's name.[39] From an economic viewpoint we have to conclude that these measures create certain 'costs' which are at least as high as the costs of the necessary investments into environmental protection, for otherwise these instruments would show no such effect. But what kind of 'costs' are these?

As a basis for an analysis let us introduce the assumption that leaders of companies – no matter whether they are owners or mere managers – value independent decision making. At least to some extent these entrepreneurs are responsible for the outcome of their business unit so they welcome the freedom to decide freely upon its further market strategy. There are authors who even assume that the satisfaction derived from intrinsic motivations such as independence and success is much more important for entrepreneurs than the financial advantages of leading positions.[40] Leaders therefore enjoy having success which can be attributed to their own performance and abilities. Continued intervention of bureaucrats into the affairs of a company thus does not only endanger financial revenues, and consequently the income of managers, but also non-material 'revenues', such as independence, power, prestige and the scope for creative business solutions, which Korndörfer describes as important components of the bundle of goals of company leadership.[41]

Apart from the above explanation one more assumption may contribute to the effectiveness of intensified official attention towards companies which disrespect environmental issues. We can assume that decision makers in Japanese companies are deeply embedded within a social network made up of representatives of competing firms, customer suppliers and even various official organizations and agencies.[42] Intensified official attention and intervention in company businesses is a sign of the inability of company officials to prevent what has caused this, and as a result the appreciation of responsible managers among members of their network diminishes. This can even reach the point where prospective business partners decide against doing business with the company because of its reputation.

Neglect of environmental issues can be taken as a sign of lacking carefulness or even technical expertise.[43] This becomes even more pronounced when the administrative guidance reaches the next step: the threat to make the name of offending companies public. From the apparent effectiveness of these measures there is only one conclusion that can be drawn: this kind of intervention – in combination with the effects of lingering fines and production shut-down – raises the social 'costs' of environmental pollution to a point where it is more expensive for the company leaders to ignore the regulation than to conform to the rules.

On the basis of the above analysis we can even go one step further. We can identify some of the social institutions which support administrative guidance as a major instrument of environmental policy in Japan. These can be listed as follows:

1   *It is socially advantageous to obey bureaucrats.* Unlike in Western cultures, where a manager who disregards the wishes of government officials or cheats taxes can even be thought of as exceptionally daring or clever, there is no heroism in Japanese company executives openly resisting administrative guidance. There is even a saying in Japanese which can be translated as 'you can never win against crying children and high officials'.[44] Although there are examples in the post-war economic history of Japan that contradict this opinion, a manager has to have very good reason to withstand official influence, and it is not likely to happen on minor occasions.

2   *Government officials have the right to interfere with everyday company affairs.* In Western thinking bureaucratic responsibilities and company management are strictly separated. Against the background of the neo-liberal tradition, we are convinced that the economy will produce the best outcome when left to itself. Any intervention raises suspicions of a state overstepping its boundaries and destroying economic stamina. In Japan, it is an everyday thing for government officials to interfere with business decisions, and bureaucrats need no special excuse for doing so, especially if the economic stance of an enterprise has become critical in any respect.

3   *Bureaucrats have insight into the industries they are dealing with.* In Germany government officials are not considered competent in business matters. They are socialized into a completely different form of organization and specialize on passing laws and issuing decrees. Because of this they are believed to be almost useless when it comes to business problems. The Japanese system of training on the job emphasizes the spreading of practical experience in handling business matters inside government agencies. For this reason, bureaucrats are often considered sufficiently equipped to decide upon business problems.[45]

A careful examination might very well reveal a lot more social institutions which are important for the effectiveness of administrative guidance in environmental protection in Japan, but these three will suffice for now. As a final step, we have to see in which direction institutional change may go and what that may mean for the future of environmental protection in Japan.

Direction and effects of institutional change

At this point the varieties and sources of institutional change could be discussed in great detail, but because of the limited space a short summary will have to suffice. Institutional change originates in differences between the existing institutions (formal and informal rules and habits) and the needs of particular individuals, social groups or society as a whole. Roughly divided it can take two forms.[46] First, so-called 'political entrepreneurs' (politicians, leaders, social innovators of any kind) can work to change existing institutions or create new ones. Second, things such as everyday decisions and law suits can act unintentionally and gradually to change institutions to better fit the changing circumstances.

In the surroundings of the Japanese environmental sector, both of these impulses can be witnessed to some extent. Whether because of the pressure exerted by foreign governments and foreign enterprises in Japan or because of the long lasting economic stagnation or because of other factors, deregulation has become a prominent issue among Japanese policymakers at the start of the twenty-first century. Moreover Japanese company officials also seem to have become tired of the tutelage of Japanese bureaucrats.[47] The question is to what extent these impulses can actually stir up institutional change in Japan. Is deregulation a real aim of Japanese politicians or is it only lip service paid to mounting internal and external pressure? How many Japanese decision makers in companies and in the government really support institutional change, and how many work against it? These are questions that cannot be answered on a solid scientific foundation and therefore must remain unanswered here, too. What can be done instead is an assessment of the possible effects of this institutional change on environmental policy in Japan.

One important point is that we can assume that the change can be expected to happen more quickly in the economic sector than in the bureaucracy. Interaction with government officials may be one important part of the training of company managers, but nevertheless it is only one among many others. For bureaucrats who have contact with economic issues, administrative guidance is a major part of their education. It almost represents the core competence of these officials. Naturally it would be much harder for them to adapt to a completely different way of policy making than it would be for company representatives. We can assume that because of the resulting resistance against institutional change many bureaucrats would rather work hard to stick to old methods and principles rather than develop new ones. On top of that, the deterioration of old rules and habits is likely to happen much more quickly than the building up of functional equivalents such as formal written regulations and their strict enforcement. These presumptions lead to one conclusion: if institutional change in the form of deregulation and the decreasing power of administrative guidance makes further progress in Japan, the protection of the environment becomes endangered. If administrative guidance becomes more and more ineffective, in the short run (and perhaps even in the longer run) no socially accepted and embedded alternatives exist for enforcing environmental protection in Japan. In the end, because of path dependency, Japan is dependent on administrative guidance in order to protect its environment, at least for the moment.

Acknowledgement

First of all I have to thank many people who made this article possible. I would like to thank those environmental experts whom I have interviewed during my stay in Japan in 1999 and 2000. They were very patient with my unusual questions. Without the information offered by them the practical insight into environmental regulation in Japan included in this chapter would never have developed. My thanks also go to the employees of the DUG office (Deutsche Umwelt- und Geotechnologie) in Kawasaki and Prof Okuno-Fujiwara at Tokyo University. They introduced me to many of the aforementioned experts, which enhanced the results of the interviews to a great extent. I would like to thank Prof Jochen Röpke and Cornelia Storz for their contributions while supervising my dissertation from which this article is derived. The latter also introduced my work to Prof Janet Hunter whom I have to thank for including this chapter in this publication.

Notes

1 This chapter is based on a forthcoming article in the Japan-Jahrbuch of the Institute for Asian Affairs in Hamburg but lays special emphasis on the importance of informal institutions in environmental regulation and the possible impact of their change.

2 Eberhard Feess, *Umweltökonomie und Umweltpolitik* (2nd edn, München: Vahlen, 1998); Anastasios Xepapadeas, *Advanced Principle in Environmental Policy* (Cheltenham: Edward Elgar, 1997).

3 Apart from these negative externalities there also exist positive externalities in economic thinking. A company that is, for example, processing highly polluted water from a river for its own usage may well create positive effects if their waste water quality is better than the original. This is called external benefit in contrast to external costs created by harmful activities.

4 Horst Zimmermann and Klaus-Dirk Henke, *Finanzwirtschaft: eine Einführung in die Lehre von der öffentlichen Finanzwirtschaft* (8th edn, München: Vahlen, 2001), pp. 443–45.

5 Ibid., pp. 45–47, 444.

6 It has to be added here that there is a controversy among economic scientists whether a central government is needed to enforce environmental protection or not. This discussion climaxed on the dispute of Pigou vs. Coase, best discussed in Coase's article 'The Problem of Social Cost' reprinted in Ronald H. Coase, *The Firm, the Market and the Law* (Chicago, IL: University of Chicago Press, 1988). Pigou was convinced that a government should levy taxes for the exact financial amount of external costs on the harmful activity. Such a tax is called a Pigou-tax. Coase, on the other hand, thought that environmental protection could be realized through private negotiations if proprietary rights could be distributed completely. If that could be done all environmental pollution would harm the property of a human being who could sue the polluting person or negotiate towards a compensation for the emitting party in order to stop the pollution. It can be shown that under the circumstances of the neoclassical economic model both solutions create a situation with optimal allocation of pollution and production. In reality the governmental approach to internalize the external costs by various means of central power are dominant on the national level while on the international level only negotiations remain.

7 The previous section also explains the basic problem behind environmental protection on an international level. According to the logic governing Table 10.1 every country wants to maximize its own profit by avoiding the costs of environmental protection and

enjoying the natural goods preserved by the other countries who shoulder the necessary investments. Individually rational, this stance – if shared by too many governments – results in the least global benefit.

8 Ecological taxes are never meant to reduce emissions to zero but to achieve an environmentally and economically reasonable amount of pollution.

9 Zimmermann and Henke, *Finanzwirtschaft*, pp. 450–51.

10 Peter H. Hall, 'The Theory and Practice of Innovation Policy: an Overview', in Hall (ed.), *Technology, Innovation and Economic Policy* (Oxford: Philip Allan Publishers, 1986), pp. 21–22.

11 There are other instruments for environmental policy, such as the use of the governmental purchasing power, educational programmes in order to strengthen environmental consciousness or even the creation of international standards such as ISO 14000, but it would lead too far away from the initial intention of this chapter to discuss them in full. Interested readers should see Ilona Koester, *Steuerbarkeit gesamtwirtschaftlicher Entwicklung aus systemtheoretischer Sicht* (Mafex vol. 6, Marburg: Marburger Förderzentrum für Existenzgründer aus der Universität, 2004).

12 Xepapadeas, *Advanced Principles in Environmental Policy*, p. 69.

13 Peter-Christoph Storm, 'Einführung', in Storm (ed.), *Umweltrecht* (München: dtv, 2001), pp. xii–xiii.

14 Yoshio Miyazaki, 'Neuere Tendenzen in der japanischen Umweltpolitik unter besonderer Berücksichtigung des Umweltrahmengesetzes', in Gesine Foljanty-Jost (ed.), *Ökologische Strategien Deutschland/Japan – Umweltverträgliches Wirtschaften im Vergleich* (Opladen: Leske & Budrich, 1996), pp. 146–49.

15 Ibid., p. 146; interview with Tsunetō Akira, Ministry of International Trade and Industry, Bureau for Industrial Policy, Section for Industrial Structure, 9 February 2000 in Tokyo.

16 Interview with Tsunetō Akira of MITI, 9 February 2000; interview with Nakui Kōji, Ministry of International Trade and Industry, Agency for Industrial Location Planning, 9 February 2000, Tokyo.

17 Interview with Ōmori Keiko, Environmental Agency of Japan, Department of Planning Coordination, 10 March 2000, Tokyo.

18 Interview with Ōno Toshiyuki, Chief Engineer of the R&D Department of NKK Plant Engineering Corp., 23 March 2000, Yokohama; Nihon Bijinesu Kaihatsu KK (NBK) (ed.), *Kankyō bijinesu Hakusho* (Osaka: NBK, 1998), p. 29.

19 For a detailed presentation of the Minamata case see Sadami Maruyama, 'Die Reaktion von wirtschaft, Staat und lokaler Gesellschaft auf die Minamata-Krankheit', in Foljanty-Jost, *Ökologische Strategien Deutschland/Japan*.

20 Interview with Shimizu Hitoshi, Head of the Sales Department of Shōwa Enjiniaringu KK, 12 March 1998, Kawasaki.

21 Nihon Kankyō Kyōkai (NKK) (ed.), *Mizu Kankyō o Kangaeru* (Kankyō Shiriizu 66, Tokyo: Tōin Kikaku Insatsu, 1994), p. 7.

22 Interview with Ōgaki Shin'ichirō and Ōtaki Masahiro, professors of the Graduate School of the University of Tokyo, Faculty of Engineering, 25 November 1997, Tokyo.

23 Okuda, Masayuki, *Mizu to Gomi no Kankyō Mondai* (Tokyo: Tōtō Shuppan, 1995), pp. 26–27. The complex situation concerning environmental standards with regard to nature is particularly rarely included in publications concerning environmental policy in Japan. For a quite detailed presentation see Ishibashi, Ken, *Suishitsu Kankei no Kiso Chishiki: Kōgai Bōshi Kanrisha* (Tokyo: Tōkyō Kyōiku Jōhō Sentaa, 1996) and Okuda, *Mizu to Gomi no Kankyō Mondai*. In fact there exist more forms of regulation concerning the protection of water quality than are mentioned here. First there is a regulation concerning the whole amount of biologically active pollutants emitted into three closed maritime regions. And second local governments are entitled to set stricter or additional standards for their region. Since an inquiry into the situation in major municipalities (Tokyo, Osaka, Kyoto, Yokohama and Shizuoka) conducted by

the author suggests that the latter possibility is rarely used, these regulations are for practical reasons omitted in this chapter.

24 Ishibashi, *Suishitsu Kankei no Kiso Chishiki*, p. 91.

25 Interview with various members of the Agency for Water Supply of the City of Shizuoka, Waste Water Department, 8 December 1997, Shizuoka.

26 Ibid.; Ishibashi, *Suishitsu Kankei no Kiso Chishiki*, p. 90; interview with Hiraga Naoki, Tanaka Shigeyuki and Yamamoto Satoshi, Municipality of Osaka, Construction Department, Planning Section, 16 December 1997, Osaka.

27 Interviews with Hiraga, Tanaka and Yamamoto, Municipality of Osaka, 16 December 1997; interview with members of Agency for Water Supply for City of Shizuoka, 8 December 1997; interview with Suzuki Hideo and Watanabe Naoyuki, Associates of the Waste Water Department of the City of Kyoto, 8 December 1997, Kyoto.

28 Interview with Hiraga *et al.*, 16 December 1997.

29 Xepapadeas, *Advanced Principles in Environmental Policy*.

30 Rational in the sense of the neoclassical equilibrium model which is not, of course, unanimous in economic science. This rationality could be called 'hyper-rational' if we consider the underlying assumptions but this is not the place for a detailed discussion.

31 Critics of the neoclassical model would argue that this is happenstance because common sense and neoclassical theory agree on this point.

32 These interviews included those with Hiraga *et al.* from Osaka, the officials from Shizuoka, Suzuki and Watanabe in Kyoto. Additional interviews where this information was sought were those with Hirano Shozō, Ōno Koichi and Suzuki Kōzō, Sewage Department of the City of Yokohama, 18 December 1997, Yokohama; and with various members of the Department for Sewerage of the City of Tokyo, 19 December 1997, Tokyo.

33 At least following the neoclassical logic. As described later there might well be other incentives not covered by neoclassical assumptions.

34 In the case of emissions endangering human health any company can be subjected to fines and shut-downs in order to stop illegal emissions, but for waste waters harming the natural environment this holds true only for 'designated' facilities, as indicated above.

35 It can be taken as a hint of the unwillingness of bureaucrats to use this last and most formal instrument, or it can be a hint of the shrewdness of Japanese managers when it comes to avoiding this point of no return for both sides, as is proposed by neoclassical thinking.

36 Interview with Shizuoka officials, 17 December 1997; interview with Osaka officials Hiraga *et al.*, 16 December 1997.

37 At least in departments dealing directly with regulation.

38 Interview with Tsunetō Akira, MITI, 9 February 2000.

39 Interviews with officials from Shizuoka and Osaka as earlier.

40 An entrepreneur after the definition of Jochen Röpke (*Die Strategie der Innovation* (Tübingen: Mohr, 1977)) and Josef Schumpeter ('Unternehmer', in *Handwörterbuch der Staatswissenschaften* (vol. 8, Jena, 1928)) is a person who thinks up and carries out innovations in a given company or other organization. This functional definition is not necessarily connected with ownership of production facilities or even with a leading position in a firm. Moreover, entrepreneurship should not be confused with invention which means the search for new technological or scientific knowledge. Innovation can be carried out with or without invention, just as inventions can lead up to innovations but do not have to do so. See Röpke, *Die Strategie der Innovation*, pp. 136–38, 148–49, based on David C. McClelland, *The Achieving Society* (Princeton, NJ: van Nostrand, 1961).

41 Wolfgang Körndorfer, *Unternehmensführungslehre: Einführung, Entscheidungslogik, soziale Kompetenzen* (Wiesbaden: Gabler, 1999), pp. 38–39.

42 It can be assumed that such a network exists also for company representatives in other countries. From the experiences in various interviews (interview with Fujimori Keizō, former Managing Director of NEC, 15 March 2000, Kanagawa; interview with Hara Kiyoshi, Head of the Bureau of the Industrial Conference for Ozone Layer Protection

(JICOP), 6 March 2000, Tokyo; interview with Inoue Tsukasa, Head of the Nagasaki Deutsch Industrial Society (NDIS), 22 August 1997, Nagasaki; interview with Mizokami Atsuo and Okuyama Masaji, of Nihon Sangyō Kikai Kōgyō Kai (Japan Society of Industrial Machinery Manufacturers – JSIM), 25 August 1997; interview with Shimizu Hitoshi, 12 March 1998; interview with Tsunetô Akira, 9 February 2000; interview with Unno Mizue, Managing Director of So-Tech Management Consulting, 10 March 1998, as well as many others, the author can positively testify to its existence in Japan.

43 Interview with Fujimori Keizō, 15 March 2000.
44 Ōmiya, Tomonobu, *Keizai to Gyōsei no Kankei ga Hitome de Wakaru Jiten* (Tokyo: Asuka, 1993), p. 50.
45 Interview with Tsunetō Akira, 9 February 2000.
46 Compare, for example, Douglass North, *Institutions, Institutional Change and Economic Performance* (Cambridge: Cambridge University Press, 1990).
47 Interview with Tsunetō Akira, 9 February 2000; interview with Ōno Toshiyuki, 23 February 2000.

11 Changes in conducting foresight in Japan

Kerstin Cuhls

Introduction

The following contribution describes changes in conducting foresight in Japan, as well as organisational changes in science and technology policy-making. Foresight is defined as the attempt to look systematically into the longer-term future of science, technology, the economy and society. It aims to identify those areas of strategic research and the emergence of generic technologies which will have a large impact on economic and social benefits. In Japan, there is a special focus on identifying future technologies that might enable policy-making to adapt existing conditions for a better performance in science and technology. The process of looking into the future is undertaken using different methods, most of them aimed at stimulating communication about future events. The process as such is, therefore, often as important as the results. The results of foresight are normally used for policy-making or strategic planning in science, technology and innovation. They are therefore of interest to companies, to decision-makers, and to the media and those private persons who want to know what lies ahead.

Foresight has been a 'tradition' in Japan for 35 years now, as will be outlined in the following section. However, during the last 10 years, with international co-operation in the field and new methodological developments giving new impulses, the interest in looking into the future and drawing conclusions for the present has increased in Japan and in many other countries in the world, along with greater expectations as to what foresight itself can be assumed to deliver. Sometimes these expectations are too high, and foresight is expected to fulfil too many purposes at once. We have to keep in mind the fact that foresight is a systematic approach towards looking into the future, but that the future as such is still unknown to us. Moreover, even if we are relatively sure about developments during the coming years, we are still likely to have difficulties in estimating what the market might be, that is, if technologies will be applied and accepted by society. The question of what people really need and want is increasingly taken into account in new foresight approaches, but it is difficult to anticipate this in the long run. The impact of new developments on the economy can only be predicted. Nevertheless, it is assumed that these exercises will have a positive impact on innovations, and therefore on the future markets for new products, which will in turn lead to better market positions. This will have a direct impact on the economy, too.

The following section provides a more detailed definition of foresight, along with an account of its objectives. The subsequent section illustrates the history of foresight in Japan, focussing on the national Delphi forecast/foresight surveys. A major part of this section will explain changes in the context of national organisational re-structuring (e.g. in the organisation of the ministries), policy shifts and changes in the foresight process itself as derived from policy and organisational changes. It can be stated here at the outset that there is a future for foresight in Japan, and its relevance in the science and technology policy context is increasing.

What is Foresight?

The 'classical' definition of 'Foresight' was made by Ben Martin and can be paraphrased as follows:

> (Technology) foresight is the process involved in systematically attempting to look into the longer-term future of science, technology, the economy and society with the aim of identifying the areas of strategic research and the emerging of generic technologies likely to yield the greatest economic and social benefits.[1]

Coates formulated it more broadly:

> Foresight is the overall process of creating an understanding and appreciation of information generated by looking ahead. Foresight includes qualitative and quantitative means for monitoring clues and indicators of evolving trends and developments and is best and most useful when directly linked to the analysis of policy implications. Foresight prepares us to meet the needs and opportunities of the future. Foresight in government cannot define policy, but it can help condition policies to more appropriate, more flexible, and more robust in their implementation, as times and circumstances change. Foresight is, therefore, closely tied to planning. It is not planning – merely a step in planning.[2]

This also means the identification of strategic research. 'Picking the winners', as symbolised by the title of Irvine and Martin's famous book,[3] does not mean merely glancing into the future but the preparation of initial decisions concerning the future. Foresight is not only about 'picking the winners', it can also be used strategically to pick out the losers. Foresight draws conclusions for the present and is therefore a broad-range policy instrument that can serve various objectives.[4] There is no *one* user or *the* definite participant in foresight approaches but different participants and different users contribute to the success of a foresight exercise.[5]

Foresight is definitely needs-oriented. The communication effect of pre-assessing future options or decisions, as well as mobilising and bringing together the different stakeholders of the innovation system (or 'wiring up' in Martin and Johnston's terms), seems to be as important as empirical results.[6]

The end of the twentieth century has witnessed the advent of many new foresight methods for envisaging the future and any combinations thereof. Most of the experiences of organised experiments applying various foresight initiatives concerning future issues in science, technology or society have been evaluated as very positive. Companies have made use of the data, the media have published a large number of articles, ministries have reflected once more about their research priorities and a research institution has even based an evaluation on Delphi results.[7]

In many countries, foresight activities have been supported by ministries responsible for science and technology or for research or by other public bodies. All foresight concepts try to implement communicative processes which integrate the different actors in the innovation system.[8] Many activities have also attracted interest from the general public – either because of the approaching year 2000 (though this was less true in Japan) or because of the felt need to gain more 'information' by thinking about the future (one has to keep in mind that this information is not facts but flexible data, often no more than opinions). The targets of foresight activities have changed accordingly.

Thus, foresight is conducted in order to gain more knowledge about things to come, so that today's decisions can be based more solidly on available expertise than before. Foresight is more than prognosis or prediction. It 'holds the promise of *managing* uncertainty through intensive interaction between stakeholders'.[9] Fink *et al.* go even further, proposing the tool of Scenario Management for strategic foresight activities.[10] Implicitly, this means taking an active role in shaping the future. A possible result can be that our prognosis of today will be falsified because of our new orientation and the decisions we base on foresight information. Former attempts to plan the future or to develop heuristic models of the future (in the sense of some futurological concepts) were based on the assumption that the future is pre-defined as a linear continuation of present trends.[11] These approaches were not regarded as successful because they were on the one hand too simplified – and evaluated mainly by their predictive accuracy (e.g. if the prediction turned out to be 'right' or 'wrong'). Some methods included different variables to match the complexity of the dynamics of actual social, economic and technological developments, but this was also insufficient from the prognosis point of view. Nevertheless, some of these studies provoked a lively discussion about the future.[12] In foresight and forecasting, the methodology is not fixed, and a mix of methods and instruments seems to be most promising.

Foresight is by now well-established as a useful instrument for incorporating awareness of long-term challenges and opportunities into more immediate decision-making. The current definition from the EU describes foresight as 'a systematic, participatory, future intelligence gathering and medium-to-long-term vision-building process aimed at present-day decisions and mobilising joint actions. The term "Foresight" therefore represents the processes focusing on the interaction between science, technology and society'.[13]

Foresight is therefore about

- thinking
- debating
- shaping the future.[14]

It is thus not a single methodology, but different methods can be and are mixed together to fulfil the intended purposes. This can be done more formally with surveys, Delphi studies or with different types of workshop. There is also a range of formal and more informal methods to carry out the task of looking into the future. In foresight activities, it is important to bring together actors from different sectors and from different thematic and societal backgrounds, so that different ideas are brought in and judged from different points of view.

As we have said, therefore, foresight is not prediction and not prognosis. Pure prediction is not based on communication or on systematic processes, and prognoses are generally extrapolations from already existing data aggregated in the past. Whether the model is a dynamic or linear one, the assumption in both these cases is that the future is just a prolongation of the past. Foresight in the new sense is also different from forecasting, although the difference is often regarded as a semantic one. In fact, in the USA, there is no difference in the wording at all, but in Europe and other countries of the world such as Japan, the differences are defined by the set of factors identified in Table 11.1.[15]

There is also a link from forecasting and foresight to planning. Some parts even overlap, but to reiterate Coates' earlier statement, 'Foresight is not planning. It is merely a step in planning.'[16] With foresight (and forecasting), information about the future can be provided on which the planning can be based, but it is not the plans themselves.

There are different objectives in foresight, which range from priority-setting in science and technology to vision-building and networking. The new approaches in (technology) foresight can have many objectives, but since foresight cannot meet them all, specific targets have to be set. In the context of policy-making, the most important can be identified as[17]

- to enlarge the choice of opportunities, to set priorities and to assess impact and chances;
- to explore the impact of current research and technology policy;
- to ascertain new needs, new demands and new possibilities as well as new ideas;
- to focus selectively on economic, technological, social and ecological areas, as well as starting to monitor detailed research in these fields;
- to define desirable and undesirable futures;
- to start and stimulate continuous processes of discussion.

The future is largely shaped by reciprocal underlying influences. The development of one field often influences another field more, and more indirectly, than anticipated. For example, developments in electronics influence biotechnology or culture. These influences cannot at first sight be assessed. It is only the parts,

Table 11.1 Summary of some major differences between forecasting and foresight

Foresight	Forecasting
• Basic points: needs, research questions are still open and looked for as part of the foresight process	• Basic points: topics and research questions have to be clarified in advance
• More qualitative than quantitative	• More quantitative than qualitative
• Looks for 'information' about the future for priority-setting	• Questions how the future in the selected area might look like
• Brings people together for discussions about the future and for networking, makes use of the distributed intelligence	• More result-oriented, can also be performed by individuals or in single studies (depending on the methodology)
• The development of criteria for assessments and preparation for decisions is one of the objectives	• Assessments, different options and choices or the preparation for decisions are not necessarily (but sometimes) an objective
• Has objective of disseminating information about the future	• Describes future options; more driven by results than about disseminating information
• Long-, middle- and short-term orientation with implications for today	• Long-, middle- and short-term orientation as well as the path into the future
• Seeks to ascertain if there is consensus on subjects/topics regarding future development	• No consensus necessary
• Participation of 'experts' as well as other participants is crucial	• Dependent on 'experts' and/or precise methodologies, less dependent on opinions

structures or framework conditions that are visible or acknowledged that can be understood or to some extent influenced. If the knowledge incorporated in systems theory is also taken into account, then we also have to reckon with the mutual influences of the systems and rules in which the actions of persons are embedded. An awareness of uncertainty was brought to futures research when new formulations of chaos theory emerged. The new ideas about foresight that emerged in the 1990s, starting with Irvine and Martin, did not say that the future cannot be influenced directly but made it clear that any influence on future developments is strictly limited and that the impact can be only partly estimated.[18] Nevertheless, the future can be 'prospectively monitored'. The accelerating changes that a person has to adapt to socially and psychologically make it necessary to anticipate these changes before they become reality.[19] This, therefore, is the current state-of-the-art of foresight, especially in Europe. In Japan, however, as we shall see, the predictive element in foresight still has a significant weight.

History of foresight in Japan

Japan started developing science and technology later than many other countries, but it is clear that she has nevertheless been immensely successful. Many factors explain this success story, one of them being the adaptation of large foresight or forecasting studies at the end of the 1960s. In Japan, the *Delphi method* has often been used for foresight activities. Delphi is a survey method which utilises feedback in two or more so-called rounds. Experts, defined very broadly, are asked about future issues which are then formulated in statements. In the first round, these statements are assessed according to a set of criteria, for example importance for the economy, for society, for the environment, as well as measures to be taken or which is the leading country in the particular field. One major assessment is always concerning the time by which something may become actuality. However, as nobody can know the future, people look for psychological anchors. Therefore, the second round entails asking the same experts the same questions, but this time with feedback from the first round, that is they get the results of the first round. As the survey is conducted anonymously, the experts can now either stick to their previous opinion or change their minds without losing face. After the second (or additional) round it is possible to observe whether any consensus is emerging concerning the issue under discussion.[20]

The Delphi method belongs to subjective-intuitive methods of foresight. Delphi was developed in the 1950s by the Rand Corporation of Santa Monica, California, in operations research. The name can be traced back to the Delphic oracle, as Woudenberg reports that the name 'Delphi' was intentionally coined by Kaplan, an associate professor of philosophy at University of California Los Angeles (UCLA) working for the Rand corporation in a research effort directed at improving the use of expert predictions in policy-making.[21] Back in 1950 Kaplan *et al.* referred to the 'principle of the oracle' as a 'non-falsifiable prediction', a statement that does not have the property of being 'true' or 'false'.[22] Thus coining the term 'Delphi' for the modern foresight method seems to be more than a simple brand name.

The founding of the temple at Delphi and its oracle took place before recorded history, but thanks to archaeologists and historians we have extensive knowledge about the functions and benefits of the oracle.[23] For a thousand years of recorded history the Greeks and other peoples, sometimes as private individuals, sometimes as official ambassadors, came to Delphi to consult the prophetess who was called Pythia. Her words were taken to reveal the rules of the Gods. These prophecies were not usually intended simply to be a prediction of the future as such. Pythia's function was to tell the divine purpose in a normative way in order to shape coming events. This is similar to the current approach.

In Figure 11.1, offering a new illustration of the 'genealogical tree' of the Delphi technique from a Japanese perspective, the major steps achieved in a chronological manner are listed. Major national endeavours using the Delphi technique are taken into account but not, for example, the many experimental or scientific applications of the Delphi process, in which, say, 20 students are engaged on such work within the context of a master's or doctoral thesis. Also not included are business applications on a more focused and less sophisticated level. It has to be stressed here that the focus lies intentionally on large holistic surveys with a likely impact on society. For information on the other types of Delphi application, we need to turn to business management textbooks or monographs on strategic planning, in which Delphi applications are mentioned as one of a number of tools.[24]

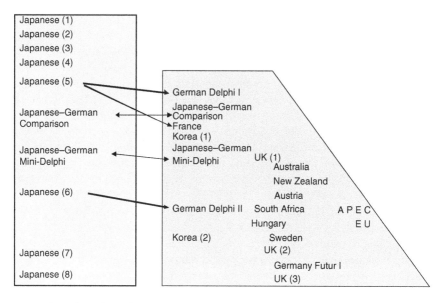

Figure 11.1 Genealogical tree of Delphi.

Sources: Terutaka Kuwahara, NISTEP Foresight Workshop, Tokyo 2004; for earlier versions from a German–Japanese perspective, see also Cuhls, *et al.*, 'Innovations for our Future'.

As already stated, the initial work was performed at Rand after 1948. In 1964, for the first time, the report from a huge Delphi survey in the civil sector was published.[25] Shortly after this, the lead in further development and broader application of the Delphi technique was taken over by Japan. In 1969, Japan's Science and Technology Agency started to conduct a large study on the future of science and technology. Before this there had been a systematic attempt to acquire foresight knowledge from the USA. Although the first large Delphi study in Japan did not correctly foresee the oil price shock, being conducted and published just before that happened, the Japanese Delphi process thereafter continued every five years.[26] The process is regarded as an updating of data concerning the future. The eighth survey is now in preparation, and an interim report is available.[27]

Although in most other countries foresight activities fell into oblivion in the 1970s because they had not foreseen the oil shock and the kind of 'limits to growth' that it presented, the Japanese Delphi process persisted. In Japan, it was observed that it was more important to make the future happen and to shape it actively by using the information gained in foresight activities, setting stable framework conditions for development in certain fields and making use of foresight procedures to update the information. Given the unknowability of the future, it was considered important to update the knowledge and the information that was available about it.

The Delphi surveys completed and published on a quinquennial basis since 1971 have been discussed in different circles. Let me give one example. The first Delphi report looked at areas like the development of society, information, medicine and health, nutrition and agriculture as well as industry and resources. In all these fields, the issues for consideration were formulated by experts. The assessment made was about the timescale for things to be realised, the techno- logical potential and where catch-up with other countries would be necessary. There were three rounds in the survey and 2,428 experts participated in all of them.

The second Delphi report in 1976 covered seven fields with 20 sub-fields, and 1,317 experts were involved throughout the study. More criteria were specified, including not just the time of realisation but such things as the importance of the topic and measures to be taken. From the second report on, only two rounds were conducted. In the third study, 1,727 experts participated, and the number of areas as well as the number of topics increased further. The fourth survey involved 2,002 experts and 1,071 topics, with the criteria remaining nearly unchanged. The same was true for the fifth study which had 16 areas, 1,150 topics and 2,385 experts. By this time the methodology was well-established, but the organisers at National Institute of Science and Technology Policy (NISTEP) were of the opinion that improvements were necessary. It was at this time, therefore, that the co-operation with the German Fraunhofer Institute for Systems and Innovation Research was initiated.[28] Over the following years, through Mini-Delphi studies, the co-operation was enhanced and the Delphi methodology improved. The sixth Delphi study was also performed in co-operation with Germany, about 30 per cent of the topics and some criteria were the same. Nevertheless, there were separate German and Japanese reports.[29]

For the public and for companies, there was from the fourth Delphi survey on an easy to read publication. Later on it even included *manga* (comics). The sixth study of 1997 now has the potential to be used for new strategic priority-setting aimed at finding ways out of the current mood of depression, which has also spread to science and technology policy. Following completion of the seventh study in 2001, the eighth study will be a large foresight approach with different parts (see p. 198), in which the Delphi study is the major component but which also makes use of other methodologies such as scenarios.

Parallel to its development in Japan, with the recent resurrection of foresight in general and the possibilities that were made available through the filter of all the 'options' of different actors, the Delphi technique has been taken out of the toolbox and implemented in Europe in a manner rather different from that in which it was applied in the early years. There appeared a new wave of large-scale government foresight studies in Europe, with Dutch and German government agencies and sim- ilar bodies taking the lead, followed quickly afterwards by France and the United Kingdom. The Germans organised a learning phase, starting both from the 'mediating' publication of Irvine and Martin's *Foresight in Science* and from Japanese experiences, co-operating in their first Delphi with Japan's fifth exercise.[30]

France followed in turn, copying the German approach. In none of these countries was a resort solely to the Delphi technique considered useful. In the Netherlands, Delphi methods were not embarked upon at all, whereas in Germany there were reported to be parallel approaches, some using the Delphi method, others not (like 'critical technologies approaches', scenarios etc.). The same is true for France where a Delphi survey and the critical technologies approach were pursued in parallel and organised by different, even competing ministries.[31] As part of further co-operation between Japanese and German institutions, joint methodological developments were achieved in the frame of a 'Mini-Delphi'. Even in Eastern European countries, such as Hungary or the Czech Republic and in Turkey, Delphi studies based on the Japanese approach were performed. In Germany, large public national Delphi studies are no longer being currently conducted, but there is a foresight approach based on workshops called Futur – The German Research Dialogue.[32]

What are the changes?

Institutional and organisational changes

Among the most significant changes taking place in Japan since the year 2000 have been organisational changes in the government. A reduction in the large number of ministries had been discussed over a long period of time. It was also considered necessary to clarify the status of 'agencies' which embraced some of the functions of ministries but were not officially ministries. A third argument was that tasks in ministries and agencies sometimes overlapped, making the situation difficult to comprehend, and this required clarification. Such a re-arrangement had long been considered particularly necessary in order to strengthen policies relating to science, technology and economic issues.

With the reorganisation of the ministries and the ministerial system officially in January 2000, a change in the innovation system and the making of Japan's science and technology policy also took place. The major change relevant to foresight activities was the merger of the former Science and Technology Agency (STA, *Kagaku Gijutsu Chō*) with the Ministry of Education (*Monbushō*) to form the new Ministry of Education, Culture, Sports, Science and Technology (MEXT). Parts of the STA were taken over by the Ministry of Trade and Industry, which changed its name to Ministry of Economy, Trade and Industry (METI), giving it additional functions relating to the economy more broadly.

Not all the changes can be described here, but Figure 11.2 summarises the ministerial reorganisation in the context of Japan's Science and Technology Policy. It is too early to judge the impact of these changes, but a significant result of this move is that the number of ministries was reduced and the agencies were integrated into ministries. The functions have been clarified to a certain extent, although certain overlaps remain. For instance, MEXT is responsible for Science and Technology in general, while METI retains some competing and complementary responsibilities such as those relating to energy, innovation and other close-to-market research. In the opinion of some innovation researchers in Japan, power has

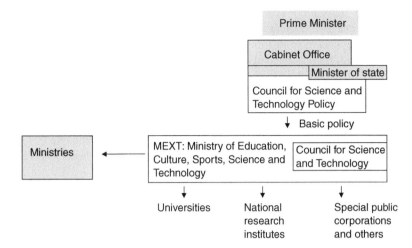

Figure 11.2 Who was involved in Japan's science and technology policy in 2003.

Source: MEXT, see http://www.mext.go.jp/english/org/science/34.htm, own modifications.

shifted towards METI. Securing the necessary attention for science and technology in a larger ministry like MEXT is also regarded as a problem, because MEXT is also responsible for culture and sports, and these seem to have little in common with science and technology. The direct connection to the prime minister previously enjoyed by the agency (the prime minister's office was responsible for the STA, meaning that it was directly represented in the cabinet by the prime minister) was severed, and science and technology policy is now under ministerial responsibility.

The re-arrangement of the different councils for the ministries is relevant to foresight, too. Most important is a new Council for Science and Technology Policy located directly within the Cabinet Office. It was intended to merge all science and technology councils together, but this goal remains unrealised. This failure has significant implications for current foresight activities, as the appearance of such a merged council would have given the activities more impetus and more visibility as well as a better financial base.

Parallel to this re-structuring, national institutions were also re-arranged. The NISTEP, which is responsible for conducting foresight through the Delphi surveys, used to report directly to the STA. Since the reorganisation, the institute has been the responsibility of MEXT.

The reorganisation was also the opportunity for a reorganisation inside NISTEP. With the departments as they are now, the 'Science and Technology Foresight Centre' was founded as a special kind of NISTEP department with permanent staff and some staff rotating from MEXT, other ministries and from industry. The Japanese name of the centre is somewhat different, being *Kagaku Gijutsu Dōkō Kenkyū Sentā* (Research Centre for Science and Technology Directions), but in the context of the development of new kinds of 'foresight activities', including demand-oriented research and new methodologies with participative elements, the English translation was regarded as more adequate internationally.[33] The previous Japanese expression *gijutsu yosoku* (technology forecasting) was regarded as too narrow in this context, especially as a differentiation between 'foresight' and 'forecasting' was attempted.[34] The major activities of NISTEP are defined in this context as the collection and analysis of information on science and technology trends through expert networks, research into trends in major science and technology fields and Technology Foresight and S&T benchmarking surveys. NISTEP, here especially the new STFC (Foresight Centre), reports directly to the Council for Science and Technology Policy. On the one hand, this makes all foresight activities more visible, and on the other hand, it gives the policy-makers direct access to knowledge about the future.[35]

New national foresight activities

A new survey and foresight activity agenda was developed for the reporting of foresight activities. With this in mind, in 2001 NISTEP conducted interviews with foresight experts all around the world to learn how to fulfil these tasks pragmatically. These included interviews at the Fraunhofer Institute for Systems and Innovation Research (ISI), in Germany and the Institute for Prospective Technological Studies (IPTS) in Seville. Accordingly, it was decided to continue with Delphi studies which had been conducted every five years since NISTEP had taken over the fourth Delphi forecast survey from the STA planning bureau. An added incentive was to broaden the scope of their activities according to the new developments in foresight methodology that had occurred especially in Europe. One decision was that the Delphi studies should be conducted according to a different timing, in order to make better and more strategic use of the data gained for Japan's five-year plans in science and technology. That meant an earlier start to the eighth Delphi survey, not in 2004 or 2005 but in 2003 instead. This meant that in March 2004 the eighth study was in general introduced to an international audience at a conference in Tokyo, and the publication of the final report was set for April 2005. This exercise sustained the trend initiated with the seventh survey of looking at demand-oriented and society-driven questions.

In addition, the results of the studies have been used directly to inform the Council for Science and Technology Policy at the Cabinet Office. Not only direct analyses from the survey have been used for this purpose, but a monitoring system for new trends, tendencies, technologies and other relevant developments has been established. A monthly newsletter contributes to this aim, in which well-known scientists report about developments in their fields. The newsletter, *Science and Technology Trends*, is also available in English every three months, both in printed form and online (www.nistep.go.jp).

Changes in the national Delphi surveys

The national Delphi surveys themselves have changed steadily.[36] The seventh Delphi survey was conducted in 2001 on behalf of the MEXT. NISTEP performed the task together with the Institute for Future Technologies (IFTECH, *Miraiken*). The time horizon of this study was 30 years like the previous ones. Again, the questions that were asked related to the importance of more than 1,000 individual topics in different fields of innovation, their time of realisation, the international level of research and measures to be taken for implementation. The topics concerned research in general, not just the technologies themselves but also organisational and other matters linked with them. There were some differences, however. Up to that point, mainly panel work had been used to prepare the selection of topics that would be included in the questionnaire. In line with the Delphi procedure, they were sent to experts twice, and the end results were analysed and discussed in different expert groups. The report was provided to all interested persons.

For the seventh Delphi survey, new aims and new methods were applied. Although the Delphi procedure was still the backbone of the foresight activity, some additional analyses and surveys were added. These included

1   An examination of social and economic needs;
2   A survey of rapidly developing fields of science and technology;
3   The development of scenarios for the most important fields of science and technology;
4   Innovation fields and single topics adapted as usual for the Delphi survey.

The results are being included in the new Five Year Plan for Science and Technology. It is worth noting that the fields in the seventh Delphi survey totalled 1,065 topics under the following headings:

- Information and communications
- Electronics
- Life science
- Health and medical care
- Agriculture, forestry, fisheries and food
- Marine science and earth science
- Space
- Resources and energy
- Environment
- Materials and processes
- Manufacturing
- Distribution
- Business and management
- Urbanisation and construction
- Transportation
- Services.

In previous surveys, the selection of experts had been confined to a relatively unchanging database, but for the seventh survey more experts were considered via co-nomination and publicly available data bases.

The eighth Delphi survey, as mentioned earlier, has been conducted earlier than usual and includes more topics oriented to social issues and demand. The official publication of the results of this survey was expected in April 2005, but an intermediate report is available from NISTEP, as indicated earlier. Figure 11.3 illustrates the different 'pillars' of foresight in this eighth national foresight exercise, which has sought to broaden the methodology utilised, to include more participation by people from 'society' and to apply a greater variety of methods, including scenarios.

The first pillar is the screening of databases, applying a kind of bibliometric methodology. From these databases, upcoming and new topics as well as rapidly developing fields relevant for science and technology have been identified. It is the initial results from this exercise that are available in the intermediate report. The second pillar is the Delphi survey. As in the previous studies, this is an expert survey. Expert committees have prepared a list of topics relating to science and technology, getting them assessed in two rounds. Most fields have been technology-oriented, but topics of societal interest have also been included. The topic fields are

- Information and communication
- Electronics
- Life sciences
- Health, medical care and welfare
- Agriculture and forestry, fisheries as well as nutrition
- Frontiers: space, marine and earth sciences
- Energy and resources
- Environment
- Nanotechnology and materials
- Manufacturing
- Industrial infrastructure
- Social infrastructure
- Science and technology for society.

The third pillar is the development of scenarios and scenario analysis. There are individual scenarios by recommended authors, normative scenarios on the basis of science and technology visions and the environment and in-depth scenarios for each field in focus. Around 50 scenarios have been written by co-nominated authors. The scenarios are understood as complementary to the Delphi analysis and themes such as emerging technologies, basic research and solution of social problems have been able to be discussed in the context of these scenarios.

The fourth pillar has been socio-economic needs analysis, for which data has been gathered and trends analysed. Important issues identified were, for example, safety and security, the ageing society and the knowledge society. Needs were listed and verified via expert interviews, a participatory process (workshops) and a questionnaire survey. As indicated earlier, overall results are expected in 2005.

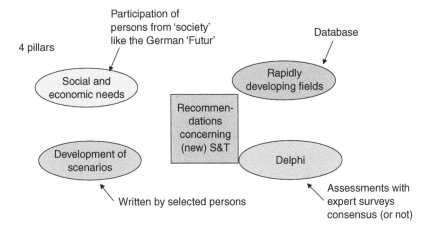

Figure 11.3 The four methodological pillars of foresight in Japan.

Source: Based on Kuwahara, 'Social Needs in Japan', own design.

Changes in policy implications

Policy concerning foresight is also changing. Reasons for this can be attributed to the worsened economic situation in Japan, challenges such as demographic change that require longer range thinking and the current situation of Japan's somewhat peripheral position in relation to some areas of innovation, science and technology. Catching-up strategies and learning from others are no longer solutions, and Japan needs to take the initiative, set priorities and steer budgets more carefully. The other factor that requires more careful consideration in longer term science and technology policy is human capital, given the lack of young people who decide to study natural sciences and become researchers. As a result, human resources in these fields are already insufficient and will be inadequate in the future if no measures are taken to address the problem.

Japan has always been considered to be very technology-friendly, although this has been questioned in some surveys,[37] but it is clear that this 'belief' in technological solutions is now at least decreasing. Japan, therefore, faces the same dilemmas as other countries, namely coping with the reality of what is feasible and desired. Science and technology policy, therefore, has to take much more into account what society really needs, requires and wishes. Long-term investments without considering the implications (e.g. without an assessment of technology) are no longer possible. Thus, before investing in science and technology, these desires have to be taken into account in order not to make the mistake of investing in fields which are unwanted and bitterly opposed later on. The anti-nuclear movement and related developments show clearly that it is no longer possible to build new nuclear power plants without the acceptance of the population.[38]

On the other hand, the future remains unknown. No one can know which technology will be interesting, creating a booming market, become the lead technology or be accepted, and our methodologies to find out the 'need' of the population are still limited mainly to surveys and participatory workshops. Therefore, there is still room for development, as shown by one of the current international experiments, the German foresight process Futur.

Another change is the new way of integrating the results of foresight activities into policy planning. In the past, it was often assumed that the Japanese had national strategies to become the world leader or number one.[39] However, in fact no concerted strategy for science and technology existed. The assumption that foresight was directly linked to such strategic national planning is no more than a hypothesis put forward by international observers and cannot be proven. There were always different users of foresight/forecasting or the Delphi results, and no coherent national technology planning existed. The STA was not a ministry but only an agency, not powerful enough to 'dictate' or 'force' anyone to stick to planning activities based on foresight. The usage was always voluntary – and many companies or institutions just ignored this offer, whereas others were very keen on participating in the exercises, learning through them, communicating them and making use of the results for their own strategic planning. The aim of using foresight more strategically is therefore understandable. We should note, moreover, that over the past few years there have been many claims that science and technology in Japan need to be better linked to society, thus the new attempts to take a needs perspective into account is in line with international developments in science and technology policy.

Another new aim is to inform policy-makers at different levels more directly than before. In previous years, this happened more on an *ad hoc* basis and via the leading participants in the surveys, experts, reports and other publications, but now the Council for Science and Technology Policy in particular is informed directly. The information is diffused via newsletters, and more direct information is available for the different committees in different ministries and in companies.

Summary

The impact of foresight on real science and technology policy-making has been somewhat nebulous up to now. Some impact on companies has been recorded,[40] and also on the policies of ministries as well as on research programmes, but since the channel of such influence is often human agency, it is clearly very difficult to 'prove' this with empirical evidence.

Both at the organisational and at the policy level the changes in Japan have gone further towards the inclusion of the people's opinions. Therefore, especially in the development of science and technology policy, with all the problems ahead and the necessity of gaining a better understanding and support from students and ordinary people, new methodologies and means are called for to integrate people's opinions and gain their support at an early stage. This is being attempted with a mix of foresight methodologies and other public acceptance tools. Without this early support and knowledge about a potential market or resistance against a specific development, it is very difficult to estimate the risk of developing a costly new technology or product and to free up funds for investing in cost-intensive future fields. One of the major aims of foresight is to identify these fields and to gain support for investing in them. This will help to produce a consensus on the major directions for these developments, something that has to be achieved by people, and is necessary for the realisation of the objectives that are to be laid down. Especially important is the participation of unusual actors in the system or 'experts', those who were until now often ignored, notably participation by the younger people who will actually experience the future or by 'normal people from the street', so that those undertaking the foresight exercise can know what these people will need, thereby gaining further insight into foresight processes and their methodology.

Nevertheless, these processes can be very expensive, depending on the approach chosen, so they must be result-oriented as well. It is not just the goal that is important but also the result that is achieved. The undertakers of foresight have to show that it is worthwhile undertaking such a process and investing the money in it, some element of value-added. For this purpose, evaluation processes also still need to be developed. In Germany and the United Kingdom, the initial steps to develop such kinds of evaluation are being taken and are likely to be instructive.[41] The Japanese foresight approach and its real impact on science and technology policy-making, on science, technology and innovation or even the economy, is difficult to prove and has not been evaluated formally up to now. Nevertheless, it certainly had the effect of making people think about the future – and in some cases even influenced the strategic planning of companies or certain projects. What can with confidence be stated at the end of this chapter is that after more than thirty years of activities, there is still a future for foresight in Japan.

Notes

1 Ben R. Martin, 'Foresight in Science and Technology', *Technology Analysis and Strategic Management* 7, 2, 1995.
2 Joseph F. Coates, 'Foresight in Federal Government Policymaking', *Futures Research Quarterly*, Summer 1985, p. 30.
3 John Irvine and Ben R. Martin, *Foresight in Science: Picking the Winners* (London: Pinter, 1984).
4 Kerstin Cuhls, 'Opening up Foresight Processes: Participation and Networking', *Économies et Sociétés* (Paris: Cahiers de L'Ismea, 2000).
5 Kerstin Cuhls, 'Participative foresight – How to Involve Stakeholders in the Modelling Process', in *Future Directions of Innovation Policy in Europe*, Proceedings of the Innovation Policy Workshop held in Brussels July 2002 by the Innovation Policy Unit of the European Commission (Brussels: Directorate-General Enterprise, 2002).
6 Kerstin Cuhls, *Technikvorausschau in Japan: ein Rückblick auf 30 Jahre Delphi-Expertenbefragungen* (Heidelberg: Physica, 1998); Kerstin Cuhls, 'Opening up Foresight Processes'; Ben R. Martin and Ron Johnston, 'Technology Foresight for Wiring Up the National Innovation System: Experiences in Britain, Australia and New Zealand', in Hariolf Grupp (ed.), *Special Issue on National Foresight Projects for Technological Forecasting and Social Change* 60, 1999.
7 Kerstin Cuhls, Knut Blind and Hariolf Grupp (eds), *Delphi 98 Umfrage: Zukunft nachgefragt Studie zur globalen Entwicklung von Wissenschaft und Technik* (Karlsruhe: ISI, 1998); Kerstin Cuhls, Knut Blind and Hariolf Grupp, *Innovations for our Future: Delphi '98: New Foresight on Science and Technology*, Technology, Innovation and Policy, Book Series of the Fraunhofer Institute for Systems and Innovation Research ISI no.13 (Heidelberg: Physica, 2002).

8 For 'strategic' or 'distributed' intelligence, see Stefan Kuhlmann, Patries Boekholt, Luke Georghiou, Ken Guy, Jean-Alain Héraud, Philippe Laredo, Tarmo Lemola, Denis Loveridge, Terttu Lukkonen, Wolfgang Polt, Arie Rip, Luis Sanz-Menendez, Ruud Smits 'Improving Distributed Intelligence in Complex Innovation Systems', Final Report of the Advanced Science and Technology Policy Planning Network (ASTPP), (Karlsruhe: ISI, 1999).

9 Barend van der Meulen, Jan De Wilt and Jan Rutten, 'Developing a Future for Agriculture in the Netherlands', in special issue of *Journal of Forecasting* edited by Cuhls and Salo, 22, 2003.

10 Andreas Fink, Oliver Schlake and Andreas Siebe, *Erfolg durch Szenario-Management: Prinzip und Werkzeuge der strategischen Vorausschau* (Frankfurt: Campus, 2001).

11 For an overview see Harold A. Linstone, *Decision Making for Technology Executives: Using Multiple Perspectives to Improve Performance* (Boston, MA: Artech House 1999); Karlheinz Steinmüller, *Beiträge zu Grundfragen der Zukunftsforschung* (Gelsenkirchen: Werkstattbericht des Sekretariats für Zukunftsforschung 2/95, 1995). See also Ossip K. Flechtheim, *Futurologie: Möglichkeiten und Grenzen* (Frankfurt am Main: Edition Voltaire, 1968); Olaf Helmer, *Analysis of the Future: the Delphi Method* (Santa Monica, CA: Rand Corporation, 1967); Olaf Helmer, *Social Technology* (Los Angeles, CA: Rand Corporation, 1966).

12 For example Dennis L. Meadows, Donella H. Meadows, E. Zahn and P. Milling, *Die Grenzen des Wachstums* (German edition of *The Limits to Growth*; Stuttgart: DVA, 1972); Jay Wright Forrester, *Der teuflische Regelkreis: das Globalmodell der Menschheitskrise* (Stuttgart: DVA, 1971) or *Industrial Dynamics* (Boston, MA: MIT Press, 1961).

13 'Strengthening the dimension of foresight in the European Research Area', www.cordis.lu/rtd2002/foresight/home.html

14 Ibid.

15 For a more detailed differentiation see Kerstin Cuhls, 'From Forecasting to Foresight processes – New Participative Foresight Activities in Germany', in special issue of *Journal of Forecasting*, edited by Cuhls and Salo, 22, 2003.

16 Cuhls, 'From Forecasting to Foresight processes'; Coates, 'Foresight in Federal Government Policymaking'.

17 Cuhls, *Technikvorausschau in Japan*.

18 Steinmüller, *Beiträge zu Grundfragen der Zukunftsforschung*; Irvine and Martin, *Foresight in Science*.

19 Helmer, *Analysis of the Future*.

20 For details see Cuhls, *Technikvorausschau in Japan*, also Kerstin Cuhls and Terutaka Kuwahara *Outlook for Japanese and German Future Technology, Comparing Technology Forecast Surveys* (Heidelberg: Physica, 1994).

21 Fred Woudenberg, 'An Evaluation of Delphi', *Technological Forecasting and Social Change* 40, 1991, p.132.

22 Alan Kaplan, A.L. Skogstad and M.A. Girshick, 'The Prediction of Social and Technological Events', *Public Opinion Quarterly* XIV, 1950, p. 94.

23 Herbert W. Parke and Donald Ernest Wilson Wormell, *The Delphic Oracle* (Oxford: Basil Blackwell, 1956).

24 Compare Harold A. Linstone and Murray Turoff (eds), *The Delphi Method: Techniques and Applications* (Reading, MA: Addison-Wesley, 1975); Joseph P. Martino, *Technological Forecasting for Decision Making* (New York: North Holland c.1983); Erich Jantsch, *Technological Forecasting in Perspective* (Paris: OECD, 1967); Cuhls, *Technikvorausschau in Japan*.

25 Theodore J. Gordon and Olaf Helmer, *Report on a Long-Range Forecasting Study* (Santa Monica, CA: Rand Corporation, 1964).

26 For the first four Delphi surveys see Kagaku Gijutsuchō Keikakukyoku (STA), *Gijutsu Yosoku Hōkokusho* (Tokyo, 1972); Ibid., 1977 and 1982; Kagaku Gijutsuchō Kagaku Gijutsu Seisakukyoku (ed.), *Wagakuni ni okeru Gijutsuhatten no Hōkō ni kansuru*

Chōsa: Gijutsu Yosoku Hōkokusho (Tokyo, 1986). A short version of the fourth report was published as Institute for Future Technology (IFTECH), *Future Technology in Japan, Forecast to the Year 2015* (Tokyo, 1988). Subsequent surveys are Kagaku Gijutsuchō Kagaku Gijutsu Seisaku Kenkyūjo (NISTEP) and Mirai Kōgaku Kenkyūjo (IFTECH), *2020nen no Kagaku Gijutsu, Dai 5kai Kagaku Gijutsuchō Gijutsu Yosoku Chōsa* (Tokyo, 1992) (short version NISTEP, *The Fifth Technology Forecast Survey, Future Technology in Japan*); NISTEP, *The 6th Technology Foresight – Future Technology in Japan toward the Year 2025* (Tokyo, 1997); NISTEP, *The 7th Technology Foresight – Future Technology in Japan toward the Year 2030* (NISTEP Report no.71, Tokyo, 2001).

27 NISTEP, Science and Technology Foresight Centre, MEXT, *Kagaku Gijutsu no Chūchōki Hatten ni kakawaru Fukanteki Yosoku Chōsa* (Interim Report, Survey Material no.105, Tokyo, June 2004).

28 The author of this chapter was employed as part of this cooperation to conduct a copy of the Japanese study in Germany.

29 Cuhls and Kuwahara *Outlook for Japanese and German Future Technology*; Kerstin Cuhls, Sibylle Breiner and Hariolf Grupp, *Delphi–Bericht 1995 zur Entwicklung von Wissenschaft und Technik – Mini-Delphi* (Karlsruhe: ISI, 1995), later appearing as brochure of the Federal Ministry for Research and Education, BMBF (Bonn: BMBF, 1996); NISTEP, *6th Technology Foresight*; Cuhls, Blind and Grupp, *Delphi '98 Umfrage*.

30 Cuhls and Kuwahara, *Outlook for Japanese and German Future Technology*.

31 For the critical technologies approach, see several articles in the special issue of *Technological Forecasting and Social Change* on national foresight projects, edited by Hariolf Grupp, 60, 1, 1999.

32 See www.futur.de. For more details on previous foresight studies see earlier work by Cuhls for an evaluation. See also Kerstin Cuhls and Luke Georghiou, 'Evaluating a participative foresight process: Futur – the German research dialogue', *Research Evaluation*, 13, 3, December 2004; or Kerstin Cuhls, 'Development and Perspectives of Foresight in Germany', in Institut für Technikfolgenabschätzung and Systemanalyse (ITAS) (eds), *Technikfolgenabschätzung. Theorie und Praxis*, 12, 2, Karlsruhe, 2003, pp. 20–29.

33 For these recent developments see Cuhls, 'Future Trends in Science and Technology' or Cuhls, 'From Forecasting to Foresight processes'.

34 Ibid.

35 see www.nistep.go.jp

36 For an overview see Cuhls, *Technikvorausschau in Japan*; Kerstin Cuhls, 'Foresight with Delphi Surveys in Japan', *Technology Analysis and Strategic Management* 13, 4, December 2001.

37 Kerstin Cuhls, 'Interesse an Technik in Japan', *Internationale Forschungs-, Technologie- und Innovationspolitik* (ITB-Berichte, March 1999).

38 Anonymous, 'White Paper on Nuclear Energy', *STA Today*, 7, 11, 1995, p. 3 (concerning the Atomic Energy Commission (ed.): *White Paper on Nuclear Energy*, 1995 Edition, Tokyo, 1995).

39 Ezra F. Vogel, *Japan as Number One: Lessons for America* (Cambridge, MA: Harvard University Press, 1979); Karel van Wolferen, *The Enigma of Japanese Power* (*Vom Mythos der Unbesiegbaren*, German Version, München: Droemer Knaur, 1989); Marvin J. Wolf, *The Japanese Conspiracy: their Plot to Dominate Industry Worldwide, and how to Deal with it* (New York: Empire Books, 1983). Also Chalmers Johnson, *MITI and the Japanese Miracle: the Growth of Industrial Policy 1925–1975* (Stanford, CA: Stanford University Press, 1982) for the Japan Inc. theory.

40 Satoru Kondō, *R&D Senryaku Ritsuan no tame no 'Gijutsu Yosoku' Katsuyō Gaido Bukku* (Tokyo: Urban Produce, 1993), for other countries like Germany see Cuhls, Blind and Grupp, *Innovations for our Future*.

41 Cuhls and Georghiou, 'Evaluating a participative foresight process: Futur – the German research dialogue'.

Index

T - #0011 - 230425 - C0 - 234/156/13 [15] - CB - 9780415368223 - Gloss Lamination